6/05 6/12

Prisoners of Ritual

*An Odyssey
into Female Genital Circumcision
in Africa*

About the Author

Hanny Lightfoot-Klein studied the topic of female genital circumcision during a six-year trek through Sudan, Kenya, and Egypt, during which time she lived with African families. An educator and family counselor, she is the author of numerous articles on the subject of female genital circumcision that have been published in scientific and popular publications in England, the United States, Germany, Denmark, Norway, and Sweden. She is a member of the Society for the Scientific Study of Sex and the Association for Women in Psychology. Ms. Lightfoot-Klein received her MA in social psychology from the American University in Washington, DC.

Prisoners of Ritual

*An Odyssey
into Female Genital Circumcision
in Africa*

Hanny Lightfoot-Klein

The Haworth Press
New York • London

Prisoners of Ritual: An Odyssey into Female Genital Circumcision in Africa is #2 in The Haworth Series on Women.

The Haworth Press, Inc., 10 Alice Street, Binghamton, NY 13904-1580
EUROSPAN/Haworth, 3 Henrietta Street, London WC2E 8LU England

Library of Congress Cataloging-in-Publication Data

Lightfoot-Klein, Hanny.
    Prisoners of ritual : an odyssey into female genital circumcision in Africa / Hanny Lightfoot-Klein.
        p.   cm. — (Haworth series on women, ISSN: 1040-7359 ; 2)
    Includes bibliographical references and Index.
    ISBN 0-86656-877-8
    1. Clitoridectomy. 2. Infibulation. 3. Circumcision. 4. Clitoridectomy — Sudan (Region) 5. Infibulation — Sudan (Region) 6. Circumcision — Sudan (Region) I. Title. II. Series: Haworth series on women ; v. 2.
GN484.L53   1989
392 — dc20
                                                                                    89-15639
                                                                                    CIP

To those who gave me food and shelter,
Bound up my wounds,
And helped me on my way.

To those who told me their stories.

To Stephanie, my daughter,
To Daniel, my son,
And to all children,
This work is lovingly dedicated.

CONTENTS

Preface

In February of 1979, a World Health Organization (WHO) conference on "Traditional Practices Affecting the Health of Women" was held in Khartoum, the capital of Sudan. Thus began a cautious campaign against the little known and even less discussed but widespread practice of female sexual mutilation in Africa. This practice predominates in approximately 40% of that vast continent's geographical area. It is known to exist to a far lesser degree in other parts of the Third World, in the Gulf States (Hosken, 1982), in Yemen (Saadawi, 1982; Hosken, 1982), among some Islamic peoples in Indonesia and Malaysia (Hosken, 1982; Ganesha Society, 1979), and in Sri Lanka (Linnander, 1986).

The number of these mutilations was at that time estimated to be 30 million (Brisset, 1979), carried out ritually on girls, women, and female infants. As more information has become available on the subject, this estimate has been revised to over 80 million (Hosken, 1982). In view of these overwhelming figures, the initial conference, attended by 65 health officials, most of them Africans, can only be described as exceedingly modest.

When I first arrived in Khartoum in 1979, I was totally unaware of the World Health Organization conference being held there at the same time. I was equally unaware of the rituals I write about here. I learned about these things later, gradually, a bit at a time over a period of several years.

The roads I have traveled and the information I have gathered represent merely one woman's lone trek through some of the less frequented areas of Africa. Mine was a quest for understanding. I lived among the African populace, ate their food with them — often from one common bowl — and traveled extensively throughout a nearly trackless expanse of desert terrain, much as they do — endlessly on foot, carrying large loads, along antiquated colonial railroad routes, atop the freight of ramshackle lorries and on camel back. Wherever I went, I was welcomed. I smiled and I asked questions, searching and deeply personal questions, questions for which I had hardly even expected answers. But the answers were nearly always given, truly given, as gifts are given. I looked for villains in this conundrum, and I found none. I found instead men and women entrapped in an antiquated ritual, dating heaven only knows how far back into history, unable to free themselves from its centuries-old enmeshment, all of them its prisoners.

This book tells the story of my personal travels among these people, along the tortuous road to understanding why these practices continue so tenaciously to exist.

Acknowledgment

The subject matter of this book is somewhat out of the ordinary. It involves a body of information that has not been obtained with the ordinary research techniques, and it deals with a topic that people anywhere could not be expected to talk about readily. The fact that I was able to research this topic so thoroughly in a country such as Sudan still remains a puzzle to me, and I am certain that it would never have been possible without the extraordinary goodwill, trust, and openness of the many people who helped me or who took part in my research and contributed their own particular story.

I wish to express my thanks to these many remarkable people, professional and lay, who enabled me to conduct this research. They are too numerous to cite individually here, but I will never forget their kindness, their incredible generosity of spirit, and the many truly memorable, significant, individual acts by which they aided and sustained me.

I am particularly grateful to Dr. Salah Abu Bakr and to Dr. Aziz Malik for making me welcome in their gynecological hospitals and allowing me to do my work there. Fardous Ahmed Eltyeb and Awatef Adam Ali were wonderfully articulate translators who helped me in great measure to understand the implications of the information I obtained, and I owe them a debt of gratitude as well.

It is difficult to imagine this book ever coming to fruition without the unflagging support of my mentor, Dr. John Money of Johns Hopkins University, who has given so generously of his valuable time, and whose encyclopedic knowledge and wise counsel have been so essential and invaluable to me. I count myself exceedingly fortunate that he has found my self-instigated work to be of sufficient merit to warrant this kind of support.

I am grateful also to Berit Ås, the Norwegian legislator who mobilized women in that small and socially progressive country to contribute parital funding for my research when I had run out of personal monies to continue it and no funding could be found by me from any other source. This donation was important to me not only materially, but psychologically as well, because it validated in me a belief in the value of what I was doing. Ellen Cole and Esther Rothblum, my editors, who, by intuiting the merit inherent in this book put an end to my weary search for a publisher, have earned my most special appreciation, as has Kathy Rutz, my copy editor, who wept over its pages, as she worked on them.

My special thanks to my son, Daniel Victor Klein, who lovingly helped me with seemingly endless revisions, corrections, and re-writings of the manuscript, and to Dr. Herta Haas, whose strong, level-headed intelligence and warm-hearted support reinforced and helped me to maintain my sense of perspective.

All of these people, in helping me, were each in his or her own individual way expressing their concern and compassion for the unfortunate Sudanese children who are subjected to female circumcision. I, as author, am only acting as their collective voice. It is folly to expect that anything of immediate significance will be accomplished by this book to cause the practice of female circumcision to be abandoned. However, it is hoped that this book will bring about a greater understanding of the problem and of the people involved in it, and perhaps contribute to its eventual solution.

PART I

Introduction

The first time I heard about the practice of what is euphemistically called "female circumcision" was one night at a Khartoum youth hostel. It was 1979 and the fact that I was in this hostel at all had evolved by sheer chance. I was then a middle-aged English teacher on a 1-year sabbatical, and I had already backpacked and hitchhiked my way through a good part of Europe. By the time I arrived in Greece, I was sufficiently seasoned as a traveler to attempt the well-frequented overland route through Turkey, Iran, and into India. However, just as I was about to make my move, the political scene in Turkey deteriorated, and shortly thereafter the ordeal of the American hostages in Iran began. To go overland became unthinkable and since this had been my chosen mode of travel, I decided to abandon my original plans. I turned south instead of east and began my African journey, starting in Egypt. I knew very little about the geography or politics of Africa. All I really knew was that some travelers followed a route that began in Cairo, went on through Luxor and Aswan in Egypt, wound its way through the Sudan and Uganda, and ultimately arrived in Kenya. I decided that this was for me, and after a long and harrowing barge trip up the Nile into Sudan, I made my way as far as Khartoum, the capital.

The last leg of the journey was also a harrowing experience. I was on a train packed with people which traveled through an ancient desert route. The locomotive continually broke down, stopped and awaited repair, and soon broke down again. The men escaped to the train's roof, there to bake in the hot desert sun. I attempted to join them but was driven back to the cars by the dust and the heat. Under cattle-car conditions, it took 4 days and nights of arduous travel through a seemingly endless wasteland of wind-driven dust to arrive in Khartoum, and at the end of this journey I staggered, exhausted and sleep deprived, into the hostel.

Overland backpackers spend much of their time exchanging bits of information about the places they have been to, the routes and modes of transportation they have taken, the experiences they have had, and the conditions they have encountered. This exchange is indispensable to them since conditions in parts of the Third World, particularly in Africa, are apt to change quite suddenly and dramatically, and what appeared possible or impossible a short while ago is likely to reverse overnight. This information exchange is the best and most reliable way to keep current. Tour books are useless.

In the hostel I made the rounds, looking for people with more Africa experience than I, and pretty soon I was conversing with an American from New York City well journeyed through many parts of Africa, who was on his way to Zaire, and who had a great deal of information to impart. After a rather lengthy discussion of travel in the Sudan, the conversation turned to more personal matters, and he began to discuss the sexual experiences he had had in the rigidly Islamic country of Sudan. He referred to some experiences with Sudanese prostitutes. "Those poor women," he said, shaking his head. At first I misinterpreted his pity as being directed toward their having to be prostitutes, which, I was certain, was no light matter in a Muslim country. However he quickly enlightened me. "You know what they do to women here, don't you?" he asked. I pleaded ignorance. "They completely cut off all the external sex organs when they are little girls, and then sew them shut. They leave only a tiny, tiny opening."

"But surely they do this only among very primitive tribes in the bush," I exclaimed.

"Not at all," he said. "It is done to every one of them here, at all levels of society, from the very top on down."

"Good heavens," I muttered and then fell into stricken silence while I digested the implications of this statement. Finally I managed to ask, "Is it possible to talk to people here about this subject?"

"Of course not," he replied emphatically. "They won't talk to you. There is a very powerful taboo against it."

Although I accepted his answer at the time, I later learned that he could not have been more wrong, and quite understandably so. He was a man. Of course no one would talk to him about it, not even the prostitutes he had known. As a Western woman of mature years, I was later to discover, I was to be privy to all sorts of personal information that women could not reveal even to their own husbands.

I spent the next 2 weeks in a deeply troubled state, wanting to know more but not knowing how to go about it. I began to travel to the small towns and villages that lay along the railway route between Khartoum and Port Sudan. One afternoon I found myself in a place called New Halfa, a dismal, barren, and dusty desert town to which those inhabitants of the lush, green Nile valley villages flooded out by the Nasser Dam up river had been relocated. In this town I was told about a large sugar factory a few miles away in the desert. I wandered in its direction, approached the guards at the gate, and was brought after some hesitation and under arms to the installation itself. There, to my great surprise and pleasure, I was welcomed profusely by the Sudanese scientific staff. I was given the red carpet treatment, even though I had turned up out of nowhere, carrying with me no more credentials than those possessed by any other eager sightseer.

The sugar mill itself was an ancient German-made installation of another era, unquestionably a residue of English colonial days. It churned away with Germanic efficiency, run entirely by Sudanese personnel. After showing me through the factory, the senior chemist invited me to his home, and I was to spend the heat of the day there.

The hospitality, kindness, and openness of the Sudanese are rightfully legendary, as I was to discover more and more as my journey evolved. My newly found friend was a highly intelligent individual, who had graduated summa cum laude from the University of Khartoum. His name was Mohammed. He spoke excellent, high-level English , which I was surprised to learn was largely self-taught. His wife Isha, a quiet, self-effacing woman, was an agriculturist who had also graduated from the university with honors. She spoke only rarely. They had a one-year-old daughter who tottered about the room joyously, just having found her legs.

The long, blisteringly hot afternoon wore on as we discussed our widely divergent lives, our interests, our feelings. Suddenly the moment seemed right. I looked at Mohammed's gentle, acutely perceptive face, and lost all my fear. I took a deep breath and began.

"Mohammed, there is something that I must know about, that you can tell me. I have also been told that it is something I must not ask about, since the subject is taboo. If you cannot speak about it, please just tell me so, and try to forgive and forget that I have asked you."

I sat forward in my chair and looked at him appealingly. In answer he spread his hands, palms upward, toward me, his face open and alert, waiting.

"Ask," he said.

I took another deep breath, phrasing my words carefully. "I want to know about what they do to little girls here when their time comes to be cut."

I heard him exhale sharply. For a brief moment his gaze dropped. There was pain in his eyes when he looked at me again. His hand swept toward Isha, who was quietly nursing their child.

"Ask that woman," he said tonelessly. "She has suffered that thing."

I shall never forget that answer or the turbulence I experienced then. For a moment I was too moved to speak. Then I fumbled for paper and pen in my pack, straightened my spine, sought and found the small beginnings of a detachment that was to sustain me in the many months of quest that were to follow, and went to work.

Most women in Sudan are circumcised pharaonically. This type of circumcision involves the excision of the clitoris, labia minora, and fleshy inner layers of the labia majora. The remaining skin is then fused over the wound and sutured down to a pinhole opening. This fusion is called infibulation.

A far lesser number of Sudanese women are circumcised in a

modified way. That is to say, a one centimeter opening may be left, and/or the outer labia may remain intact. Occasionally parts of the inner labia or clitoris remain. In Sudan, these modified procedures are called *sunna* after the teachings of the prophet Mohammed. This is a misnomer. True *sunna* as defined by Islamic teaching involves only the excision of the clitoral prepuce, and is analogous to the removal of the penile prepuce in males. True *sunna* is virtually unknown as a procedure in Sudan.

When I first expressed interest in the subject to the educated people I reached by way of Mohammed's letters of introduction in Port Sudan, I was invited almost immediately to attend a circumcision at a house in a middle-class neighborhood. I arrived only 5 minutes after the actual surgery had taken place. There was a party atmosphere, much gaiety, chatter, and many delicious refreshments. A few men were in the outer room, looking ill at ease and conversing nervously. In the inner room a number of festively dressed women were sitting around a bed. On it, a frail, bloodless-looking 10-year-old, her hands painted with henna (like those of a bride), was lying motionless, her eyes wide and stunned. A smiling midwife, proudly efficient, dressed in white, was plainly the heroine of this tableau and was greeted with great respect by everyone entering the room.

One of the neighbors told me that there had been a modified circumcision only. The child, she said, had had an injection of analgesic directly into the clitoris and as yet felt no pain. She would feel a great deal of pain later, however, she added. Had the child been told what would happen to her? Yes, and she had been happy, because she had received many gifts. She would be given antibiotics if she needed them.

The woman who told me this, a young teacher of English at a secondary school, related the circumstances of her own pharaonic circumcision at the age of four. She had been given no anesthetic, she said, and the pain had been enormous. When she realized what was happening to her, she had been "truly frightened." Three women had held her down and there was nothing she could do. After it was over, she felt very strange. She had thought "it would grow back." She had not thought it would be like that. She had asked her mother, "When will I get back to normal?" They used to laugh at her. Everything felt so different. Even passing water was difficult, the opening was so very small. It would take her a half hour to empty her bladder. Later, when she was married, sex had been extremely frightening. She had known there would be more pain, but the reality had by far exceeded her imagination. It took 5 months to achieve penetration. She still did not care for sex even now, although it had not been too painful after that. Giving birth had not been difficult by Sudanese standards. (I was later to witness the horrors of Sudanese birth.) She did not allow herself to be sewn shut again as most women do after giving birth, because she did not want to suffer any more.

She had three daughters of her own. One had been circumcised; a modified operation. She said she had discussed the need for the operation with a local female "doctor" after reading many books, and the doctor had told her that she felt the operation was medically necessary for all women, that the child would otherwise be "too sensitive sexually," and that the operation would prevent malodorous discharges and make the sex organs cleaner. She had read religious writings about *sunna* and knew that the Prophet was in favor of it.

What would she do about her other daughters? Perhaps she would not have it done to them. She did not think that being sensitive was a bad thing, and would have preferred it if she had not been circumcised herself. She felt that she was missing something in marriage and that she was not enjoying life as she could. Some men complained of women being cold; her husband never said anything.

Sudan, she believed (mistakenly), was the only country where the operation was still performed. There was so much talk about it now, she said bitterly, but it did not help. The Sudanese were still proud of the pharaonic. They thought it protected girls from shame, but it didn't. Some women still had sex before marriage, and there was infidelity among married women. Her own family disapproved strongly when she had only a *sunna* done on her eldest. She had delayed until the girl was 13, which was practically unheard of. Finally she had given in. Now her second daughter was mortally afraid, and every night would come to lie down with her and ask: "Will I be circumcised? If I don't have it, will they laugh at me?" She would tell her that it need not be done, knowing that it was not a promise, but knowing that if she did not say something of the kind, the child would not sleep.

A middle-aged, Moscow-educated Sudanese economist discussed the two types of circumcision with me. He agreed that the pharaonic circumcision was "a terrible thing for women," and cited a psychological text he had read. It was about a woman who became paralyzed whenever her husband wanted to have intercourse. The psychiatrist attributed this to the extreme mutilation she had suffered. Some families cut away only half the clitoris, the economist informed me. Would this not have some psychological effects as well? Perhaps, he shrugged, but he didn't see why it should. It was only a little piece. Did he not think that cutting off even a little piece of his penis would have a psychological effect on him? He looked shocked and agreed that it definitely would.

A teacher at a Port Sudan secondary school for boys told me he had five daughters. Yes, they had all been pharaonized, because he (erroneously) thought that this was demanded by his religion. It was good for them, he said. It would help them to conceive. How did he feel about the pain that they had suffered? He chose not to understand, and abruptly changed the subject.

An Indonesian woman married to a Sudanese businessman related a conversation she had had with some Sudanese teenagers. They assumed that she too had been circumcised and were horrified to discover that she had not. "Oh you must have it done!" they pleaded. "If you do not, your husband will take a second wife, or he will go to prostitutes!"

A Sudanese sea captain educated in Yugoslavia told me he much preferred European, unmutilated women to pharaonized, Sudanese women. The sight of a pharaonized female organ disgusted him, he said, and he failed to see how any man could even function sexually with such women. No, he would never do such a thing to his children. It was "absolutely barbaric." However, further questioning revealed that he saw nothing wrong with clitoridectomy. The woman could still feel, after all, he said.

A headmaster at a boys' school spoke of his marriage to a pharaonized woman. It had taken him 3 weeks to achieve penetration and it was very painful for his wife. She bled a great deal. When asked how he felt about this, a look of guilt and self-loathing came over his face, and he said that the suffering of a sexual partner was stimulating to some men in a strange way, because it was preferable to no reaction at all. When his wife gave birth they slit her open, and after the child had been delivered, the grandmother called in a special midwife to resew her wounded vagina closed even tighter than before. This, her grandmother felt, would enhance her womanhood, make her more like a virgin, and stimulate her husband even more. The penetration after the birth of their two children had been even more agonizing for his wife than the initial penetration. She now took pills so that she would not have another child. She was very frightened. He felt that *all* circumcision was wrong and he longed to find a way to avoid circumcising his children. He had thought of breaking communication with his family for 1 or 2 years during the time of his daughters' supposed circumcision. He would later pretend that they had been circumcised as expected.

I talked with one physician of a small girl who had come to her attention, who had been given a mild form of *sunna*. She had experienced so much shaming by her peers for this that she was constantly bothering her mother to be "properly circumcised" like the others.

Dr. Sidahamed, a physician, told me he found the practice of circumcision totally indefensible on medical grounds and described some of the manifold consequences of the operation he encountered in his daily practice. Circumcision, he said, was absolutely hindering female emancipation, and was preventing the development of the country. On the other hand he felt that sexually sensitive women were a detriment to society, and said that women would be more responsible citizens under the pressure of Western influences if they were not sexually sensitive. He was married to two pharaonized women, and felt that the operation made life smoother for him by removing sexual tensions. He was busy with his medical practice and could not devote himself to his wives too often. This way he could have sex with them when *he* wanted, but they made no demands on him. He acknowledged that the sexual response of a mutilated woman could not be compared with that of an unmutilated one and he preferred uncircumcised women himself.

He had five daughters by his two wives, and finding himself in a dilemma, had withdrawn from the decision of what was to be done with them. The grandmothers had decided, and four daughters had been pharaonized so far. There had been "no complications except for some fever and sepsis," he informed me in a detached manner, but they were still "premenstrual."

I asked him to describe the procedure and he replied in a matter-of-fact voice, but with some nervousness. It was done during the summer at a special house at a resort. The children were taken there on holiday by their mothers, and the arrangements had been made beforehand by the grandmothers. "The children are not told what is to happen to them. They are taken by force and without anesthesia. It is all quite brutal and primitive," he said. What were the children like when they returned? How had they changed? "They are less hyperactive," he replied. That was the only change he noticed. Nothing was ever discussed between him and his daughters afterward. He preferred it that way. "After all," he said, "it is women's business." He presented his mother as the wisest woman in the house and said he would not oppose her, not even to intercede on behalf of his remaining uncircumcised daughter.

This doctor's mother, a totally unschooled woman of about 70 years, whose face was lined with deep tribal scars, had been pharaonized at the age of seven. She vividly described the details of an unanesthetized village operation. The pain had been so great that when they gave her a piece of wood to bite on, she bit it in half. She remembered having been sewn so tightly that the opening closed three times, and she had had to be reopened each time to permit urination. Scarring was so severe that her husband was unable to penetrate her, and she finally had to be cut open. Still she felt that circumcision was a good thing, and that it should be done to the children because "it would keep them clean and prevent the uterus from dropping out." She was afraid they would "get dirt and worms in the vagina" if they were not circumcised. She also told me that men would not accept an uncut wife, and that they would be more pleased if the girl was sewn shut, because it was proof of virginity. In her village, the chief had told the men that it would be better to have *sunna* done on their daughters, but they had all refused.

Sofia, the second of the doctor's wives and a teacher at the girls' secondary school, said she had been subjected to pharaonic circumcision at the age of six. She remembered being very happy at the prospect, expecting something good to happen. She had been given many gifts of new clothes and perfumes. When they cut her there were five women to hold her down — one at the head, one each at the arms and legs. She had been given no anesthetic of any sort, and had not realized the enormity of what was happening to her until the midwife began cutting. The operation took a quarter of an hour. She did not remember her feelings or thoughts, she said. She had just wanted the pain to stop, but it had remained with her for a long time.

Sex had been extremely painful to her at first, she told me, and it took 10 days to achieve penetration. She said she now enjoyed sex but did not understand the question when I asked her if she was able to achieve orgasm. When I explained what an orgasm was, she said no, she had no sexual sensation whatsoever, but she enjoyed her husband coming to her, because she was very jealous of the other wife. She was curious about orgasm. Did her inability have anything to do with the operation? Some women she knew had an appetite for men, she said, but to her it was only a duty.

She has had seven children, enduring great pain with each birth. Each time she had to be sewn shut and "reopened" by her husband. She wanted three more children. She asked if the birth pain was related to her circumcision. When I told her that some normal women experience little pain in giving birth, she expressed total disbelief. She expected a lot of resistance from her family when she decided she did not want to circumcise the last of her three girls. She had not discussed the matter with her husband because she was afraid that he would give her no support, and she realized the best she might hope for was the compromise of a *sunna*. She personally knew of no family where the girls had been left uncut. People said that sewing the girls shut would protect them against rape.

A young school teacher described the pharaonic circumcision she had at the age of six. Her sisters had all been *sunnaed*, she said, but when her turn came a very famous midwife who was an expert in the pharaonic procedure was visiting the area, so her family had her pharaonized.

Dr. El Tahir Abdel Rahim, a psychiatrist and genial gentleman of the old school, discoursed freely on the generalized psychiatric problems he encountered in his daily practice. It was obvious, he said, that when you removed one of the important parts of the body at such an early age, that in itself was associated with all of the anxiety of a child, quite apart from the pain. The screaming at the time of surgery frightened the other children and heightened the atmosphere of terror. When a girl grew up knowing that a vital part of her body had been removed, puberty was not a happy experience. When a girl first menstruated, she experienced much physical and psychic pain. The orifice was not large enough to pass the menstrual blood. Apathy and depression were much more extreme than among normal adolescents.

When a marriage commenced, he said, sexual contact was associated with much pain and anxiety, and this blighted the relationship. The entire family was anxious—the girl, her husband, the parents. Men often had potency problems. They were equally afraid. They were really doing something abnormal and painful to them as well, and many actually did fail because of the fear that they would be inadequate to the task of penetrating their wives. It was a great shame to a Sudanese man not to achieve penetration.

The psychiatrist told me of a case he had recently treated. A young man, a prison guard, had married a remote relative. He failed to penetrate correctly, and after continued frantic efforts caused much injury around the wife's sexual organs, eventually creating an opening. He thought his relationship was normal, but he had actually been using an open wound. The girl had experienced tremendous pain each time the couple had intercourse, and eventually, after 5 years of this, had come to the psychiatrist's attention with severe suicidal depression. She had never discussed the situation with her husband. She had been too ashamed, and had not wanted to discourage him. At the hospital her vagina had been opened surgically and the wound allowed to heal. Such surgical procedures were done secretly, the psychiatrist said, "to save the reputation of the husband."

The paradox, as he described it, was that women felt guilty because they could not function normally. Men themselves often felt guilt at experiencing pleasure at the expense of their wives' pain. Feelings of rejection and alienation were common to both. He said he could tell most easily whether a girl was circumcised or not simply by her bearing, by the way she spoke, by her manner, by her confidence. It affected the total growth of her personality, her will, her self-image. He felt terribly sorry for women.

Circumcision was "a criminal act," he went on to say. That was why his own daughters would be *sunnaed*. He would allow only half the clitoris to be taken—the part that protruded. He felt that a large clitoris causes a lot of trouble. Girls fell from their bicycles because of sexual overstimulation if their clitorises were not cut. He told me that they were "constantly being brought into the hospital having fallen off in a sexual swoon." (I would like to comment here that during my many months in Sudan I failed to encounter even a single girl on a bicycle. I can only conclude therefore that girls are simply not allowed bicycles there, or that they had indeed all fallen off.) Cutting off a centimeter or so of the clitoris did not affect their ability to have pleasure, he said. They did not feel they had lost anything. When asked whether he might not experience a sense of loss if a centimeter or so of his penis were cut off, he looked pained, and conceded he would. But he stuck to his guns. He was certain that a girl who was completely uncut was not very marriageable.

Dr. Mohamed Said El Rayah, gynecologist, described his frustration as a physician. The pharaonic could hide a lot of diseases—prolapses, tumors, anything. These women could not be properly diagnosed because it was impossible to introduce instruments to examine them. So they remained untreated or had to submit to operations simply to permit diagnosis.

Dr. Aziz Malik, another gynecologist, showed me a 7-year-old girl who had been brought into the hospital two days previously, hemorrhaging profusely after a village pharaonic. She had required a full 36 hours of transfusions. The wild-eyed, babbling child was carried into the room in the arms of a woman attendant, her legs flexed and painfully spread apart. She cried out as she was placed as gently and carefully as possible on the examining table. As the doctor exposed her enormously swollen outer labia, she tensed her body, trying to cover herself, spasmodically warding him off with her frail arms. Between the swollen labia, dark sutures were barely visible; otherwise nothing abnormal could be seen.

At Dr. Malik's house I met three of his five daughters. There was no mistaking that they were uncircumcised. Their entire stance, their expression, the quality of their movements were totally different from those of any other Sudanese girls I had seen.

Nairah Movarra, a Czech-educated young doctor, appeared to be a remarkably competent and energetic young lady. She told me that she saw frequent infections, tetanus, hemorrhage, and fever resulting from circumcision. She felt that the notion of circumcision protecting a girl's virtue was total nonsense. A girl who was not a virgin at marriage needed only to have herself sewn shut again to create the appearance that she was.

She had been pharaonized at the age of 7, without any anesthetic. She had blocked the experience out of her mind and remembered very little except the pain, especially at first urination. She planned to be married eventually and knew that there would be more pain and other complications. I commented on the matter-of-fact way in which she spoke of this. "Well," she said, "my mother has suffered so much more; she had eight children and had been sewn shut after each one. I know that I won't have to suffer that." She vowed she would definitely leave any of her own children uncircumcised.

Hajah Kashaif Bedri, one of the founders of the organized women's movement in Sudan, appeared to be a most assertive and strong-willed lady. She too had been pharaonized. She said she would not have her daughters cut, not even to have their ears pierced. She had told her family in plain terms she would put anyone who touched them in jail. Her mother-in-law complained bitterly, but she was adamant. She had persuaded some of her friends also to leave their daughters uncut, and there was much secrecy involved in these maneuvers. The mothers worried terribly when the girls reached marriageable age, but in fact educated Sudanese men were often delighted to find that their brides were uncircumcised. Speaking of her own experience, she said she knew it was difficult for a man to satisfy a pharaonized woman sexually, but that with patience, effort, and understanding, it definitely could be done.

Finally, I spoke to Mr. Nakasoub, an influential Muslim leader in Port Sudan. He assured me that there was nothing in the Koran about the pharaonic. It was "a custom brought over from Egypt in ancient times," and had "nothing whatsoever to do with religion." There was a religious book called the *Sunna* from the works of the

Prophet, "which mentioned eight degrees of circumcision short of the pharaonic, the first degree being no more than a ritual scratch, which satisfies the requirements of the religion completely." He himself was "very much against that barbarous practice, the pharaonic," and in his religious capacity advocated the mildest form of the *sunna*. Did he have any daughters? Indeed he had. What had been done about them? They had all been pharaonized. How was this possible in view of his stated beliefs? One could not go against custom, he said. Custom was too strong in the people. *No one* could defy custom.

1. The Interviews:
Procedure and Rationale

My report is the result of three separate studies carried out in Sudan between 1979 and 1983. Each of these studies was conducted over a period of approximately 6 months. In each about half of the time was spent in Khartoum, the present capital, and adjoining Omdurman, the old capital of the country. Khartoum can be described as *relatively* modern and progressive; Omdurman is an aggregation of old-style villages, and is extremely conservative. The remaining three months were spent trekking through the hinterlands of more remote towns and villages all over the country.

Between 1983 and 1984 I followed a similar, if far less arduous, travel pattern in Kenya for more than 1 year. I found the two countries to contrast sharply. Sudan is one of the least developed countries in Africa, and paved roads are totally nonexistent except for one relatively short stretch between Khartoum and Port Sudan in the northeast corner. The rest are deeply rutted, bone-wrenching dirt roads, especially formidable if one is traveling, as I did, on the top of lorry freight. Travel overland is totally impossible during the wet season and for some time after, nearly half of the year.

As a country, Sudan has virtually nothing to attract the tourist. Kenya, on the other hand, is the foremost showplace for African progress. Travel there is no more difficult than in most European countries, and the land's economy flourishes under the ever-escalating influx of tourists from Western countries into its game preserves.

The Sudanese are by and large a devoutly Islamic people, for the most part quite untouched by Western influences and technology, with the exception of modern weapons. Most people in this country still live largely in the Iron Age, and in some of the Nuban and Darfur villages of the interior where I stayed, I saw no evidence of metal tools whatsoever. Even the true incursors of our own way of life, the plastic bag and transistor radio, that one finds in all sorts of places of the Third World, were nowhere in evidence in these villages.

Khartoum, the only metropolitan center in Sudan, boasts some modern plumbing, but only in a few government edifices and the European sector, built and inhabited by Europeans exclusively. No such refinements exist anywhere else in the country.

Garbage disposal seems to exist only in the form of herds of starving goats, which roam freely everywhere in the city, devouring everything dumped into the streets, including the ubiquitous plastic bags. Streets are deeply rutted and unpaved, even in downtown Khartoum, whipped by searing dust storms (*haboobs*) most of the year. Conditions in general are so primitive by our own standards that all of Sudan is considered to be a hardship area by such companies as the Lockheed Corporation, so that their representatives based there receive in addition to their regular salaries a fairly large sum of "hardship pay."

With few exceptions, the Sudanese are quite naive and curious about other, and especially Western, cultures, and are obviously charmed by them. In Sudan it was staggeringly easy for me to obtain replies to the most intimate questions by simply indicating a sincere willingness to answer all of theirs. The Sudanese struck me as remarkably friendly, honest, and touchingly eager to help. Not only did they answer all my questions, but they expressed open delight at my being there in general, having come such a long way, and showing such an interest in the details of their simple lives.

Lodging was never a problem. People readily took me into their houses. My bus fares were often mysteriously paid for. Innumerable times my tea or food was paid for in the tea shacks, and I was never able to find out who had paid for them. Whenever I positioned myself at the end of a long line at the bakery, waiting for bread to come, piping hot, from the ovens, I was shuffled forward, on and on, until to everyone's visible delight, I was at the very head of the line, and received my bread ahead of all others.

I can only explain their willingness to answer all my questions as yet another facet of this joy in hospitality and kindness to strangers, and the fact that strangers, especially of my variety, are still exciting and rare. In Sudan I got used to being the circus come to town, the parade going down Main Street, and I made the most of it.

Kenya, by contrast, has been virtually overrun by all manner and types of camera-toting tourists, and a large segment of the population is European in origin. Many of these people are unfortunately quite arrogant in their attitudes, and often shockingly insensitive toward the black Kenyans. Researchers of all sorts have descended upon them to study all manner of aspects of their existence, very rarely to their readily apparent benefit, and no doubt well past their level of endurance. With a very few notable exceptions, I found Kenyans to be anything but eager to be interviewed, and I did not attempt it often.

Furthermore, it was quite easy to obtain official permission to enter and inspect medical installations and even to take photographs of them in Sudan, but such a thing proved impossible in Kenya. Whatever information I gathered there was obtained by bits and scraps, mostly by word of mouth, from non-Kenyans working there in various medical capacities.

The object of my studies was to find out as much about the subject of female circumcision as possible, with emphasis on its social and psychosexual aspects. The methods employed were interviews, discussions, personal observation and inspection in operating theaters and delivery rooms, and eyewitness accounts by knowledgeable non-Africans. An attempt was made to cover as much geographical ground as possible, from city to town to village, through all levels of medical installations.

Information was obtained from all types of medical personnel, i.e., local doctors, paramedics, nurses, midwives, gynecologists, pediatricians, and psychiatrists, as well as knowledgeable non-Sudanese (generally Western or Western-educated doctors, nurses, or midwives). Nonmedical people such as religious leaders, teachers, social scientists, and historians were also consulted. The bulk of the interviews was with Sudanese women of all ages and social standing, and addressed personal experiences, feelings, and attitudes toward the practice. They were obtained mostly on a catch-as-catch-can basis: in private homes, on trains, in villages, clinics, schools, inns, at the universities—wherever conversation was possible.

Some interviews were carried out within an hour's time. Others were more on the order of conversations with people I got to know intimately over a period of weeks, months, and in the case of one Port Sudan family, even years. (See "Sofia and Sidahamed," pp. 105-111.)

At first I was puzzled by the willingness of people to discuss highly personal matters with me, but I soon discovered that there was often a great eagerness, particularly on the part of young married couples and parents of little girls, to unburden themselves once they discovered that they were dealing with a knowledgeable person who was able to listen without passing judgment.

The interviews often took on a cathartic quality for people who were tormented by conflict and who were seeking support. People often expressed surprise at my ready admission that neither I, my daughter, nor any woman of my acquaintance in the West was circumcised. The entire concept was strange to them in the utmost, and they were generally charmed by what they appeared to regard as a disarming honesty, and so they responded in kind.

In view of the delicacy of the subject (and as I proceeded, I soon began to ask more and more intimate questions about their marital lives), it always came as a great surprise when some woman or man thanked me profusely and with obvious sincerity. Whenever I asked why they were thanking me, the answer was generally, "Because you want to help."

In all, about 400 interviews were conducted. A series of about 100 interviews was carried out at Bulluk Hospital in Omdurman, under the kind auspices of Dr. Salah Abu Bakr, its director. He not only gave me the run of his hospital, but provided me with two excellent translators as well. These two married Sudanese women, Fardous and Awatif, were registered nurses who had trained in London, and they were, of course, circumcised pharaonically themselves. They had considerable insight into both cultures, and were able to translate not only linguistically, but in terms of the cultural and emotional overtones of what was being asked and what replies we received. We formed the habit of a three-way consultation at the end of each interview to check our impressions of the validity of the information we received. I can recall no single instance when our impressions failed to match. At worst, we all agreed that a particular interview had to be discarded as inconclusive. This, however, was rare. Generally, once a subject got past the initial discomfort of being with strangers, it was a matter of being "all girls together," and we were able to let our hair down to an amazing degree.

Another series of interviews carried out in a far less organized manner was with men, most of whom had never had a conversation with an educated Western woman before, and certainly not one that dealt with their sexual and marital histories.

Had I attempted to carry out a similar study in Kenya it would have been difficult, if not impossible, to get past the local taboos and the total denial that such a thing as female circumcision exists at all. This is true in spite of recent legislation in Kenya which forbids the sexual mutilation of women.

By way of illustration I can relate the following: Two Danish female doctors of my acquaintance working in the maternity wards and delivery rooms of sizable Kenyan hospitals reported that no one, not even Kenyan gynecologists, was willing to discuss the subject with them. When one of these young women first commented on the obvious fact that a Kenyan maternity patient was having difficulty in delivering due to her massive circumcision scarring, she was told by the male Kenyan doctor that she did not know what she was talking about, that the patient was perfectly normal. When she insisted by pointing out that the woman had obviously been deprived of her clitoris and inner labia, the doctor once more told her that she was talking nonsense. Both Danish doctors concurred that this denial took place consistently whenever the subject was mentioned to any of the Kenyan staff during the entire year they worked there. It was simply impossible to discuss the matter.

It is probably safe to assume that even in Sudan, most of the data collected could not have been obtained had the researcher not been female. Most women in this culture are not even able to obtain the benefits of medical services if only a male doctor is available, even in the presence of a husband, and female doctors are exceedingly few in number. Men simply will not allow their wives to be examined or treated by another man.

Dr. Salah Abu Bakr, Director of Bulluk Hospital in Omdurman, appeared on Sudanese television in 1981 and not only discussed his findings on the denervation of genital tissue in pharaonically circumcised women, but also showed pertinent slides. The latter

made him the subject of a great deal of criticism. One other peripheral consequence of this television program was that I searched him
out, appeared unannounced at his hospital (telephones are generally
no better than nonfunctional desk ornaments in Sudan), stated the
nature of my research, and requested his assistance.[1]

He immediately called a staff conference and instructed all of his
staff to cooperate with me and to answer all of my questions, which
would largely deal with their personal lives and sexual experiences.
The women in turn made the condition that I answer all their questions about mine. I did as they asked, and the bargain was struck.
From them I earned the nickname "El Shadida," The Strong One.
Rapport with this particular group was excellent. (See "The Midwives," pp. 245-246.)

In addition to staff members, I also interviewed some mothers of
pediatric patients. These women stayed at the hospital with their
children, in the customary way, and had a great deal of time on their
hands when the children were sleeping, thus making them a well-
motivated group. This group consisted almost entirely of unschooled village women, as did a small group of pregnant women
waiting to deliver. Other women were also interviewed in towns
and villages of the interior. These women were largely uneducated,
but several had had between 2 and 4 years of schooling. In contrast,
students and teachers interviewed at the Ahfat College for Women
were exceptionally well educated by Sudanese standards. The hospital staffs fell somewhere in between.

A number of histories is presented herein (see Appendices I and
II). In reviewing the histories, one must be aware that a high percentage of them has been drawn from the only two groups of
women and men that are questioning the practice of female circumcision, and more specifically pharaonic circumcision at all: the educated and those working in some medical capacity. One encounters
among the cases presented, therefore, *far more* opposition to the
practice and more purported intentions not to circumcise or to do

---

1. Dr. Salah, as he is called, has since succumbed to the overwhelming frustrations involved in running a gynecological hospital in Sudan and to the lack of
support received from the government in his endeavors, and to their great loss has
joined the brain-drain into Saudi Arabia.

less drastic procedures than one would find in the population at large. The body of the population at large, to date, is not questioning the practice of female circumcision at all. To get a more representative overview of what is really going on in the country at large at this time, one must concentrate on the case histories of the uneducated, which make up the vast bulk of the population.

Although the general educational level in the population interviewed was far higher than that of the population at large, women of all educational levels are represented, having had anywhere between 0 and 19 years of schooling. The women ranged in age from 17 to 68. City, town, and village dwellers are represented among the women, city and town dwellers among the men.

Some women who were asked to serve as subjects did not agree to do so. Those who did agree, however, appeared to enjoy the interview and often asked questions themselves. No hostility was encountered. Only two interviews were terminated, when it became obvious that the woman felt she was treading on unsafe ground, which I interpreted as being due to some personal situation.

Some village women refused because they interpreted our request to talk about their circumcision to mean that we wanted to see it, and could not be persuaded that our intent was otherwise.

None of the men I approached refused to be interviewed.

The most salient feature noted in most of the women was what might best be described as their "survivor quality": a kind of stoic, indestructable, realistic good humor. One tale after another unravelled, each with its full measure of pain and suffering. Yet strangely, we laughed a great deal together as we exchanged our widely disparate information, and I often felt humbled in contemplation of their dignity, their insuppressible zest, their ability to experience joy, to express love, to speak of passion, and the amazing inner balance they projected.

About one-third of the interviews were held without a translator, which is to say, in English, with a smattering of Arabic. The remainder were conducted with various translators, of which two were English-trained Sudanese nurses (married and female), one a college graduate (unmarried and female) with no exposure to other cultures, and one social worker (unmarried and female) with no exposure to other cultures. Some of the interviews with men were conducted with the help of a Sudanese doctor (unmarried and male). This doctor also translated for three interviews with women. Even though I managed to learn enough Arabic to get by in the capital, the dialects in the outlying areas were so different and varied that it would have been inconceivable not to use a translator.

It is interesting to note that the quality of the answers obtained from the interviews essentially did not vary in each of the above described situations. When I asked one of the (educated) women for whom the male doctor translated how she was able to be so candid in the presence of a male, she replied: "Because he is my doctor."

In obtaining the information in the hospital series, a line of questioning was begun which became progressively more refined and precise as the study evolved. We would call a woman into the room and make her comfortable. She would have been told beforehand that the interview would deal with her circumcision and her marriage. The first few questions dealt with age, place of birth, years of education, circumcision age and type, and other surrounding circumstances. The first modification that we had to make was in defining the exact procedure she had undergone. Sudanese tend to give the name *sunna* to any procedure short of a complete pharaonic with pinhole infibulation. Also they do not have a clear picture of what a normal female organ looks like. The woman would therefore not be asked what type of circumcision had been done to her, but rather was asked to describe *what she had left*, and how large an opening was allowed to her.

In asking women what complications they had suffered as a result of their circumcision, I frequently received the answer that there had been none. Women generally were not able to ascribe their frequent health problems to circumcision, due to ignorance of a cause and effect relationship between the two. Another source of confusion was the definition of what was "normal." For example: When I asked whether there had been any problem with urination as a result of tight infibulation, I was frequently told that everything had been "normal." Then I changed the question to "How many minutes did it take you to urinate?" This resulted in the discovery that anything up to 15 minutes was considered to be completely normal. (Discrepancies in the time perception of unschooled village women are discussed in a later chapter.)

In order to determine areas of erogenous sensitivity, I asked "What parts of your body are the most sensitive?" Women would freely name nearly any part of their body, but the sex organs were never mentioned voluntarily. The question that followed then had to be: "What about the area of your scar?" and next: "What about inside?" This sequence was generally acceptable and elicited the desired information.

Some women insisted that there had been little or no pain involved in their circumcision. When this happened, I questioned the women more closely on other painful events in her life, and whether in the place she came from it was considered shameful to admit pain concerning circumcision. A variety of reasons appeared to exist, and generally more insight was obtained into the individual background for this rather strange response.

One of the chief reasons given for the practice of female circumcision is that it is believed to attenuate or abolish sexual desire in women. To test the veracity of this, I asked the question, "Do you ever ask your husband to have sex?" The answer was almost invariably an emphatic "No!" When asked why, the reason given was that it was "exceedingly shameful for a woman to do that." Somehow the strong "No!" often seemed to have a false ring to it, and often I was aware of a suppressed amusement. I was greatly puzzled and discussed the matter with my interpreters, who had received the same impression. Finally one of them suggested, "Ask them if they use smoke." I was unaware of what this meant until she took me to her home and showed me. She placed some pieces of sandalwood in a burner, and lighted them. Soon a fragrant smoke issued from the wood. When the flames died down, she took off all her clothes and squatted over the coals, wrapped in a tent-like blanket, while the smoke permeated her skin. She then rubbed herself all over with a strongly fragrant oil, and when she had finished, held out her arm and asked me to smell it. The odor was quite powerful. I remember having smelled it on many occasions, wherever there were women in Sudan. "That is what she does," I was told. "That is what we *all* do when we want intercourse with our husbands. When he smells that odor, he knows exactly what it means."

The question was thereafter changed to, "Do you use smoke and oil?" There was hardly a woman who did not admit to using them, after either some embarrassed or delighted laughter at my being "wise" to her. I made it clear that I was as ready to answer questions about myself and my own sexual life as I was to ask them about theirs, and after that, communications tended to flow. It was always the source of the greatest wonderment to them that I freely admitted to being completely uncircumcised, since everyone knew that only small children, mental defectives, and the daughters of prostitutes remained in such a state in Sudan. The first two were easy to eliminate but I was frequently asked if my mother had been a prostitute, and when I answered in the negative, I was asked why she had left me in such a state. Whenever a woman denied the use of the smoke ceremony, as well as any sexual interest or pleasure, other cues, such as a depressed demeanor and the total absence of laughter or even smiles, nearly always verified this.

When asking women whether they experienced orgasm, I got the impression that most knew exactly what I was asking about. After discussing intensity, frequency, and time required, I asked them to describe what they felt when they had orgasm. Although a good number were understandably at a loss to describe this, an even greater number obliged with some very telling and often colorful descriptions of what they experienced (see pp. 85-86.)

Men were not asked whether they had at any time in the process of penetrating their wives experienced impotence. Although in some cases it was quite evident that such failure to function had been likely, this could in no way be admitted by any man in that culture, especially to a woman, and the question was consequently omitted.

It is common knowledge in Sudan that women there, as in other places in the world, sometimes have sexual relations before marriage in spite of the rigid cultural taboo against this. In order to feign virginity, they have themselves refibulated by a midwife before marriage. It does not appear to be very common, however, and in any event it is not a practice that one might expect them to talk about. The females interviewed were confined, therefore, entirely to married women, and the questions asked dealt exclusively with sexual experiences they had had with their husbands. Further, no attempt was made to obtain information on extramarital experiences. Fortunately it was possible to interview a small number of women who had been married twice, and some very telling differences in the individual relationships and sexual experiences were noted, and are shown in Appendix I. Since the information received tends to be repetitive in nature, only a select number of interviews are presented in Appendices I and II.

I began my study with an assumption that circumcised women, particularly those who had been circumcised in the extreme, pharaonic fashion, would be incapable of a normal sexual response. How far afield this original supposition had been was brought home to me most forcibly by one unforgettable preliminary interview, which sent me thinking along totally different lines.

She was a woman of about 40, with a strong featured face and alert eyes that she kept in continuous, intense contact with mine as we talked. She gave the impression of intelligence, and told me that to her great regret, her father had allowed her to complete only two years of schooling. I began the interview with a series of questions on routine personal data. When I finished with these, I switched into a more personal line of questioning, and in the course of this asked her: "Are you able to enjoy sexual intercourse?" Until then the responses I had received to this question had frankly puzzled me. They were evasive and confusing. Some women showed amusement, others gave a pious denial which somehow did not ring true, some manifested honest sadness, others believable denial or even puzzlement.

This woman's eyes opened wide, and she gave an incredulous guffaw. What followed was a most amazing performance. She doubled up with laughter, began slapping her thighs, and finally fell off her seat onto the floor, where she continued to rock with explosive and uncontrollable laughter. My translator at first gaped at her, and when the woman attempted to gasp out an answer, started laughing wildly herself. Ultimately she, too, was wallowing on the floor with laughter, both of them shrieking and slapping at each other. Each utterance brought on renewed mirth. Finally I too was on the floor with both of them, laughing and hooting at I knew not what, trying to get some comprehension of the whole thing.

In the end, my translator calmed down sufficiently to enlighten me. "She says," she managed to gasp, "She says that you must be completely *mad* to ask her a question like that! She says: '*A body is a body*, and no circumcision can change that! No matter what they cut away from you — they cannot change that!' ''

It was a sobering experience in that it reminded me to remain aware at all times that I was interacting with real human beings with real lives and real relationships with a multitude of dimensions, not simply with female genitalia in various states of mutilation. I earnestly attempted to hone my sensitivities as a consequence, and began to revise a lot of my questions in the interviews and conversations that followed.

2. Female Circumcision
in African Countries in General,
and Sudan in Particular

ORIGINS

The practice of female circumcision dates back to antiquity, and although various theories have been advanced, its origins are obscure. Excision practices can be assumed to date back thousands of years, conceivably to the early beginnings of mankind. Quite conceivably also, circumcisions at some early point in human history replaced human sacrifices as a way of placating hostile forces and spirits. At what period these practices came into conjunction with the obsessive preoccupation with virginity and chastity that today still characterizes Islamic-Arabic cultures is not known, but infibulation clearly appears to be a result of that meeting.

Herodotus, the famous historian, reported female circumcision in ancient Egypt in the 5th century B.C. He was of the opinion that the custom originated in Ethiopia or Egypt, as it was being done by the Ethiopians as well as Phoenicians and Hittites (Taba, 1979).

A Greek papyrus in the British Museum dated 163 B.C. mentions circumcisions performed on girls at the age when they received their dowries. The Greek geographer Strabo further reported the custom in 25 B.C. when he journeyed to Egypt (Hosken, 1982a). He concluded that it was first performed on women of high caste and seems to have been an essential premarital rite. Mummies from an earlier period, thought by some to have been circumcised and infibulated (Huber, 1969), were actually not in a state of preservation that would lead to substantiation of that theory.

Various authors have shown that female circumcision was practiced as well by early Romans and Arabs. In some groups it appears to have been a mark of distinction, in others a mark of enslavement and subjugation.

While clitoridectomy appears to have been restricted to those of high social rank, infibulation, on the other hand, seems to have been reserved for slave girls, many of whom were transported from Sudan and Nubia (Widstrand, 1965). This was to prevent their getting pregnant. An infibulated virgin fetched a far higher price on the slave market.

From its probable origin in Egypt and the Nile valley, female circumcision is thought to have diffused to the Red Sea coastal tribes with Arab traders, and from there into eastern Sudan (Modawi, 1974). The first indisputable account of this comes from the historian Pietro Bembo, which was published posthumously in the early 1550s (Widstrand, 1965; Abdalla, 1982; Cloudsley, 1983). There are various reports on the practice of infibulation by a number of 18th century travelers, who reported its performance on slave girls by slave traders who traveled along the Nile (Widstrand, 1965; Cloudsley, 1983).

Available historical resources and anthropological findings can furnish us only with educated guesses on how the practices actually originated, and on whether there were one or several origins. It is impossible to do more than speculate, but in the many areas that are so water poor that they can in no way support even the minutest population increase (as for example in Darfur, the northwestern desert area of Sudan), it is not difficult to envision infibulation practices arising from a driving need for population control, which developed in conjunction with drought and desertization of formerly fertile areas.

It has also been theorized that the practice of excision resulted from primitive man's desire to gain mastery over the mystery of female sexual function. By excision of the clitoris, sexual freedom in women could be curbed and women were changed from common to private property, the property of their husbands alone. Excision, since it removed the organ most easily stimulated, was thought to reduce a woman's sexual desire. Giorgis (1981, p. 15) maintains that the origin of the practice can be traced to the patriarchal family system, which dictated that a woman could have only one husband although a man could have several wives. Along with other elaborate formal and informal sanctions, strong patriarchal systems fostered female circumcision, which restricted women's sexuality for the preservation of the male's lineage. To keep intact this monogamous system imposed on women, infibulation was performed not only on virgins but also on widows, divorcees, and women whose husbands were away on journeys (Saadawi, 1980, p. 39).

In ancient Egypt, girls could not marry, inherit property, or enter a mosque unless they were circumcised (Giorgis, 1981, p. 9). The Egyptian pharaonic belief in the bisexuality of the gods offers a further explanation:

> Now just as certain gods are believed to be bisexual, so every person is believed to be endowed with the masculine and feminine "souls". These "souls" reveal their respective physiological characteristics in and through the procreative organs. Thus the feminine "soul" of the man, so it is maintained, is located in the prepuce, whereas the masculine "soul" of the woman is situated in the clitoris. This means that as the young boy grows up and finally is admitted into the masculine society he has to shed his feminine properties. This is accomplished by the removal of the prepuce, the feminine portion of his original sexual state. The same is true with a young girl, who upon entering the feminine society is delivered from her masculine properties by having her clitoris or her clitoris and labia excised. Only thus circumcised can the girl claim to be fully a woman and thus capable of the sexual life. (Shaalan, 1982, p. 271)

GEOGRAPHIC DISTRIBUTION

The Sudan is Africa's largest country. The northern two-thirds of the country is generally referred to as Northern Sudan, and the remainder as Southern Sudan. There are tremendous differences in ethnic origin, culture, and religion between the two. The former is inhabited by Arabic-speaking tribes who are a mixture of the original Hamitic races and Arab migrants who came to the region bringing with them the Islamic culture from the Middle East. In appearance they are best described as black Arabs, in whom the interbreeding with Southern negroid tribes at some point in history is quite evident.

The South is inhabited by negroid tribes who were isolated until the massive slave trade of the 19th century. Christianity was spread in this area by missionaries at the beginning of the 20th century. Apart from a few localities in the South where intermarriage has occurred, female circumcision and infibulation are not practiced among these southern tribes.

Female circumcision as a practice is primarily an ethnic one, and has no relation to political boundaries. As people move back and forth across borders or migrate from one country to another, they carry their customs with them. Thus for example, the Rischaida, desert nomads in the Red Sea Province of Sudan who originally migrated from Saudi Arabia about 150 years ago, do not practice female circumcision even though the other inhabitants of Red Sea Province, and particularly the Hadendewah, perform a severe pharaonic. This is equally true in Kenya where the Luo, the country's second largest population group, do not practice circumcision (Kouba and Muasher, 1985, p. 97), whereas the Kikuyu, the largest group, as well as other smaller tribes practice excision. In the eastern part of Sudan the most severe types of infibulation are practiced by the Beja, Hadendewah, Beni Amir, Amarar, and Bushairiya tribes (Modawi, 1974; Hosken, 1982a; Dareer, 1982a). The Beja and Beni Amir tribes tend to circumcise girl babies between 7 and 40 days of age (Dareer, 1982b). The reasons given are that the infant "feels nothing" and that the wound heals quickly at that age.

In Western Sudan the Kinin tribe does not circumcise its females. However the Fellata, Hausa, and Fur, who previously practiced *Sunna* circumcision or did not circumcise at all, have recently adopted extreme forms of the operation. This has come about because of urbanization and increased contact or intermarriage with Arab Sudanese who practice pharaonic circumcision. The Nubians in Kordofan have behaved in a similar fashion. The Zaghawa and Shanabla tribes in the west practice the severest form of circumcision. In the latter a v-shaped cut is made below the introitus and the sides stitched together to give a very small hole. This type of circumcision is called "Khitan" (Dareer, 1982a).

In the predominantly Christian southern part of Sudan females are not circumcised, with the exception of a few localities where the inhabitants have come into contact with Arab traders, as for example in Wau (Shamma, 1949).

Estimates of the number of females of all ages in Africa who have been circumcised range from 30 million (Brisset, 1979) to 80 million (Hosken, 1982a) to 100 million (Gleviczy, 1980). Hosken, whose estimate is likely to be the most accurate, has done exhaustive research on the subject and is generally accepted as the foremost authority. At the 2.9 per annum population growth rate in Africa, as reported by the Population Reference Bureau in Washington, D.C., this would place the present figure closer to 94,000,000.

The practice of female circumcision is found across Africa in a broad, triangular east-west band that stretches from Egypt in the northeast and Tanzania in the southeast to Senegal in the west (see Map 1). Excision is practiced in the mountainous regions of Ethiopia (Hosken, 1982a). In Nigeria, the Ibo, Hausa, and Yoruba, that country's three main ethnic groups, also excise their females (McLean, 1980), as does most of Mali (Epelboin and Epelboin, 1979, p. 27). The majority of women are excised in Burkina Faso (Hosken, 1982a). Most population groups in Senegal also practice excision. Infibulation occurs especially in the Horn of Africa, namely in the lowlands of Ethiopia, Djibouti, Somalia, and Sudan. Somalis living in Ethiopia and northwestern Kenya also practice infibulation. It is known to exist also in Mali, Northern Nigeria, and Senegal (Hosken, 1982a).

In Sudan, where indigenous people do not practice circumcision at all in less than a third of the country, virtually all women in the affected remaining areas, constituting 85% of the female population of the country at large, are circumcised. Dareer (1982a, p. 1) found that in Sudan, out of a total sample of 3,210 women, 3,171 (98.8%) were circumcised, and only 39 (1.2%) were uncircumcised. Out of these, 2,636 (83.13%) were pharaonically circumcised, 386 (12.7%) had the intermediate or modified type, and only 80 had what they called "sunna." The remaining 69 could not be classified because they said they did not know which type they had undergone.

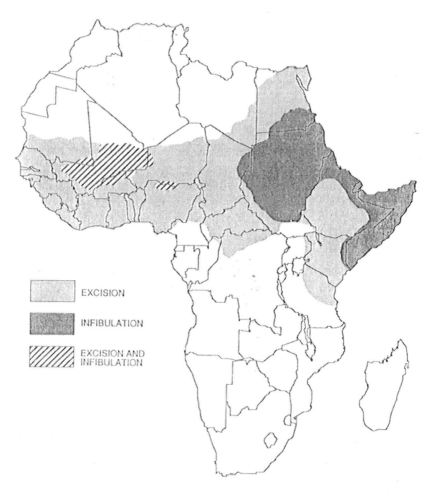

EXCISION

INFIBULATION

EXCISION AND
INFIBULATION

Map by Daniel V. Klein

THE PROCEDURES

Female circumcision is not to be equated with male circumcision, since it generally involves far more extensive damage to the sexual organs, and more often has far reaching effects on the health of the individuals subjected to it. Of the five types listed below, the first and least damaging type is the only exception (Verzin, 1975; Shandall, 1979; Hosken, 1982a).

* *Mild sunna*: the pricking, slitting, or removal of the prepuce of the clitoris, leaving little or no damage. *Sunna* is an Arabic word meaning "tradition."
* *Modified sunna*: the partial or total excision of the body of the clitoris.
* *Clitoridectomy/excision*: the removal of part or all of the clitoris as well as all or part of the labia minora. This operation often results in scar tissue that is so extensive that it occludes the vaginal opening. In Sudan this operation is also called *sunna*.
* *Infibulation/pharaonic circumcision*: consists of clitoridectomy and the excision of the labia minora as well as the inner layers of the labia majora. The raw edges are then sewn together with cat gut or made to adhere to each other by means of thorns. The suturing together is done so that the remaining skin of the labia majora will heal together and form a bridge of scar tissue over the vaginal opening. A small sliver of wood or straw is inserted into the vagina to prevent complete occlusion, and to leave a passage for urine and the menstrual flow.
* *Introcision*: the enlargement of the vaginal orifice by means of tearing it downward. This practice is common in Somalia.

While all of these types have been reported in Africa, excision and infibulation are by far the most commonly practiced forms.
To this list two more types that are of special importance in the Sudan should be added: (Modawi, 1974; Dareer, 1982a):

* *Intermediate*: a modification of the pharaonic circumcision, which consists of removal of the clitoris and part of the labia minora, leaving the labia majora intact. The introitus is then narrowed by suturing with cat gut. Local anesthetics and often antibiotics are used. Extreme forms of the intermediate type are often difficult to distinguish from the pharaonic type. Milder forms on the other hand are mistakenly called *sunna* by the Sudanese. There are two types: one is called *sunna kashfa* (uncovered *sunna*) where only the top or half of the clitoris is

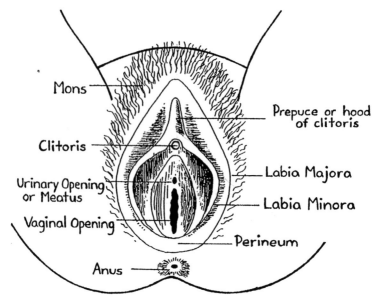

Mons

Prepuce or hood
of clitoris

Clitoris

Labia Majora

Urinary Opening
or Meatus

Labia Minora

Vaginal Opening

Perineum

Anus

FIGURE 1. Normal Female anatomy

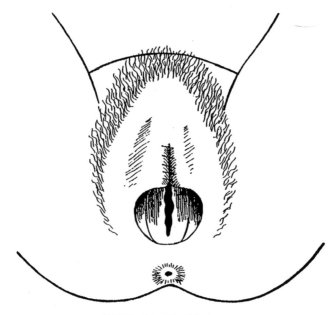

FIGURE 2. Modified *sunna*.

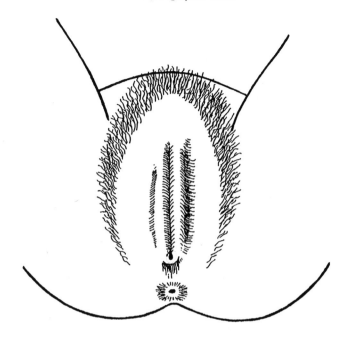

FIGURE 3. Pharaonic circumcision

excised. The second type is *sunna magatia* where in addition
to excision of the clitoris the surface of each lip of the labia
minora is roughened to allow the insertion of a few stitches,
causing the labia to heal together. In Khartoum this is also
referred to as "sandwich" among the midwife trade.

• *Recircumcision or refibulation*: Performed on women who
  have given birth, are widowed, or divorced, to simulate a virginal vagina. It is called *adla* (tightening) and is mostly performed on those women who have had a previous pharaonic or
  intermediate circumcision. The edges of the scar are pared and
  sewn together. Alternatively the loose redundant tissue around
  the fourchette is stitched (Dareer, 1982a). The end result is a
  tight introitus. Refibulation is sometimes also referred to as
  Adlat El Rujal (men's circumcision) because it is designed to
  create greater sexual pleasure for men.

Girls are now being circumcised at an early age in most African societies. There are a number of reasons for this. A younger girl is more easily controlled, and being unaware of what is going to happen to her, puts up no resistance. Koso-Thomas (1987, p. 23) comments that performance of the operation on a younger girl is said to be less psychologically traumatic. Some of these children cannot remember what it felt like, as the genitalia had not fully developed at the time of circumcision. Although memory of an event is hardly a valid measure of the amount of psychological trauma received, it is known that there is likely to be less damage to the genital area, as a small child can easily be forcibly held down to minimize her movement.

THE PRACTITIONERS

Traditional practitioners vary among different African ethnic groups. Most of the procedures are performed by traditional midwives. Apart from midwives, roving "gypsies" and "fortune tellers" also perform the operations (Assaad, 1980, p. 8). Among the Fula Bande of eastern Senegal, the traditional practitioners are old women of the blacksmith caste (Epelboin and Epelboin, 1979, p. 26). In northern Nigeria among the Hausa, barbers perform the surgery (Ogunmodede, 1979, p. 31). In northern Zaire, the traditional circumciser is a male "priest" (Kouba and Muasher, 1985, p. 100), and in Egypt both *dayas* (traditional midwives) and barbers perform circumcision (Assaad, 1980, p. 8). Instruments include razor blades, scissors, kitchen knives, and less frequently, pieces of glass. Antiseptic techniques and anesthesia are generally not employed, or for that matter known.

In an urban setting, and particularly among the elite, the procedures are now performed by doctors or trained nurses or midwives in a clinic-like setting, under sterile conditions, using anesthesia. Although this appears on the surface to be a far less dangerous and more humane way of performing these operations, Ismail (1982, p. 311) reports that when anesthesia is used, more tissue is apt to be cut away, as the child tends to struggle less.

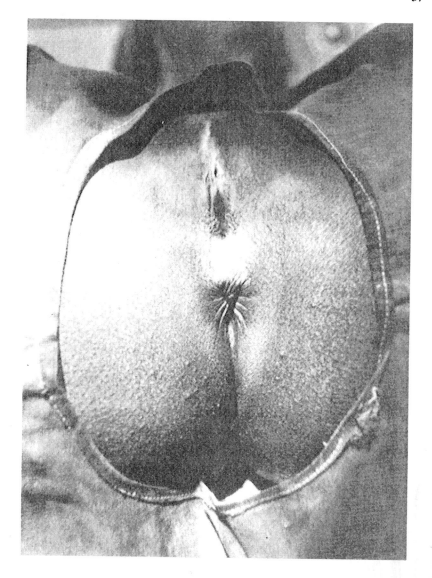

PHOTO 2.1. Genital-rectal area of a 25-year-old married woman, showing introitus, urethral opening, and pharaonic circumicison scar. This photo was taken after she had received general anesthesia in preparation for an exploratory operation. Her vaginal opening was too narrow and inelastic to permit the introduction of instruments needed to examine her internally.

RATIONALE

One might well ask why such a damaging practice continues unabated in the 20th century. The most common answer is that it is
simply custom, and everyone must bow to custom. The penalty for
defiance is total ostracism. Other reasons given for female circumcision seem to be consistent in most African societies, and are for
the most part based on myths, an ignorance of biological and medical facts, and religion.

Tribal myths justify the need for circumcision to distinguish the
sex of a child. The Dogon and Bambara of Mali believe that:

> When human beings first arrive in the world, they are both
> male and female and possess twin souls. The boy's "female
> soul" is in the prepuce, the female element of the genitals, and
> the girl's "male soul" is in the clitoris, the male element.
> From the moment of birth, the Bambara child is inhabited by
> the *Wanzo*, an evil power which is in his blood and skin, and a
> force of disorder within the individual. The *Wanzo* prevents
> fecundity. The prepuce and the clitoris, seats of the *Wanzo*,
> must be severed to destroy that malefic power. (Epelboin and
> Epelboin, 1979, p. 28)

The Bambara believe that the clitoris is poisonous, and will kill a
man if it comes in contact with his penis during intercourse (Epelboin and Epelboin, 1979, p. 28). The clitoris is considered unpleasant to both sight and touch, and it is a sign of maturity when an
Egyptian woman's "ugly genitalia" have been removed (Assaad,
1980, p. 6). The Mandingo believe that circumcision enhances fertility (Worsley, 1938, p. 690). Another common belief is that excision enlarges the vagina and makes childbearing easier (Kouba and
Muasher, 1985, p. 104). Actually the reverse is true. Among the
Ogbaru of Nigeria, tradition forbids uncircumcised women to deliver a baby, and they are therefore circumcised during their first
pregnancy, often complicating birth with severe hemorrhage and
genital infection.

Koso-Thomas (1987, p. 9) points out that it is often argued that
circumcision maintains good health in a woman. Evidence is often
quoted of girls who were always sick, but after being circumcised

became healthy, hale, and hearty. When circumcised women do fall ill, it is assumed that this is brought on by supernatural causes. Moreover, circumcision is often credited with healing powers. It is claimed to have cured women suffering from melancholia, nymphomania, hysteria, insanity, and epilepsy, as well as kleptomania and proneness to truancy. Dareer (1982a) reports that in rural areas of Western Sudan, if a girl is ill and not gaining weight she is assumed to have the "worm disease." Female circumcision is believed to cure this malady by releasing the worm.

The notion that female circumcision of any kind increases male sexual pleasure is widespread among the populace in both Sudan and Egypt (Ammar, 1954). Among the people of Nigeria it is widely believed that the clitoris is an aggressive organ and that, should the baby's head touch it during delivery, such a baby will die or develop a hydrocephalic head (Oduntan and Onadeko, 1984, p. 98). In some areas of Sudan and Ethiopia it is thought that if the female genitalia are not removed, they will dangle between the legs like a man's. The Tagouana of the Ivory Coast believe that a nonexcised woman cannot conceive. The clitoris is said to interfere with a woman's menstruation, impregnation, and childbirth. In Burkina Faso it is believed that it has the power to render men impotent (Hosken, 1982a, p. 2).

The Yoruba practice excision as a form of contraception. They believe that sperm may enter into a nursing mother's milk and cause harm to the child. They maintain that excision enables the nursing mother to abstain from sex, so that she avoids having her milk contaminated (McLean, 1980, p. 7). In many African countries, a woman who is not excised is considered illegitimate and cannot inherit money, cattle, or land (Hosken, 1982a, p. 3). Even more compelling, uncircumcised females of the East African Nandi know that their children will be strangled (Lenzi, 1970).

Circumcision serves not only to protect a woman from aggressive males, but to protect her from her own sexuality. The belief that uncircumcised women cannot help but exhibit an unbridled and voracious appetite for promiscuous sex is prevalent in all societies that practice female circumcision (Giorgis, 1981, p. 17). "To keep the young girl pure and the married woman faithful, genital operations are maintained as one of Africa's most valued traditions'' (Ogun-modede, 1979, p. 30).

Female circumcision is reputed by many to enhance fertility. (People, 1978, p. 28) Children are one of the few resources that women control in male-dominated societies. The high rate of infant mortality in Africa — 250 deaths per 1,000 live births in some areas (draft report of the Meeting on Women and Family, Health, 1978), and an even higher rate during the first years of life — has compelled women to have as many children as possible to ensure the survival of a few. Fertility is therefore extremely important to women, and they subject themselves and their daughters to procedures that they believe will ensure it.

Female circumcision and infibulation are also viewed as a way of socializing female fertility. Boddy (1982, p. 695) argues that women are not so much preventing their own sexual pleasure as enhancing their own femininity. Circumcision brings the fertility potential of women sharply into focus by dramatically de-emphasizing their sexuality. Thus women insist on circumcision for their daughters in order to assert their indispensability as the potential mothers of men, rather than being mere sex objects or servants. In these highly segregated Islamic societies, women do not achieve social recognition by becoming more like men, but by becoming less like men physically, sexually, and socially (Assaad, 1982). In these societies women are able to advance their social positions only by giving birth to sons. An uncircumcised woman who has not been "purified" and is thus unable to marry may not bear legitimate children and attain a position of respect in her old age.

Several studies in recent years have shown some of the firmly held beliefs associated with female circumcision to be without foundation. It has long been reputed by African men that gross clitoral hypertrophy is common among African women, and that they have correspondingly insatiable sexual appetites. Hosken reports that thousands of Ethiopian women examined in family planning clinics revealed no such clitoral hypertrophy. Nor have the many African women who have not submitted to circumcision in recent years exhibited bizarre sexual behavior (Hosken, 1982a, p. 26).

Koso-Thomas (1987, p. 11) reports that she interviewed 50 urban women in Sierra Leone who had had sexual experience before circumcision. She found that none of these women were able to reach the level of satisfaction they had known before circumcision, and were unaware before the interview that this deficiency was a result of circumcision. During these interviews she was told of women who had striven to find the ideal partner through trial and error until they had lost their husbands and their homes. Koso-Thomas comments that it seems ironic that the operation intended to eliminate promiscuity in fact could have the opposite effect.

Megafu (1983) finds that premarital coitus among the Nigerian Ibos is on the rise in almost equal proportions among circumcised as well as uncircumcised women, and he speculates that Western influences are likely to be the cause of this change in sexual behavior for both groups.

Karim and Ammar (1965) studied circumcised women in Egypt and found that female circumcision did not seem to decrease sexual desire, but it did affect orgasmic ability. Megafu's study of the Nigerian Ibos (1983) also concluded that the sexual urge is not necessarily impaired by removal of the clitoris.

THE ROLE OF RELIGION

The custom of female circumcision does not appear to have originated in Islam, but was accepted by it. Hansen (1972/73, p. 19) believes clitoridectomy to be an original African institution adopted by Islam at the conquest of Egypt in 742 A.D. The Prophet Mohammed is reputed to have attempted to ameliorate the harshness of the custom at around this same time, but without success.

Islam's stern emphasis on chastity and its general suppression of sexuality have no doubt provided a fertile ground for the development of the extreme excisions and most of all the infibulations that characterize the Sudanese pharaonic. It is nonetheless worth noting the virtual absence of female circumcision in most Islamic countries today. In 80% of the Islamic world today, the practice is unknown, notably also in Saudi Arabia and Iran. In Egypt it is largely confined to the Nile valley, suggesting a Pharaonic rather than Islamic origin. It is found to a lesser extent as well among other religious groups, such as Animists, African Coptic Christians, and a small sect of Ethiopian Jews, the Fallashas, many of whom have recently emigrated to Israel.

As in all religions, different factions in Islam hold different beliefs. Thus Assad points out (1980, p. 14) that although Islam does not condone female circumcision, the official position of Islamic jurists in the countries that practice it is as follows:

> Female circumcision is an Islamic tradition mentioned in the tradition of the Prophet, and sanctioned by Imams [religious leaders] and Jurists in spite of their differences on whether it is a duty of *sunna* (tradition). We support the practice and sanction it in view of its effect on attenuating the sexual desire of women and directing it to desirable moderation.

She also points out that the custom was perpetuated by such Moslems because it strengthens their control on virginity and chastity.

Female circumcision is mentioned nowhere in the Koran, but since the predominantly illiterate population of Sudan is largely ignorant of the precepts of its own religion, most people believe the pharaonic to be one of its demands. Nor is the incorporation of primitive custom into the prevailing religion in Sudan unique to that country alone. In Kenya, where clitoridectomy is practiced among tribes that have been converted to Christianity, the custom has also assumed religious significance. Young girls submit to the mutilation at puberty in the full belief that if they do not, they will be condemned to eternal hell fire. The teachings of missionaries in Africa, although well meaning, have often succeeded only in reinforcing existing practices and in providing a more clear-cut ground on which to base the reasons for these practices.

It is known that in Ethiopia in the 16th century, when missionaries tried to stop the rites among their converts, all the men refused to marry girls that were not circumcised. Circumcision was eventually allowed again on the urgent advice of Rome, so that the ground gained by the missionaries would not be lost as converts failed to marry and reproduce (Baasher, 1982, p. 176). Reports indicate that some medical missionaries now clitoridectomized tribal women in hospitals under aseptic conditions, using anesthesia (Hosken, 1977/78, p. 494).

CIRCUMCISION AND THE LAW

In recent colonial history, Sudan was jointly ruled by England and Egypt. In 1946 a British law forbade all forms of female sexual mutilation. This law proved not only ineffectual, but actually caused a political backlash under the leadership of Mahmud Mohammed Taha against colonial control. The population promptly pharaonized its daughters, many still in infancy and with a considerable number of fatalities. In 1956 Sudan shook off colonial control, and in 1974 passed its own law forbidding the pharaonic procedure. Excision of the clitoris remained permissible under this law.

Gains made to the civil rights of women are never on a very stable footing in Africa, and are apt to suffer reversals at any time. I interviewed the aforementioned Mahmud Mohammed Taha, spiritual leader of the Republican Brothers, a progressive Islamic sect, in 1983. He described the philosophy of his group as total spiritual enlightenment for *all* members of Islam, regardless of sex. Once such enlightenment was attained, he was convinced that humanitarian social reform would follow. Although Taha's philosophy attracted a number of dedicated followers, it was not very popular. In 1984 President Numeiri of Sudan reinstated the reactionary Shariah laws (quite possibly to ingratiate himself with Saudi Arabia, where these laws are rigidly adhered to), which reinstated public executions and punitive cutting off of hands, and which revoked whatever legislation had been passed guaranteeing civil rights to women in Sudan. Taha was thrown into prison, and early in 1985 he was publically hanged for his heretical views. Shortly thereafter, President Numeiri was deposed in a bloodless coup, when he was not readmitted to his country after a visit with President Reagan.

Pharaonic circumcision in Sudan continues unabated. Youseff (1973) observes, "In Sudan, the laws against infibulation have not been obeyed because the custom is still an integral, positive-functioning component of the familial complex, and so, indirectly of the entire socio-cultural system."

In Egypt in 1959, a resolution by the Minister of Health recommended that partial clitoridectomy performed by doctors take the place of the more extreme procedures performed by the *dayas* (midwives). Another resolution in 1978 forbade *dayas* to perform the operations (Hosken, 1982a). The practices have continued unchanged.

Kenya has a long, bitter history of colonial British opposition to circumcision. Recently, President Daniel Moi, successor to Kenyatta, who favored circumcision practices, has taken a strong stand against the rites. In July 1982 he condemned them and stated that "whoever will be found committing the act or encouraging it will be prosecuted." Calling it a money-making scheme, he advised Kenyans to maintain cultural values that are beneficial and to discard those that are useless (*Nairobi Times*, 1982). Moi's position has not been implemented, however, and the Kenyan government has now recognized the need for a slower approach which utilizes "tact and prudence" (Kouba and Muasher, 1985, p. 105).

The greatest stumbling block to those working toward the abolition of what they recognize to be a medically disastrous and inhumane practice is the fact that these procedures are performed by families in the firm belief that what they are doing is good and necessary and in the child's as well as the family's best interests. Thus laws forbidding female circumcision, even if they are chartered by African governments, cannot be enforced if they are ignored by the entire population and there is no one to implement them.

Nonetheless, it must be realized that such a law is not without some potential for bringing about change where the desire to abandon the practice already exists. It can certainly be invoked successfully in instances where a girl's parents do not wish to circumcise her but are bitterly opposed by members of the older generation in their decision. Since there is a fair number of instances on record where grandmothers took it upon themselves to circumcise a girl in the absence of her parents, such actions must be guarded against by the enlightened parent. Invoking the law and threatening all members of the family with jail should the girl be circumcised against the parents' wishes may be a drastic measure, but it has already been effective in a number of cases.

It should also be realized that such laws present a double-edged sword, and may in far more cases be self-defeating since it might prevent parents from bringing their damaged daughters to a medical installation when things go wrong after a badly managed circumcision. The child may bleed to death in preference to the parents' naming the perpetrator and facing subsequent ostracism. In Sudan, where such a law exists, girls are only very rarely brought to medical installations for repair. This is not so in countries where such a law does not exist. Assaad (1979, p. 12) points out that legislation in Egypt has driven the practice underground in that country as well. She voices the opinion that it would have been better not to legislate against the custom since complications such as hemorrhage, which have become commonplace, now cannot be reported.

AFRICAN NATIONALS IN EUROPE

In European countries a number of cases have recently come to the attention of authorities and there are unquestionably far more that have not been detected. Some of these have been the offspring of African diplomats residing in European countries who have been circumcised by European surgeons at the request of African parents. Others have been the children of laborers who have undergone the rite in the home at the hands of some medically unskilled member of the family.

Instances of genital operations performed on the daughters of African immigrants have been reported in Sweden and Italy, and excisors are being brought from Senegal and Mali to operate on African girls residing in France (McLean, 1980, p. 6). In London private doctors have admitted that they perform clitoridectomies on immigrants at fees as high as $1,700 (*Newsweek*, 1982).

As African "guest workers" continue to pour into Europe, there can be little doubt that the number of female circumcisions performed there increases proportionally. The effect on female offspring that are the product of mixed marriages between Africans and Europeans is a matter for conjecture and is becoming a matter of concern. The problem has become sufficiently alarming in Europe so that Sweden, England, Denmark, and Norway have proposed legislation prohibiting these procedures to be performed there. Other European countries are also considering remedial laws to stop the practice within their jurisdiction.

3. Sudan:
The Current Situation

CIRCUMCISION IN SUDAN TODAY

The World Health Organization conference in February 1979 held in Khartoum, the capital of Sudan, was attended primarily by health officials active in those countries where female circumcision is practiced. These participants unanimously condemned the mutilations as disastrous to women's health and as indefensible on medical as well as humane grounds.

Contrary to what generally was believed by those few Westerners who knew about the practice at all, female circumcision is being carried out not only in remote areas of the bush or among primitive desert tribes, but also in the cities and capitals of those countries. It is carried out at all levels of society—from the elite class, the intelligentsia, and professional classes on down to the simplest villager.

Baasher (1977) comments: "Although many families doubt the ethical role which female circumcision may play in the control of sexual desire, they readily perform the operation in order to conform to the social milieu and spare their daughters the contempt which may be shown by the more conservative members of the community." In Egypt things are much the same, as Assaad (1982) describes them: "Motivated by love and concern for their daughters' future, well meaning women have perpetuated the custom and have inflicted much pain and suffering on their daughters out of a firm belief in the physical and moral benefits of this operation as the sure guarantee of marriage and consequent economic and social security."

Some of the Sudanese health officials, midwives, and other citizens voiced the opinions that things have changed considerably since the passing of the 1974 law against pharaonic circumcision, and that educated people are now making only token scratches on their daughters, or leaving them entirely uncut. A study by Modawi (1974) reported that the practice is rapidly approaching extinction. But predictions of even greater imminent change were contradicted by two European woman doctors practicing in Sudanese cities. Things are essentially the same as before, reported Munk of Port Sudan and Williams of Khartoum (1979, 1981, 1983). They found that even their Sudanese medical colleagues were circumcising their daughters as before, and they did not recall ever examining any Sudanese female patients over the age of 11 who had not been circumcised pharaonically, or at best in the modified fashion. They assert that a researcher can count on finding good intentions, wishful thinking, rationalizations, self-deception, and outright lies, but not actual change.

Dr. Salah Abu Bakr (1981), director and chief of gynecology at Bulluk Hospital in Omdurman, corroborates that instances of noncircumcision and noninfibulation are still exceedingly rare. This was further substantiated by my personal inspection of women at a number of hospitals and clinics, and by the testimony of two Italian nun nurses and an Indian nurse midwife, all of whom had been in practice for a number of years in various gynecological wards in Sudan.

In point of fact, the practice is actually spreading or has already spread into indigenously populated areas in southern and western Sudan, as these territories become progressively Arabized. As unschooled Islamic people who erroneously believe female circumcision to be part of their religion spread into these indigenous areas, they bring with them their customs which are eventually adopted by the less socially and economically advantaged indigenous population in order to make their daughters more marriageable. When these are asked why they have adopted this practice they reply that it is the "modern and hygienic" way that educated people do it. In the manner of all *nouveaux* they not only imitate the settlers, but perform the most extreme type of the pharaonic known in all of Sudan. They refer to their version of the procedure as "scraping the girls clean," and they do in fact leave nothing, not even skin.

The spread of the practice is so complete that I found that in the city of Nyala in the west of Sudan, where the pharaonic was completely unknown 50 years ago, it now saturates the area completely. The same is true of the somewhat more remote town of Nyertete where it was first introduced 20 years ago and where all of the population now practice it.

To understand why such a practice is so readily adopted, one must be aware that other mutilating practices exist in much of Africa to this day, and there is already a pre-existing tendency to modify the body surgically. Facial tribal scarring is practiced on both men and women in all of Sudan and usually takes the characteristic form of three vertical strips of flesh gouged deeply from the cheeks, beginning just below the lower eyelid and running the length of the cheek to the jaw line. These markings were called "one-eleven" scars by the British colonials because of their characteristic configuration. Other types are found less commonly, notably the characteristic vertical scarring of the forehead among the Dinka in south Sudan, and the "*E*" configuration in the west.

Among the superficially Westernized youth in Khartoum today, facial scarring has fallen somewhat into disrepute and when it is not altogether abandoned, three small token cuts at the temples usually take the place of the dramatic and drastic one-eleven scars. The scarring practice differs from ritual circumcision in at least two major ways. It is *highly visible* and it is *optional*, or at least has become so in recent years. For women it was formerly considered a sign of great beauty to be thus marked and when a girl now opts not to have her face scarred, it is no shame to the family. The girl is merely considered to have forfeited a degree of beauty. Blue tatooing of women's lower lips, also considered a mark of beauty but in fact a way of desensitizing yet another erogenous zone, seems to fall into a similar category and is now seen less frequently, particularly among educated young women.

Where circumcision *which is invisible to the public eye* is concerned, conservative forces appear to be gaining steadily. This is unequivocally related in Sudan to the massive "brain drain" of trained medical personnel and other intellectual resources into Saudi Arabia. Saudi Arabia offers trained individuals more than tenfold the personal economic rewards obtainable within their own countries. It is not surprising to discover that the entire graduating class of Ahfat University in Omdurman accepted jobs in Saudi Arabia in 1983 without a single exception! At the University of Khartoum, the country's only other university, a similar situation exists.

The brain drain firmly places medical services for women into the hands of medically untrained midwives, the very people who stand to gain the most by perpetuating the severest and most damaging of these procedures. The economic significance of the practice to these people cannot be overemphasized.

It has been recently reported that in Uganda, which borders on Sudan, still another spread of pharaonic circumcision is taking place in areas that have traditionally not circumcised women. Militant Africans have returned to Uganda from exile with a new awareness of their culture and are seeking to preserve those African customs and folk ways that are rapidly disappearing in the wake of progressively advancing Westernization. The aspects of Western culture supplanting the African ones are of a very low order and the concern of the aforementioned Africans can readily be understood. As the positive old ways and customs rapidly disappear, these individuals tend to cast an eye around them, looking for endangered African customs they wish to preserve. In Uganda, they do not have to look very far—no farther than to their neighbor, Sudan. Pharaonic circumcision has been introduced into Ugandan areas in this fashion, and again it is the elite class that is introducing it. In its usual fashion, it is spreading in its most extreme form. A recent newspaper report from Germany states that in areas of Uganda adolescents of both sexes have tried to escape the rites by fleeing their villages, and that they are being hunted down systematically by the village elders.

While some areas of Africa appear to be regressing alarmingly, there is cause for some possible optimism for the future of others. While little or no change toward the abandonment of this damaging custom seems to be in evidence in Sudan so far, the psychological climate in the capital certainly gives some evidence of change, if only among the educated. Those who oppose the practice are hopeful that this will be translated into action in the future.

A Sudanese conference on female circumcision under the auspices of the Babiker Bedri Foundation for Women's Studies was held in Khartoum in 1981, at the time when interviews for my study were being conducted. The conference once more unequivocally denounced all forms of female circumcision as harmful and unnecessary. Television coverage of this event reached that small segment of the population having access to a television set. Women interviewed shortly after this event tended to state that their intentions toward their as yet uncircumcised daughters had been changed in the direction of less drastic circumcision or no circumcision at all on the basis of the information they received. Whether the vast distance between intention and action will be successfully bridged remains to be seen.

Only two instances of an actual, clear-cut recession of the practice have been reported in all of Africa. They do not involve Sudan, but they are of interest here. In the long-standing conflict between Ethiopia and Eritrea along Sudan's border an area is involved where it has been customary to circumcise girls at the beginning of puberty. Here, all the young girls chose to join the Eritrean People's Liberation Front, which opposes female circumcision, and this removed them from their villages and family for some time. When they returned, they all refused to be circumcised. Within 5 years the practice was totally eradicated in that area and has not returned.

This type of phenomenon would unfortunately be possible only where the girl has a viable option and is not too young to take advantage of it. As evidence indicates that regardless of where they occur, the procedures are now being conducted at an earlier and earlier age for the simple reason that "girls are more easily managed when they are too small to put up much resistance," for the Sudanese girl who is pharaonically circumcised between the ages of 4 and 8 years, no such option exists.

From Nigeria, Megafu (1983) reports that among the Ibos a definite decline in the rate of circumcision is in evidence. He found that his sampling of 140 women between the ages of 36 and 45 showed 85% to be circumcised. By contrast, this percentage had dwindled to 33% among a sampling of 120 females between the ages of 16 and 25. The reasons for this decline are not entirely clear, but Megafu speculates that Western influences are of great significance.

Koso-Thomas (1987, p. 36) also claims that in Sierra Leone urban areas "most men will now marry uncircumcised women in cases where the marriage is no longer prearranged by their families.'∮In rural areas marriages are still prearranged and the bride must be circumcised.

THE PROCEDURES AND THEIR CONSEQUENCES

Circumcision practices for both sexes worldwide are many and vary greatly. They can be summarized as follows (Money, 1981, p. 251):

> Alteration or mutilation of healthy body organs may be designated as cosmetic or stigmatic. It may be achieved by binding, amputating, scarifying, piercing, cutting, burning and tatooing. It may be performed ritually, abusively, punitively or electively. Genital alteration in the male includes gonadectomy, penectomy, subincision, circumcision and piercing; and in the female infibulation . . . clitoridectomy, clitoral circumcision and piercing.

The following sections will deal primarily with pharaonic circumcision of females as it is practiced in Sudan. Clitoridectomy practices in Western countries as well as male circumcision will be discussed in later chapters.

In Sudan circumcisions are generally carried out on girls between the ages of 4 and 8, although they may occur as young as 2 and as old as 11 years of age when they are performed on several girls in a family at the same time. The illegal procedures are generally performed by trained midwives in cities or towns or by untrained elderly woman in the villages and settlements. When families cannot pay for their daughters' circumcisions, the operation is performed as a social service by anyone who will do it.

The procedure is described by various observers (David, 1978; Villeneuve, 1937 [see McLean, 1980]; Lantier, 1972). There are minor variations depending on the territory where it takes place, but essentially the procedure is much the same wherever it is practiced. The following takes place in Djibouti, near the eastern Sudanese border (McLean, 1980):

❋ The little girl, entirely nude, is immobilized in the sitting position on a low stool by at least three women. One of them with her arms tightly around the little girl's chest; two others hold the child's thighs apart by force, in order to open wide the vulva. The child's arms are tied behind her back, or immobilized by two other women guests. The traditional operator says a short prayer: "Allah is great and Mohammed is his Prophet. May Allah keep away all evils." Then she spreads on the floor some offerings to Allah: split maize, or, in the urban areas, eggs. Then the old woman takes her razor and excizes the clitoris. The infibulation follows: the operator cuts with her razor from top to bottom of the small lip and scrapes the flesh from the inside of the large lip. This nymphectomy and scraping are repeated on the other side of the vulva. The little girl howls and writhes in pain, although strongly held down. The operator wipes the blood from the wound, and the mother, as well as the guests, "verify" her work, sometimes putting their fingers in. The amount of scraping of the large lips depends on the "technical" ability of the operator. The opening left for urine and menstrual blood is miniscule. Then the operator applies a paste and ensures the adhesion of the large lips by means of an acacia thorn, which pierces one lip and passes through into the other. She sticks in three or four in this manner down the vulva. These thorns are then held in place either by means of sewing thread or with horsehair. Paste is again put on the wound. But all this is not sufficient to ensure the coalescence of the large lips, so the little girl is then tied up from her pelvis to her feet; strips of material rolled up into a rope immobilize her legs entirely. Exhausted, the little girl is then dressed and put on a bed. The operation lasts from fifteen to twenty minutes according to the ability of the old woman and the resistance put up by the child. ❋

In an urban setting this procedure is nowadays mitigated by locally injected analgesic, which may or may not ameliorate the immediate pain somewhat, but can hardly be adequate with such extensive surgery. A more modern variation of the procedure is reported by Boddy (1982), taking place in northern Sudan:

The girl is lying on [a native bed], her body supported by several adult kinswomen. Two of these hold her legs apart. Then she is administered a local anesthetic by injection. In the silence of the next few moments [the midwife] takes a pair of what looks to me like children's paper scissors and quickly cuts away the girl's clitoris and labia minora. . . . Then she takes a surgical needle from her midwife's kit, threads it with suture, and sews together the labia majora, leaving a small opening at the vulva. After a liberal application of antiseptic, it is all over. The young girl seems to be experiencing more shock than pain and I wonder if the anesthetic has finally taken effect.

She further recounts the procedure as it was practiced before this same midwife received government training in midwifery in 1969:

A circular palm mat with its center removed was so placed that it fit over a freshly dug hole in the ground. The girl was made to sit on the mat at the edge of the hole. Her adult female relatives held her arms and legs while the midwife, using no anesthetic and having no apparent concern for sterile procedure scraped away all of the external genitalia, including the labia majora, using a straight razor. Then she pulled together the skin that remained on either side of the wound and fastened it with two thorns inserted at right angles. These last were held in place by thread or bits of cloth wound around their ends. (Fresh acacia thorns produce numbness when they pierce the skin, and may have helped to relieve the pain.) A straw or a reed was also inserted, posteriorly, so that when the wound healed there would be a small opening in the scar tissue to allow for elimination of urine and menstrual blood. The girl's legs were then bound together, and she was made to lie on the [bed] for a month or more to promote healing. . . . When the wound was thought to have healed sufficiently, the thorns were removed and the girl unbound.

This older version of the procedure is what still takes place in towns and villages. Hayes (1975) reports that her investigation in 1970 revealed that the circumcision ceremony was still basically the same as those described above. My own research between 1979 and 1983 corroborates this. Parenthetically I would also agree with her comment that the Muslim custom of washing the genital and rectal area after defecating and urinating, rather than wiping with tissue or other material, probably has high survival value where circumcision is concerned.

Doctors do not admit to performing the operations, but there is little question that in quite a few cases among the privileged they are able to collect high fees for performing circumcisions under optimum conditions, and so of course they do. In view of the Sudanese law forbidding pharaonic circumcision, the doctor's position in regard to the authorities resembles the position of doctors in some Western countries previous to the passage of laws making abortions legal, or in those where no such laws yet exist. Those who can afford the fee can generally find a doctor willing to perform this service. The doctor's ethical position is clearly vindicated. He performs a highly demanded service with a minimum of risk to the patient, on whom it would be performed in any event. Trained nurses and doctors often willingly perform a slightly less drastic operation, with the clear knowledge that in doing so they save the child from a complete pharaonic.

Much more often the procedure is performed by midwives who have been trained in the techniques, or if those are unavailable or unaffordable, by untrained midwives. Dr. Bakr, Director of Bulluk Gynecological Hospital in Omdurman, informs me that every single member of his nursing and midwifery staff performs circumcisions and recircumcisions on the side and he describes in detail the exact procedures that each of them specializes in (1981).

The very poor, which is to say most of the people, find anyone with some purported skill or experience, or none at all. Sometimes it is even done by a member of the family who takes the task upon herself with no knowledge whatsoever of anatomy. Mostly it is done under totally unhygienic conditions, with inadequate lighting, and at the hands of old women with imperfect or failing eyesight.

Whoever performs the circumcision, whether licensed doctor or aging midwife, is able to rest assured that if anything goes wrong, the family will not reveal the operator to the authorities. Everything possible is done to protect her from exposure and punishment. A child's death is simply accepted as the will of Allah and never questioned.

It is difficult to determine the number of fatalities directly attributable to circumcision. Sudanese doctors variously tend to estimate that between 10% and 30% of fatalities occur in the country at large, particularly in the outlying areas where trained practitioners are nonexistent and antiseptic procedures unknown. It is impossible to get accurate information since the procedures are illegal and no one will admit to having a child die in this way.

It is reported that in Tanzania, the village woman performing circumcisions operates on as many as 100 girls per day during the holidays (Eresund, 1979, p. 12). A similar situation exists in other areas as well. It is hardly likely that under such conditions sterile procedure of any sort can be observed or bad mistakes due to haste avoided.

Dareer's study (1982a, p. 28) shows that 84.5% of cases needing medical intervention were unreported. (In trekking through the country and outlying areas, one receives the overall impression of a rather low ratio of females to males. This is only a personal impression and hard to prove, since women in an Islamic society are not very visible outside of the home. The exorbitant bride price or dowry required of a man before he is able to marry, of which I have heard so many Sudanese bachelors complain, would tend to lend some substance to this observation, however.)

In Sudan in 1981, I found that over 90% of approximately 300 women between the ages of 15 and 71 interviewed and/or personally inspected in delivery rooms and operating theaters were pharaonically circumcised. The remaining 9% or so comprised mostly upper-class women from relatively educated families who had been subjected to a variety of less drastic procedures. Class structure in Sudan as in other parts of the world is defined largely by education, position, and wealth. The vast majority of people is totally unschooled. When we speak of upper-class Sudanese, therefore, we are referring to those few government officials, professionals, and moneyed people who have attended a university, who generally have had some experience with the West, and their families.

Even for those less drastically mutilated women, spontaneous infibulation may nonetheless occur when the wound adheres to itself after excision, particularly after extensive cutting has been done. Although unintentional, the results of a spontaneous infibulation are identical to where the woman has been sewn.

Of the women I interviewed, more than 50% had been circumcised without any form of analgesic. The remainder had received local analgesic injections. Since most of the women interviewed were of urban origin, it must be assumed that among the population at large, the percentage of women receiving such anesthesia would be far less, since medication in general is not available in outlying areas.

Immediate health complications following circumcision take the form of infection, hemorrhage, shock, septicemia, tetanus, retention of urine due to occlusion, trauma to adjacent tissues, and psychic trauma. Antibiotics are available only in cities.

A study by Koso-Thomas (1987, p. 29) finds that 83% of all females undergoing circumcision are likely to be affected by some condition requiring medical attention at some time during their life in Sierra Leone, where excision is practiced. In countries like Sudan where infibulation is also performed, this percentage is unquestionably even higher.

The manner of walking of the infibulated woman is quite distinctive and easily recognizable. She shuffles slowly and painfully, barely lifting her legs at all, and sliding her feet along the ground. From the women themselves one learns that the consequences of the operation are with them throughout their lives. Nearly all of them reported difficulty with urination until the infibulation was forced open at marriage. The average period of time required by a pharaonically circumcised virgin to urinate, as reported by women, is 10 to 15 minutes. She must force the urine out drop by drop. Some women reported requiring up to half an hour, and one woman said that it used to take her 2 hours to empty her bladder at the end of the day. Kidney and urinary tract infections appear often. Infected implantation dermoid cysts are common. Spontaneous occlusion necessitating reopening of the aperture occurs frequently, and in some cases repeatedly. Nearly all infibulated women reported agonizingly painful menstruations, in which the menstrual flow is all but totally blocked, resulting in a build-up of clotted blood behind the infibulation, frequently requiring surgical intercession.

Because of the blockage, it generally takes 10 or more days to complete a menstruation. Quite apart from the physical pain involved, the girl is psychologically disabled for this period each month. Her embarrassment at the odor of discharging long pent-up menstrual blood is so acute that she generally does not leave her house during this period. The implications for her prospects in attaining an education or possibly even a job are not promising. In point of fact, very few women hold jobs, even among the educated classes in the capital.

At marriage, the infibulation must be forced open by her husband, who often finds it impossible to do so, even with the aid of "the little knife." Scarring and keloid formation are often so massive and hardened that even surgical scissors are not adequate to the task. One Sudanese doctor cited a case of a 20-year-old woman who was brought to his office after 2 years of marriage, during which the husband had vainly tried to penetrate her infibulation. The doctor said he broke three surgical blades in the attempt to open her vagina before he finally succeeded with a very strong pair of scissors. Many doctors report similar cases. It is the type of story that one hears over and over again, with only minor variations.

Of the women interviewed, 15% volunteered that penetration of their infibulation proved to be impossible to their husbands, and that they were opened surgically upon presenting themselves at a medical installation to be delivered of their first child, impregnation having been possible in spite of the infibulation. Others had been opened by the midwife's knife, under conditions of great secrecy. They had been married for periods of up to 8 years under both these circumstances.

Where vaginal intercourse is impossible some couples will resort to anal intercourse (Modawi, 1974). Funnel anus, anal fissures, and occasional incompetent anal sphincters have been reported as complications of this (Shandall, 1967; Modawi, 1974; Verzin, 1975). This practice is not discussed readily, and probably is far more common than is generally admitted.

All women, without exception, reported going through a great deal of suffering during the process of gradual penetration, which lasted on average 2 to 3 months. Quite a few suffered tearing of surrounding tissues; hemorrhage was common, as was infection. Many reported psychic trauma.

In Dareer's study (1982a), the time required for full penetration was 2-12 weeks in pharaonic circumcision, 2-5 weeks for the intermediate type, and 3-7 days for the *sunna* type. A complication that is not uncommon is the creation of a false vaginal canal, which may occur when a scar fails to dilate when repeated pressure at the genital site leads to stretching and invagination of the skin (Sami, 1986; Shandall, 1967; Modawi, 1974; Verzin, 1975).

At parturition women were subjected to extensive and sometimes multiple anterior cuts, necessitated by the inelasticity of their circumcision scars which made normal dilation impossible. Again hemorrhage was common. Fistulae (openings into the urinary systems or the colon due to tissue damage) were sometimes created, causing incontinence, and with it, ostracism.

Every pharaonically circumcised woman who gives birth must be cut in the way described in order to allow passage of the newborn. I observed close to 100 births in Sudanese hospital delivery rooms. Not a single one of the pharaonically circumcised women was able to dilate more than 4 cm. of the 10 cm. necessary to pass a fetal head normally. The rigidity of the scar tissue causes perineal tears and prolongs labor. This causes fetal distress, anoxia, and even death (Cook, 1979, p. 63). Defibulation during childbirth is a particularly dangerous procedure because of the large blood supply in the genital area at that time (Giorgis, 1981, p. 31).

The recurrent, manifold problems suffered by women are generally not understood to be an outgrowth of the procedures performed in early childhood. They are considered to be "normal" and the lot of all women. Since the procedures are practiced on all girls before puberty or far earlier, there are no uncircumcised, physically mature women with whom comparison is possible, and hence no challenge to erroneous beliefs.

At the Khartoum Teaching Hospital the sum of still births, neonatal deaths, maternal deaths, Cesarian sections, and forceps deliveries was recorded at over 20% of all births in 1981. This figure would, of course, be correspondingly higher in a nonhospital setting. It also does not include other complications, such as infections developing later on. Since women tend to leave the hospital on the same day that they give birth, the actual number of neonatal and maternal deaths is bound to be considerably larger. Even in Khartoum, where the best medical services to be had in the entire country are available, operating theaters shut down with depressing regularity due to tetanus epidemics. Complications to both mother and infant would not necessarily make their appearance on the day the woman gives birth, and a far higher figure can therefore be expected.

Throughout the entire country conditions of hygiene are best described as deplorable, even in the best hospitals. Resident cats crouch in the corner of delivery rooms amid uncollected bloodied cloths and discarded bandages, preying on the rodent population. Swarms and masses of flies cover the beds, the patients, the instruments, the delivery table. There is no such thing as a bed pan, and stinking ward latrines devoid of all disinfectant are choked with human ordure and yet more flies. Every few days water fails to come from the taps (in those places where there are taps, and those are few indeed) and all attempts at cleaning up anything grind to a halt. The floors remain unswabbed, the garbage mounts in the wards. Hand washing among the staff is kept to a minimum. A more perfect breeding ground for infection can hardly be imagined.

After delivery, a woman's vaginal opening is more often than not again sewn shut to pinhole size, and 40 days after she has given birth—a period of grace prescribed by the religion, and mercifully adhered to—the agonizing process of forcing the infibulation open begins once more. This refibulation, or as the Sudanese call it, "recircumcision," is a rather puzzling innovation that first made its appearance 50 years ago in Sudanese urban centers. It will be discussed further in later chapters.

Psychic problems make their appearance before and after circumcision and at various stress points in a woman's life such as menarche, marriage, and parturition, and tend to gradually recede after the crisis points are passed. Phobic behavior is common. Girls often exhibit extreme anxiety and emotional volatility before circumcision. After surgery, periods of emotional withdrawal are common. A period of relative normalcy follows this, but around the onset of menarche, depression is often seen. At penetration, pregnancy, and parturition these psychic disturbances tend to reappear.

It would not be surprising to see some personality changes commonly occurring in young girls subjected to circumcision; that is, a gay and lively child may become timid and withdrawn. Verzin (1975) reports discussing this aspect of circumcision on many occasions with teachers, psychiatrists, and other gynecologists, and all agree that this change, if it occurs at all, is not noticeable in Sudanese girls. Some other observers, however, categorically state that there is evidence that a child becomes withdrawn in the first year or two following circumcision. This, however, gives place to contentment and even pride when girls are a few years older. Major psychiatric breakdown as a result of the circumcision is rarely observed among the Sudanese.

Baasher (1982) comments further:

> In evaluating the overall psychological effects there is no doubt that the child as a result of the operative interference of female circumcision is overwhelmed, subjected to excruciating pain and real suffering. Some of the physical and psychological reactions are mitigated by social support and the special family care given the child. However, the outcome of the operation and its effect on the mental state and the well-being of the child in general depend on her psychological defenses, personality formation, past experience, the preparatory phase, the way in which the operation has been performed and the ensuing complications which may take place.

When some knowledgeable Sudanese men—and this includes two psychiatrists—advance the theory that an unusually high pain threshold is the explanation for women's ability to endure so much pain and for women's not infrequently encountered inability to remember that there *was* any pain, or for that matter any of the details of their circumcision at all, I do not believe that we are talking about pain thresholds at all. That seems to be a very convenient rationalization for educated men who are not in accord with the practice but are powerless to stop it. What we are talking about, in fact, is a highly developed ability to adapt, and thereby survive. If the adaptation involves a form of trance, self-hypnosis if you will, which allows occlusion of a horrendously painful event, or if it involves repression, or temporary withdrawal, then it should be understood that these are survival strategies at which women become more and more adept as they progress through life. One need spend only one morning in the nightmare of an obstetrical ward, witnessing one woman after another being cut open and then sewn up again by midwives, many of whom have become in the course of their lives incredibly callous, to know that the "high pain threshold" theory is utter nonsense.

In a U.S. study of African college students, Shaw (1985) found that most circumcised women from various Islamic cultures did not express pain during pelvic examination procedures. Yet all of these women, when questioned, reported severe pain. This apparent contradiction may be explained in cultural terms, and the fact that such women are often taught not to express pain involving their sexual organs.

While the pain of circumcision was often blurred or altogether screened out in the later recollection of adult women, they remembered all too clearly and were able to describe vividly the later agonizing experience of struggling to pass their menstrual flow while still in the virgin state. This is all but impossible for a girl to accomplish, and she can expect no relief from this situation until she marries, and her husband forces her infibulation open.

Here she is truly caught on the horns of a dilemma, because in order to escape the pain of infibulated menstruation, she must face and endure the ordeal of penetration. Understandably, depression in adolescent girls is common. Just how common is hard to evaluate, even for Sudanese doctors, since girls are simply not brought to them for the treatment of such an ailment. Depression is not recognized as an illness, and doctors see it as only peripheral to some other medical problem for which the girl is brought to them. Doctors report that when they treat a girl who is suffering from a tight infibulation, the symptoms of depression almost invariably recede dramatically.

SOCIAL AND PSYCHOLOGIAL CLIMATE: ATTITUDES

While the difference of opinion regarding the emotional repercussions of circumcision on girls and women is not easy to resolve, it is provocative. Like so many things concerning women in an Islamic Arab culture, emotional pathology is not highly visible there. Although I saw only occasional evidence of it among women and girls on a day to day basis in Sudan, it certainly does occur. When the phenomenon is viewed from outside the Sudanese culture, it is almost impossible to believe that some significant psychological pathology would not result from such an overwhelmingly traumatic and painful experience. However, our view of the situation is clouded by our own culturally derived standards.

Generally speaking, to observe Sudanese people of both sexes leads one to believe that they are a happy people who are satisfied with their lot in life. Their faces exude serenity and joy. They intensely love their harsh and barren land. Whenever I tell them of one of the many kindnesses that some other Sudanese has shown me, they glow with pride as if they have been personally praised. Whenever some breach of conduct is under discussion, they quickly hasten to assure me that the persons involved were not Sudanese, but from some other land. (The man who beat his child harshly was an Egyptian. The prostitutes are Syrian, or Lybian, or whatever; never Sudanese.) "Such things are not done by the Sudanese," they tell me with great seriousness, placing their hands over their hearts.

The merchants in the *suk* (market) never cheat you or take advantage of your ignorance as a foreigner. On the contrary, they nearly always give you a little something extra—an extra orange, a handful of dates, a few more inches of cloth, with an air of apparent satisfaction and good will. If they do not have exactly what you ask for, they may very well go in search of it for you, leaving you sitting by their open money box until they return to delightedly hand you what you were looking for, and then refuse any payment for their trouble. When you have difficulty finding your way to a particular place, they will walk with you a part of the way until they encounter someone else who will walk another stretch with you, and so on, until you are safely delivered at your destination. Perfect strangers are forever offering to share their little bowl of food with you, and when you give money to a beggar (who almost always looks immaculately clean), he rewards you with a touchingly happy smile, and loudly praises Allah for having sent you.

One does see a tremendous amount of religious fervour and devotion, and it can be argued that this can be interpreted as constituting a form of neurosis, but again we would be applying Western definitions, which are not valid for this culture. There is not, in any event, the kind of driven, fanatical behavior that we have come to associate with some of the other Islamic nations. There seems to be a lot of pleasure and joy involved for the Sudanese. They are deeply convinced of the infinite goodness and wisdom of Allah, and to this they trustingly resign their fates.

This is not to say that every woman you question does not answer you that if Allah had only willed it, she would rather have been a man. But is this not also still true of a goodly number of women in our own countries? And is such a statement still considered to be evidence of neurosis among us?

What enables the majority of Sudanese women to remain emotionally intact in spite of a lifetime of virtual torture and suffering, and the ever present spectre of yet more torture and suffering to come, pertaining directly to the fact that they are women, and directly to all aspects of their sexual functions? Sudanese psychiatrists may be believed when they say that the answer lies largely in the clearly defined role of the woman in society, the support of the extended family, and the circumcision ritual itself.

To understand the role of the pharaonically circumcised woman in Sudan, one must view it within the context of an Arab Islamic culture. As in other Arab Islamic societies throughout the Near East, family honor in Sudanese society is defined in greatest measure by the sexual purity of its women. Because of this, a modesty code is rigorously imposed on them, which generally includes female seclusion, veiling of the face or head in public, child betrothal, the virginity test of brides, definitive transfer of sexual rights at marriage, the early remarriage of divorcees and widows, as well as genital mutilation.

The Koran regards the sexual impulse as a natural appetite to be gratified, albeit in moderation and under particular conditions. Islam has a very positive attitude about sexual activity *for both men and women* which is accompanied by a strict insistence on fidelity and chastity (Abdalla, 1982).

The social status of the Arab Muslim family is often equated with the virginal state of its women, and any indecent behavior on the part of a woman disgraces the whole family, so that it is no longer respected by the community. Only the most stringent corrective measures will restore their honor, and this may take the form of divorce, casting the woman out, or putting her to death.

Infibulation serves to isolate the woman against her own sexual desires and the sexual aggression of others. Hayes (1975, p. 622) comments that the importance of virginity in the Sudanese ideology cannot be overemphasized. The scars of the infibulation operation are a seal attesting to an intangible and vital property of the social group's patrimony—the honor of the family and patrilineage. This seal must be transferred intact upon marriage into another lineage. If it were not intact, the lineage would not accept her.

Within this context, only a very limited number of roles are open to women, including midwife, seamstress, or vendor of minor cottage craft items. The most often enforced ideal is a woman who remains behind the high mud walls of the family compound, tending to the domestic chores, the children, and whatever livestock the family owns. When male visitors other than close relatives enter the compound, she must retire to the women's quarters until they leave.

Little girls may move freely in public until they are about 7 years old. Hence, when one visits the first two grades of a small town or village primary school, one sees that every seat in the class room holds two or even three eager students, and that every one of these participates delightedly in the class. After the age of 7, they begin covering their heads and shoulders with a veil in public, and are seen less and less outside of the family compound. Beginning with the third grade, the class rooms empty out more and more, until only a small, privileged number remains to go on to secondary school.

Separate school facilities for girls are vastly inferior to those for boys, and do not prepare them equally for the country's only coeducational state university, the University of Khartoum. Even when girls are allowed an education, the quality of their school curriculum is sharply divergent from the boys', and serves to maintain them in a definitely inferior role. A case in point: The book used nationwide to teach English to high school boys is Orwell's *Animal Farm*, a contemporary, thought-provoking novel highly critical of political dictatorships. Girls receive their English language training from Louisa May Alcott's book *Little Women*, written in Victorian America, presenting the morality of that period and women's place therein. Even the title of this book delineates women's inferior position.

After reaching puberty, a girl never appears in public unless her head and body are swathed in a *tope* (a length of intricately arranged cloth, 10 yards in length). Her public appearances are rare and closely supervised by either a grandmother or a male relative, or in the case of university students, in carefully chaperoned groups. A girl is considered to be of marriageable age around 15, although in some villages girls are married as early as 11. Just as she has been subordinate to all males and older females in her own family, she now becomes subordinate to her in-laws, and especially her mother-in-law, who now restricts her behavior and public appearances.

It is generally believed in Sudan that women are highly sexed and by nature promiscuous. Many of the people I talked to expressed the opinion that without infibulation girls would simply go wild sexually, and uninfibulated women are thought of as prostitutes. Hayes (1975, p. 624) observes:

> From the standpoint of honor and of Islamic norms of modesty, female sexuality is threatening. Socialized to believe that infibulation offers a physiological and social sanctuary from the threat inherent in their sexuality, women remain its greatest advocates, gladly subjecting their beloved daughters and granddaughters to the ordeal in order to protect them and the patrilineage. The latter result is of utmost importance to traditional women, because the patrilineage is their immediate and primary source of identity and security . . . in what they are taught to envision as a dangerous and hostile world outside the walls of the family compound. Being more vulnerable than men (i.e., without institutionalized power or authority) they have an equal, if not greater interest in safeguarding the lineage's position in the larger society.

As Sudan progresses into the jet age, there have been some changes for the elite class in recent years. Education for women was begun in 1920 and has gained quite a bit of ground since, even though it still lags greatly behind education for men. The Sudanese government (since independence from the British in 1956) has actively promoted higher education for women in order to tap that large source of potential qualified personnel. Those few women who were permitted by their families to go on to higher schooling and who were capable of passing the examinations of the state educational system are assured positions. This has created a gradually expanding variety of new professional roles for women, such as government worker, teacher, trained nurse-midwife, and doctor.

However, basically not much has changed so far. Activities permitted to the elite woman have expanded only enough to make her professional contribution to the modernizing state, little more. At the end of the workday she still retires to the confines of the harem and even as teacher or student she lives within a closely guarded, high-walled hostel. Even for the young people with the most progressive families, "dates" as we know them are inconceivable. Modesty is still as closely guarded as ever. Marriages are still arranged by the families, and unless women are accompanied by male relatives, their appearance in public places still puts their modesty and honor in question.

The married woman is still subject to the old restrictions, and her male relatives as well as all the kin of her husband are still responsible for her comportment and for punishing her transgressions. Her behavior at all times must be such that it not only stays away from all sexual misconduct, but also from the mere *suspicion* of sexual misconduct. She must at all times be careful not to become the subject of talk or speculation about her activities. Outside of her workday, she still has no public life to speak of. She never appears in restaurants, where most of the social life of men takes place. She cannot have a bank account in her own name or transact business without a male relative. It is the rare woman with considerable exposure to the West that is able to stretch the limitations her society imposes, and she does so at her own peril.

It has often been noted that in African Muslim societies a woman who fails to marry virtually does not exist.

The Islamic law determines the rights and obligations of women as follows:

1. Girls are in the custody of their fathers until they marry, at which time their husbands take over their responsibility and the women are placed under their tutelage.
2. Polygamy is allowed for men and they are permitted to have four wives at the same time, so long as they are able to pay the bride-price for each wife and treat all of them equally.
3. Divorce is the privilege of men alone. The wife has the right to divorce only in exceptional cases, such as maltreatment by the husband or if he cannot fulfill his responsibility for her physical well-being, etc. Even for these cases women rarely go to courts to reinforce their limited rights.
4. A wife's rights to the family property are unequal to her husband's and she must have his consent to dispose of it.
5. The wife's share in inheritance varies from one-eighth to one-sixteenth of the property left by the husband (depending on whether or not she has children).
6. The shares of the men's inheritance are twice as large as a woman's.
7. The testimony of two women witnesses equals that of one man and the penalty for killing a woman is only half that for killing a man.
8. Muslim men can marry not only Muslim women, but also women of the "Book" (Jews and Christians). But Muslim women are allowed to marry only Muslim men.
9. Obedience of women to men and to the canons of proper dress and modesty in their behavior are also enshrined in the law (*Sharia*).
10. Child custody, after a certain age that varies according to different legal schools of thought, goes to the father (after Abdalla, 1982).

Girls are often subjected to great peer pressure, and are known to request their own circumcisions when parents do not do this promptly enough. They are indoctrinated that they must be "properly" circumcised, which is to say, pharaonically. They are further indoctrinated that if they have children, they must have themselves resutured (recircumcised), or all sorts of terrible things will befall them, such as their husbands' resorting to prostitutes or taking a second wife. In a country where a woman has absolutely no economic power, this is no light matter. If her husband should divorce her, she also loses her children, since the children belong to him.

Even those few women who hold jobs in Sudan are not allowed to own property. Their wages belong to the husband, and when they are not married, their money must be managed by a male relative. The only property that a woman can really own outright is the gold that she wears on her body, which she receives as her share of the bride-price her husband must pay when they marry, or sometimes at circumcision. This gold is therefore of the utmost importance to any woman in Sudan.

To fail to circumcise one's daughter is to practically ensure her ruination. Among the populace, no one would marry an uncircumcised woman. (It should be noted that among the elite who have had considerable exposure to the West, there is a tendency nowadays to seek out foreign women precisely *because* they are uncircumcised. This involves only the minutest fraction of the population, but it is a phenomenon that bears watching.) It is still strongly believed by most that the more severe the procedure, the less risk that the girl will disgrace her family.

Among unschooled Sudanese, the beliefs that circumcision will keep the sexual organs clean, prevent malodorous discharges, prevent rape, prevent vaginal worms, help women conceive, facilitate giving birth, make them less sexually sensitive before marriage, but more responsive after marriage are widespread. None of these reasons have any basis in fact. (Peripherally it should also be realized that to call a man "the son of an uncircumcised woman" in Sudan is to insult him in the most shameful way possible. Historically speaking, uncircumcised women in Sudan have generally been slaves, and the epithet implies illegitimacy and a non-Arabic origin.)

Although power in Sudanese society lies ostensibly in the hands of the male, the social dynamics within the family allow for a variety of options. Men have the final word in all family matters, but they often forfeit this right where "women's business" is concerned. (I was told by an apologetic 40-year-old psychiatrist that he would have much preferred to leave his daughters uncut, but that he was "afraid of [his] mother" who would "never have permitted

70

[him] to do such a thing." Some variation on this theme was encountered with considerable frequency.)

In spite of the rigid and stringent rules imposed on girls from early childhood on, families among the Sudanese tend to be naturally loving and supportive of one another and especially of children in a major way that most Westerners can only marvel at and find enviable. Sudanese children for the most part grow up in an atmosphere of emotional security and acceptance. Far more often than children in societies where there is no extended family, Sudanese girls are able to effortlessly learn their role as mother and nurturer from many loving role models very early in life, and there is a smooth and pressureless transition into adult function, which begins as soon as she outgrows her infancy. Also, very early in life she learns about circumcision, which she comes to realize will be the rite of passage that will make her ready to marry. The parts that will be cut from her, she is told, are malodorous impurities, and once she has undergone circumcision, she will be clean, sweet smelling, and pure, and will surely be pleasing to the man she marries. Without circumcision, she is told, no man will ever want to marry her, and among the mass of uneducated men, this is certainly true. Infibulation will assure her husband of her virginity, and the more tightly she is sewn, the more he will be assured of her purity, and the more she will be able to please him sexually, and hence hold him, so that he will not want to take another wife. Her infibulated virginity will cause her to have high value in the eyes of her future husband, and will be a source of pride to her. It will bring honor to her family, to her husband, and to herself.

How fully all of this is accepted by most women is evidenced most clearly by the fact that when they are asked at what age their circumcision occurred, they are likely to answer: "This was done for me by my family when I was such and such an age." *For* me, not *to* me. Even Morgan and Steinem (1980, p. 67), dedicated feminists who deplore and decry all forms of female sexual mutilation, concede: "If a bride who lacks virginity literally risks death or renunciation on her wedding night, then a chastity belt of her own flesh is a gesture of parental concern."

Yet there are feminists in Sudan who condemn the practice as

"sexual mutilation," and view it as a cruel means of female suppression by men, a view which is shared by feminists and humanists
the world over. The medical profession speaks out strongly against
the practice because of its physical complications, and although in
northern Sudan the practice of circumcising girls is acceptable to
the majority, an increasing awareness of the needless suffering involved has provoked many questions. Dareer's study (1982a, p. 66)
indicates that out of a total of 3,210 women and 1,545 men interviewed in Sudan, 82.6% of women and 87.7% of men were in favor
of continuing the practice of female circumcision. She also found
that ignorance of consequences, fear of social criticism, and "ignorance of parents" accounted for about 3/4 of the reasons given for
favoring its continuation.

In Kenya, girls of the Kikuyu tribe sing the following song after
they have undergone clitoridectomy:

> The knife cut down the guardian of the village today.
> Now he is dead and gone.
> Before the village was dirty,
> But now without the guardian it is clean.
> So look at us, we are only women and the men have come to
>   beat the tam-tam.
> They have phalli like the elephants.
> They have come when we were bleeding.
> Now back to the village where a thick Phallus is waiting.
> Now we can make love, because our sex is clean.

The late Jomo Kenyatta, former president of Kenya, with a
Ph.D. in anthropology under Malinowski, comments in his book
Facing Mount Kenya, "No proper Kikuyu would dream of marrying a girl who has not been circumcised . . . this operation is regarded as a *conditio sine qua non* for the whole teaching of tribal
law, religion and morality" (Kenyatta, 1938). This quotation illus-
trates attitudes of women and men who are in favor of genital mutilation and of women who themselves have undergone the operation
and who consider it essential for their daughters.

As McLean observes in her 1980 Minority Rights Group Report:

Clearly, if in a community sufficient pressure is put on a child to believe that her genitals are dirty, and dangerous, or a source of irresistible temptation, she will feel relieved to be made like everyone else. To be different produces anxiety and mental conflict. An unexcised, noninfibulated girl is despised and made the target of ridicule, and no one in the community will marry her. Thus what is clearly understood to be her life's work, namely marriage and childbearing, is denied her. In a tightly-knit society where mutilation is the rule, it will be the exception who suffers psychologically, unless she has another very strong identity to substitute for the community identity which she has lost.

It is therefore small wonder that girls express gratitude for their circumcision.

As girls reach the age at which circumcision is customarily performed, they find themselves under ever-escalating peer pressure, and are often the subject of ridicule from those girls who have already undergone the ritual. They are laughed at for still having "that thing dangling between [their] legs." They are told they smell bad.

The rites themselves are couched in mystery, and although the girl generally realizes that something fearsome will happen to her, that there will be pain as something is cut from her, she is helped not to focus on this aspect of the event. Frequently the girl herself will request of her family that she be circumcised, being totally ignorant of the consequences of this act on her future health and welfare. Women often voice their feelings about this: "I had no idea. I was so young, hardly more than a baby, and they never tell you about that part of it. You don't realize what it is really all about until they do it to you, and by then it is too late."

Girls tend to look forward to their circumcision with a mixture of dread and eagerness. It is not uncommon for them to manifest severe anxiety and a generalized phobic reaction as the time approaches. They become afraid of being touched, of knives, of social gatherings, of going to sleep. This is occasioned by the fact that by the time their turn comes, they have experienced at a distance, if not actually seen, the circumcision of other girls, have heard the frantic screams, quite possibly have seen the blood of their predecessors. Still, the day of circumcision is considered to be the most important day of a girl's life.

The principal effect of the operation is to create in young girls an intense awareness of their sexuality and anxiety concerning its meaning, its social significance. In general, the practice emphasizes punishment and social control, clearly indicating to the small child a sense of the mystery and importance of sex, at the same time creating an all-consuming terror of the evils of unchaste behavior in her (Abdalla, 1982, p. 51).

All of her fear tends to be mitigated by the fact that in the period preceding their circumcision, girls are the center of all attention — heady stuff for someone so small! A joyous, festive atmosphere prevails. Loving relatives, some of whom have traveled great distances in her honor, are with the girl constantly, supporting her, encouraging her, focusing her attention away from the anticipated ordeal, and in the direction of the acceptance, love, empathy, and good will that is radiating toward her from all sides. She is given many desirable and valued presents. Her hands and feet are painted with henna, a privilege that only brides and married women are given, and that all girls appear to yearn for. Often she is circumcised along with her sisters. She is never alone during the entire time.

At the circumcision itself (I am told) she is surrounded by loved and loving faces that weep for her pain and offer sympathy and encouragement. Whether the child is able to perceive this at the time is a moot point, but I have been in anterooms while circumcisions were taking place, and have seen the personal torment women were undergoing, the frantic weeping and wailing that took place as shrieks of terror and pain issued from the other room.

When it is all over, the girl is soothed by gentle hands and is watched over constantly. If she is fortunate and develops no physical complications, she is able to heal, and since she is so young, healing is generally rapid. For a while she tends to be apathetic and withdrawn, but when the memory of the pain begins to fade, she takes her place effortlessly among marriageable young women. She feels secure in being "clean" — having been purged of her impurities, having her virginity ensured, secure in finding favor in the eyes of Allah and in the eyes of her future husband.

Of course the picture is not quite so idyllic in every case, and not all girls can be expected to escape medical complications or even disasters. Personal accounts and research findings repeatedly contain references to anxiety prior to the operation, terror at the moment of being seized, unbearable pain, a sense of tremendous humiliation, and a feeling of betrayal, particularly by the mother.

And then there is also the occasional child abuser, who finds her perfect medium in the ritual of circumcision, and who acts out to the fullest, all in the name of propriety, as in this instance cited by Dareer (1982, p. 80):

> One young lady from El Obeid, said that she would never forget the troubles she experienced and will never have her daughters circumcised. She had been circumcised three times in two years because each time her grandmother protested that her circumcision was not good. She was circumcised first at the age of six, with the intermediate type. Seven days later her grandmother decided that she should be circumcised again because she did not want that type. Unfortunately the wound became infected and she needed to have treatment. Two years later came the turn of her younger sisters. The grandmother said that she should be circumcised yet again, because the opening was too big. She had noticed this when the girl urinated. So the poor girl was subjected to the operation for a third time. In addition to all these painful operations she has had problems with menstruation and actually needed decircumcision at the time of her marriage. Incredibly, we met women who said that as they had suffered and survived, so should their daughters and granddaughters. It seems to be a form of vengeance, or a psychologically rooted reaction.

Yet there is still a large measure of truth to the idyllic picture, at least in Sudan, where people are generally characteristically loving and supportive toward one another.

Uneducated Sudanese women are unaware of alternatives to circumcision, and 98% of them still never see the inside of a school since education of women is not considered a positive value in an Afro-Islamic society. Everything is clearly defined for the Sudanese girl. There are no complicated choices that she has to make. Circumcision is a fact of her life, just as tremendous hardship, poverty, scarce water and little food, back-breaking labor, overwhelming heat, dust storms, crippling disease, unalleviated pain, and early death are facts of her life. Circumcision happens to everyone. This is the only reality, and she accepts it as everyone else accepts it. While every town has its isolated madman or madwoman, flight into unreality does not make its appearance often.

Knowledgeable women that I interviewed constantly reiterated that although they saw female circumcision and infibulation as a lamentable practice, the issue was nowhere near the top of women's priorities in Sudan. There were immeasurably more pressing problems threatening their day to day existence, which left the country at large without resources or energy to combat this relatively lesser problem.

As Koso-Thomas (1987, p. 1) points out:

> Because traditional patrilineal communities assign women a subordinate role, women feel unable to oppose community dictates, even when these affect them adversely. Many women even go to great lengths to support these dictates by organizing groups which mete out punishment to non-conforming women, and conduct hostile campaigns against passive observers. Women championing many of the cultural practices adopted by their communities do not realize that some of the practices they promote were designed to subjugate them, and more importantly, to control their sexuality and to maintain male chauvinistic attitudes in respect to marital and sexual relations. Most African women have still not developed the sensitivity to feel deprived or to see in many cultural practices a violation of their human rights. The consequence of this is that, in the mid-1980's when most women in Africa have voting rights and can influence political decisions against practices harmful to their health, they continue to uphold the dictates and mores of the communities in which they live; they seem, in fact, to regard traditional beliefs as inviolable.

It is only among the educated, in the capital, that women are becoming aware, from outside sources, that other options exist, and it is among them that a sense of outrage makes its appearance. This is where we encounter repressed rage, the rejection of the feminine role assigned to them, rejection of sexuality. It is here that a woman must grapple with the realization that she has been, if not an unconsenting victim, at least an uninformed and unconsulted one.

Moen (1983) comments that obviously only rare cases obtain psychiatric evaluation or care, but among those females who have received attention diagnoses have included loss of self-esteem; feelings of victimization; severe anxiety prior to the operations; depression associated with complications such as infection, hemorrhage, shock, septicemia, and retention of urine; chronic irritability; and sexual frustration.

Maher (1981), in a study done in Cairo comparing circumcised and uncircumcised women, showed that about 10% of the former had feelings of inferiority physically and psychosexually. The difficulties they experienced in their marital and sexual life resulted in depression in about 5%. This was 10 times the frequency reported for the uncircumcised group. Divorce occurred in 6% of the circumcised group, as opposed to less than 1% in the noncircumcised. The husbands of these women were also studied and compared (Maher, 1981). Among the husbands of the circumcised group there was a definite increase in the incidence of premature ejaculation and impotence as compared to the other group. There was also an increase in polygamy and addiction to hashish (cannabis).

Among my informants doctors report cases, especially among the educated, where women expressed the fear that they may not be sexually adequate for their husband's needs, and many, paradoxically, suffer from feelings of guilt because they are not able to function better sexually. In all women's lives there exists to some measure the ever present fear that such inadequacy will eventually cause her husband to divorce her or to take an additional wife.

For economic reasons, polygamy is relatively rare in present day Sudan, even though Islam grants any man the right to have four wives simultaneously, provided he can supply each one with a separate household. However, this present day tendency was not always so, and many Sudanese living today remember vividly their mother's suffering and their own feelings of deprivation in one of their father's multiple households.

The uneducated older women — the grandmothers — possess a deep conviction that in upholding and enforcing tradition, they hold together the fabric of a society that must at whatever cost be defended against all threat. Although they are often made out to be dictatorial, knife-wielding perpetrators of a practice for which neither they nor the men of the society will admit to having responsibility, in my opinion they are far better described as strong, proud, determined, and sad survivors of the same rites that they defend so tenaciously.

Hayes (1975, p. 632) describes the position of high status that the older women hold in the patrilineage system:

> As in many other societies, the older women achieve a status more closely resembling that of men. They have influence and authority over their daughters-in-law of the compound as well as their own daughters still living at home. Mothers are greatly respected by their sons and sons have closer emotional ties to their mothers than to their stern patriarchal fathers. Grandmothers are as respected as fathers, and great emphasis and pride is attached to the position of grandparent. At that stage of life when they would seem to approach full membership in their husband's and son's patrilineage, certainly they display an increasingly keen interest in its welfare and continuity. It is not surprising, therefore, to find that they are most often the initiators of the infibulation ceremonies for their granddaughters and that they must be considered the chief perpetrators of the practice.

Midwives are also very influential among women. Family planning proponents have found them to be a formidable obstacle in introducing modern contraceptive techniques. Since the midwives' income depends on childbirth, they view contraception as a direct threat to their socioeconomic status. A parallel situation in regard to circumcision practices exists, of course.

The position of men in regard to this practice is complex and falls into a number of categories. Among the uneducated and tradition-minded, which comprise almost the entire bulk of the population, the rule of custom is accepted and upheld without any question whatsoever. Although the procedure is arranged for and carried out by women, it is done so under the rule of a strictly patriarchal society. I was told of many cases in which women who were clitoridectomized or circumcised in a modified fashion were pharaonically circumcised on the husband's demand after marriage.

Young men often express anxiety that they will be greatly shamed by failure to penetrate their brides when they marry. Young, relatively educated men think of the practice as lamentable, and say they are trying to persuade their parents to spare their younger sisters from at least the worst procedures.

It is difficult to get accurate information on the subject of refibulation, which is a merry-go-round of assigning the blame to someone else, while everyone is involved. However, it is clear that refibulation is often done at the husband's orders at a high price, according to midwives, since evidently the degree of damage done to the woman's organs makes her an ostensibly unsatisfactory sexual partner without this. At the very least, most men accept this procedure from their wives as an act of love, or from "the grandmothers" as an act of propriety even when they do not demand it.

Since men have the benefits of more education, opposition to these practices generally come from them, or so they lead one to believe. Educated, Westernized men, as well as those who have had sexual experiences with uncircumcised or with clitoridectomized but uninfibulated women, tend to seek women in those categories for sexual partners and sometimes wives. Among the upper classes, this tendency will no doubt eventually bring about some measure of change.

It is a point of honor for men to have a child born within a year of marriage, and Dr. Mustafa Hamed Kleida (1981) reports that there is an increasing number of women who come to the Khartoum hospitals with fertility-related sexual and marital problems. They are concerned about their lack of sensation and response, and are afraid that this will prevent them from getting pregnant. They are aware, in any event, that "things are not as they should be." This is a phenomenon that is characteristic only of the past 10 years, and it is on the increase to the extent that Dr. Kleida feels it may well be a harbinger of greater change in the near future, at least in Khartoum.

It is estimated that 20% to 35% of all infertility cases in Sudan (Cook, 1979, p. 59) are attributable to the complications of infibulation. While this may have some positive value in slowing the excessively high population growth of an already overburdened economy, it would seem that family planning measures could present a better solution.

The brain drain from Sudan into Saudi Arabia is having an interesting side effect, which may eventually have some results. Female circumcision is reported not to be practiced in Saudi Arabia (Baasher, 1982; Hosken, 1982a; Grey, 1983), and with more and more Sudanese finding jobs there, the Saudi Arabian population at large is becoming aware of the practice of pharaonic circumcision in Sudan. They consider this practice of the Sudanese to be "barbaric," and "against the precepts of Islam." The interaction between the two cultures may eventually bring about some measure of change, hopefully among the Sudanese.

The following statement was made by a gynecological resident at Omdurman Hospital in Sudan about a pilot project involving the attempt to change people's attitudes toward female circumcision in the villages:

> Recently there was a workshop in Tuti, a village some distance from Khartoum, with all the women of the village attending. Doctor Salah showed his famous histological slides, proving the denervation of the vulval area as a result of pharaonic circumcision. There were a few religious men there, who told the women: "You must understand that Islam is totally against the mistreatment of women, and therefore you should not practice this terrible thing." They told them that in order to have sexual response that would please their husbands most, women should never be circumcised. Women responded nicely. I remember one woman saying to me: "I wish you had come sooner. We never knew that the pharaonic caused things like this until now.

Of course the solution to the problem is not as simple as all that. It is more than just likely that the ingrained custom and the power of sexual taboos will cause this same woman to circumcise her daughters pharaonically within a year's time of the workshop, when she has stopped thinking about it. It is practically a certainty.

SEXUAL RESPONSE AND MARITAL PROBLEMS OF CIRCUMCISED WOMEN

There is no way to objectively measure the effect of their mutilations on women's ability to have orgasm. However, by direct questioning and by observation within the culture at large, it has been possible to obtain some insight into this question.

Close to 90% of Sudanese women interviewed claimed to regularly achieve *or had at some time in their lives* achieved orgasm. It was reported by these women to occur in varying degrees of frequency and intensity. For fairly obvious reasons orgasm could not be measured in a controlled experimental setting among Islamic women. Regarding this somewhat surprising figure, we must be aware of a possible halo effect caused by a tendency on the part of women interviewed to exaggerate the sexual satisfaction obtained within a happy marriage, as part of their duty as a "good wife" and pride in their husbands, which was often very obvious. All other factors taken into account, however, this speculation is by no means certain. A further halo effect may have been obtained by the fact that only those women who were willing to be interviewed could be included in the study, and this may have skewed the results.

The sampling was not composed of a specific total population, as for instance the employees of a given hospital. Not all members of the populations used were willing to be interviewed. Only about two-thirds of the Bulluk Hospital staff cooperated. Others were obtained at random, according to their willingness to serve as subjects. Some were mothers of pediatric patients at Bulluk Hospital. Others were staff members and women about to give birth at other hospitals in El Obeid, Khartoum, and Wad Medani. A few were students and instructors at Ahfat University College for Women in Omdurman, and Khartoum University in Khartoum.

The criticism may be leveled, therefore, that the study dealt with a select population. It is entirely possible that anorgasmic women tended to exclude themselves from the interviews, and that the statistics are therefore skewed. It is far more likely, however, that those who excluded themselves had something to hide such as marital conflict, the existence of a secret liaison, or the fact that they strongly enjoyed sex but had to keep this secret from a disapproving mate. Some may well have been very private people, and others may have disapproved of the interviews on moral grounds. A number of midwives and nurses who were known for their skill at performing the illegal pharaonic circumcisions also failed to make an appearance, for rather obvious reasons.

I have deliberately stayed away from charts and tables. The figure stated above is, in my own opinion, unduly high, and no doubt out of proportion to the true state of affairs. I make no claim to describing the whole picture. There is little doubt in my mind that orgasm exists even among these drastically mutilated women to a surprising extent, and it is far from being rare.

Dareer's study of female circumcision in Sudan (1982a, p. 48), included 2,375 women, of which 2,006 were pharaonically circumcised and 295 circumcised in the modified way. Dareer reports that 50% of women interviewed

> said they had never experienced sexual pleasure and simply regarded the act as a duty; 23.3% were totally indifferent, and the remainder either found it pleasurable altogether or only sometimes. The impression received when asking whether or not they enjoyed sexual relations was that their own feelings were irrelevant and the main object was to please and satisfy their husband.

Zwang (1979) estimates that 90 to 95% of circumcised women are frigid. Abdalla (1982, p. 26) reports that "It is now believed by many medical authorities that the majority of mutilated women are frigid, especially those with "total clitoridectomy" and with other complex mutilations such as "Pharaonic circumcision."

Giorgis (1981, p. 31) comments that the correlation between female circumcision and *lack* of sexual satisfaction has been grossly exaggerated. She quotes Verzin (1975, p. 167) as a representative of the *misconceptions* that are common on this score:

Lack of sexual gratification appears to be common, the absence of the clitoris probably playing a part in this. The information is never volunteered and very rarely admitted. A blank expression, an enigmatic smile or at most an evasive reply towards a curious question, and this is irrespective of color, creed or sex of the questioner. In such a society the woman is regarded as a vassal for man's pleasure and subsequently the bearer of his offspring. It is probable that many are not even aware that there should be reciprocal enjoyment.

Assaad's study (1982) in Egypt found that 94% of 54 women interviewed by her reported that they enjoyed sex and were happy with their husbands. Among Nigerian Ibos (Megafu, 1983), who mostly practiced complete or partial excision of the clitoris, 59% of circumcised as opposed to 69% of uncircumcised women reported experiencing orgasm. Among 651 women studied by Karim and Ammar in Egypt (1965), 41.1% of circumcised women reached orgasm, as opposed to 70-77% of Kinsey's intact women. Shandall (1967), in a study involving over 4,000 women, reported that 80% of pharaonically circumcised females said that they never experienced orgasm and claimed that they had no idea what an orgasm was.

Almost all the men questioned by Dareer (1982a) said they enjoyed their sex lives and that their wives did too. However, some of them considered that a woman's compliance with the sexual act and her acceptance of pregnancy signified her pleasure.

A study on the treatment of anorgasmia (frigidity) in Egypt reports:

106 women 26 to 41 years old, married 2 to 14 years (none polygamously), mothers, and not unhappy. Their education ranged from university graduate to illiterate, their socioeconomic status from rich to very poor, and some worked in addition to being housewives. All had been genitally mutilated at around the age of 8 years. Mutilation extended from partial clitoral loss . . . to complete loss of the clitoris and labia minora and majora with anatomical distortion of the vulva and introitus. . . . In 52% there were complications, e.g. massive

scarring. None had extra marital or other sexual activities apart from routine coitus. Only 36% enjoyed coitus; 71% did it unpleasurably (sic) and painfully only to get pregnant, submitting to their husbands as a duty but not because of force, love, or the wish to become orgasmic. Some required plastic surgery, others psychological treatment and sexological reorientation only. Success (becoming orgasmic and/or enjoying coitus) was rated at 41%. Few women in Egypt receive treatment for the anatomical and psychological traumata of genital mutilation. (Christhilf, 1981, p. 253)

The discrepancies in these findings are no doubt due to cultural and other factors, and although I cannot here demonstrate their exact nature, I believe that the interviewers' own attitudes and biases as well as their personal degrees of sexual and social anxiety or the relative ease with which the material could be discussed would account for a large part of the discrepancies.

In all of these studies it is quite unusual that such a high level of response and cooperation was obtained at all, for it must be remembered that we are dealing with an extremely repressive Islamic society where sexual matters are not a subject for discussion. A sociocultural study on female circumcision carried out in adjacent Ethiopia, using questionnaires administered by trained students, reports anger and resentment from its respondents, and failure to obtain answers to its questions on a topic that they appeared to consider "too personal to discuss." Similar problems were encountered in Egypt (Bishaw and Negash, 1984), and in Burkina Faso (Kouba and Muasher, 1985). Sami (1986), in a study of female circumcision in Sudan, also complained that "people's reluctance to discuss the subject makes the task of collecting reliable information extremely difficult."

In any event, consensus in the matter of female orgasm is no greater where Western women are concerned. To quote Morgan (1972, p. 76):

Robert D. Knight says: "Perhaps 75 percent of all married women derive little or no pleasure from the sexual act." Kinsey says that only 10 percent of women are frigid. Marie Robinson hazards over 40 percent; L. H. Terman 33 percent; Weiss and English give 50 percent; Eustace Chesser only 15 percent. Bergler asserts that frigidity is a problem which concerns from 70 to 80 percent of all women; while Inge and Sten Hegeler assert "there is no such thing as a frigid woman".

In my own study it was quite clear that an impressive number of women gave the appearance of being lusty, sexually fulfilled women, in addition to the statements they made. They were able to make clear, definitive statements about how often they did or did not experience what they described as orgasm, under what circumstances they did or did not attain it, and how long a period of foreplay and intercourse it required. During the interviews these women exhibited a relaxed body posture, smiled and laughed readily and heartily, asked questions, and in general gave evidence of enjoying the exchange of information.

Some of the interviews are reproduced in Appendix I. It should be noted that a distortion in time perception — as we see it — is often evident, which is to be expected among simple Third World village women who have never owned a watch, have had little or no schooling, and who therefore do not deal in time units smaller than a minute, and then not too accurately in those. When a woman says, therefore, that orgasm lasts for 2 or 3 minutes, this answer must be seen within this context, and not taken as a statement of fact. "Two or three minutes" means in effect "a short time." This is equally true of a statement like: "After orgasm I cannot move for 15 minutes." This is also a subjective perception.

We might ask if orgasm is what we are actually talking about here. As one researcher on the subject observes, "To those who experience or have experienced orgasm regularly, it seems remarkable that females could ever have difficulty in recognizing that it has occurred" (Levin, 1981). It has been traditionally taught that the woman who experiences orgasm finds the response to be so unique that she has no hesitation in identifying the experience. Generally speaking, this probably does reliably distinguish women who have abandoned themselves to high levels of sexual excitement and orgasmic discharge from inhibited women who avoid high levels of sexual tension and who have not had full orgasmic release.

In my interviews, subjects certainly did produce some vivid and clearly recognizable descriptions which had the ring of truth and familiarity both to me and to my translators. This was equally true of those interviews (about one-third) which were conducted in English, when no translator was used.

To the question: "How often do you experience orgasm?" the following responses were representative:

> We have intercourse every two or three days. I never have orgasm during the first time, even though my husband maintains an erection for 45 minutes or an hour. When we have intercourse a second time about an hour later, I am able to reach orgasm.

> With my first husband I almost never had any pleasure, and I had orgasm only a handful of times. It was an arranged marriage, and although he was a kind man, and good to me, I did not love him. The marriage to my present husband is a love match, and I always have strong orgasm with him, except on rare occasions, when I am too tired or one of the children is sick.

> When I was younger, I used to have it happen 9 out of 10 times. Now there are so many children and grandchildren in the house that we can only have intercourse every second or third week. We have so little privacy, and we have to be very quiet about it. There are so many interruptions. Also, I have had frequent problems with urinary infections. When we have intercourse, I am able to come to orgasm once in a while now—perhaps 1 time in 10.

> I have never had any pleasure from my husband. I try to avoid sex with him whenever I can. It is not that he is brutal or that we do not love one another. It would be the same, no matter whom I married. The only thing I ever feel there is pain. I am happy when he lets me go to sleep and does not bother me.

Descriptions of orgasm were equally explicit and often quite vivid:

I feel as if I am trembling in my belly. It feels like electric shock going around my body—very sweet and pleasurable. When it finishes, I feel as if I would faint.

(*This description by a Director of Nursing.*) I feel as if I have had a shot of morphine. My body vibrates all over. Then I feel shocked and cannot move. At the end, I relax all over.

All my body begins to tingle, then I have a shock to my pelvis and in my legs. It gets very tight in my vagina. I have a tremendous feeling of pleasure, and I cannot move at all. It seems to last for about 2 minutes, and I seem to be flying, far, far up. Then my whole body relaxes, and I go completely limp for about 15 minutes.

I feel as if I am losing all consciousness, and I seem to love him most intensely at that moment. I tremble all over. My vagina contracts strongly, and I have a feeling of great joy. Then I relax all over, and I am so happy to be alive and to be married to my husband.

I feel shivery, and as if I had had anesthesia (*this description by a nurse*). I feel very happy, and I want to swallow him inside of me. It is a very sweet feeling that spreads until it takes hold of my entire body. I feel very light, and seem to float up into the air. Then I go to sleep.

I feel as if I am losing all consciousness, it is such a strong feeling. I hold on to my husband very, very tightly, and if the baby fell out of the bed, I would not be able to pick it up.

These responses were judged to be valid. However, once in a while responses appeared not to describe orgasm, but rather an anxiety reaction. "I have palpitations of the heart. There is no sensation in my pelvis. My hands feel very cold."

Among pharaonically circumcised women, and among those that have been circumcised in the modified way, both internal and external erogeneity were reported. In the question used to obtain this information, the areas were referred to as "inside" and "the area of your scar," respectively. About one-third of the women reported having pleasurable sensation in both areas, others reported only internal, yet others only external sensation, and a smaller percentage reported having no pleasurable sensation whatsoever in either area. Since no physical examinations were possible, no correlations of these data with the exact anatomical state of individual women could be obtained. The lines of demarcation between what was described as pharaonic circumcision and what was described as modified pharaonic were often hazy. The following will serve as an illustration.

Two female medical students were questioned together, and each was asked what type of procedure had been done on her. One reported that the modified procedure had been performed, the other said that she was pharaonically circumcised. When asked to describe the situation more closely, the two compared data, and it was found that the procedures they had undergone were identical.

It is apparent from the interviews that in most cases, the more severe the circumcision the woman has suffered, the weaker her feelings of pleasure and ability to have orgasm appear to be. This is particularly true of the women of Western Sudan, where the procedures are most damaging. Everything external is razed off, so that nothing remains except a fibrous mat of scar tissue upon bare bone. In most of these cases, if women relate that they have orgasm, it is described as infrequent and weak, relative to what other women describe. This was not always the case, however. Some of these women, particularly village women, claimed to have strong and frequent orgasm.

Circumcised women in general, and specifically simple, uneducated village women, are often reported by men to be enviably intact in terms of sexual lustiness, in spite of their mutilation. Sudanese women are culturally bound to hide this, and so they skillfully navigate among the demands that are placed on them by society, by their husbands, and by their own sexuality by way of a series of maneuvers and sex signals. Custom puts severe penalties on a woman's initiation of sexual intercourse; however, the uses of the "smoke ceremony" are known to every Sudanese woman, and to every Sudanese man as well. Practically every woman uses it. She signals her desire and receptivity by permeating her skin with sandalwood smoke.

Baker, the famous 19th century British explorer, describes the smoke ceremony in his notes (Moorehead, 1962, p. 234).

> A hole was made in the ground inside a tent and filled with burning embers upon which were thrown a variety of perfumes—ginger, cloves, cinnamon, frankincense, sandalwood and myrrh. The woman then crouched naked over the embers, her robe arranged like a tent round her so that none of the fumes could escape. She now begins to perspire freely in the hot-air bath, and the pores of the skin thus opened and moist, the volatile oil from the smoke of the burning perfumes is immediately absorbed.

Afterwards generous quantities of fat were rubbed into the skin and hair. Baker claimed he could smell a woman who had performed this ceremony from 100 yards away.

The intent of the signal is clearly understood by all Sudanese men, and they act upon it. The meaning of the ceremony is tacitly agreed upon, and no verbalization or other act of agreement is needed. The woman can now behave in a way that totally negates her intent. She can now act out the role of the ravaged, while he acts out the role of the ravager, or she can be dutifully acquiescent to her husband's sexual demands while seeming to have no interest or pleasure whatsoever herself.

A young German woman traveling through Sudan told me the following experience: She had been staying for some weeks with a young Sudanese couple, and felt that she had developed a good rapport with both of them. One evening she watched the wife perform the smoke ceremony, had found it interesting, and not understanding its meaning, had followed suit. The husband thereupon promptly sent his wife to her mother's house in the next village on an errand, and when she left, commenced immediately to make unequivocal sexual overtures to the girl. Her reaction was one of surprise, hurt, and indignation. She tried to convince him that she was not in the least bit interested in having sexual relations with him, but to no avail. Eventually his overtures became outright onslaughts, and she fled the house in panic. She was utterly shocked when I explained to her how she herself had precipitated the incident.

I was told by several Sudanese women that if their husbands did not pick up on their signals, they would wake them from their sleep in the middle of the night by dropping dishes or banging pots around. (Dishes in Sudan are generally made of plastic.) After this had the desired result, the husband could resume his sleep.

Custom decrees that a Sudanese woman remain totally passive during the sex act. She must lie like a "block of wood" and participate in no way whatsoever. Sudanese men confirm that in nearly all cases she does just that. Sexual pleasure is considered to be entirely a male prerogative, and if it is felt by women, it is felt in secret. Nearly all women interviewed reported that showing sexual interest and pleasure openly is "extremely shameful."

A young Syrian engineer who was on contract to Sudan told me that he was extremely unhappy and that he longed for home. He was utterly confused by what he interpreted as "completely inconsistent behavior" on the part of his Sudanese girlfriends. "They come to my bed of their own free will," he complained, "and then, when I try to initiate intercourse, they say, 'What do you want in that place? You have no business there!' And if I insist, they lie there like stones. It is terribly frustrating. Why do they come to my bed at all, if that is not what they want?"

I asked him if at those times he had noted the odor of sandalwood smoke. He most certainly had. The odor was always strong enough to knock you down, he said. I explained the behavior of his girlfriends in terms of what was culturally allowed and what was not allowed, and that the signals of sexual desire and receptivity had been given most clearly, no matter what contradictory behavior followed.

Sexually, the woman must exhibit an unnatural immobility. She is not required to be sexually active, "like an animal." Only passive behavior will enable her to fulfill the demand for modesty imposed on her. If the woman has an orgasm, she tries not to show it, and if she is unable to control her reaction, she denies that it was brought on by sexual ecstasy. One woman who told me she had frequent, intense orgasms commented that she "moved about a great deal during intercourse," and she had given her husband to understand that this was because she liked to change position frequently.

Even though women generally do not admit to their husbands that they experience sexual pleasure and orgasm, most men know when their wife's orgasm takes place. Nonetheless, outright initiation or active participation in the sex act are considered grounds for immediate divorce. Many women can tell you of at least one case of their acquaintance where this has happened. A woman who gives herself away and shows interest or pleasure openly is generally thought of as being licentious and lewd, and is dealt with accordingly. There were nonetheless some exceptions, where occasionally couples were in such deep accord with one another that anything was permissible, and where communication was open on every facet of the mutual experience. Needless to say, these were generally unusual people, by any measure. This phenomenon, as might be expected, occurred mostly among the educated.

Marital adjustment of Sudanese couples is reported to be unusually good, but as anywhere else, can range from excellent to very poor. As elsewhere, it is only as good as the emotional maturity, stability, and physical health of the partners, familial pressures, and social demands allow it to be.

According to various Sudanese psychiatrists I spoke to (all male, since there are no female psychiatrists in Sudan — even the male psychiatrist is a rare breed), the various crippling effects of pharaonic circumcision can be counteracted only by an unusually strong bonding between marriage partners, and in the opinion of most, the sexual response of Sudanese women is largely nothing more than a kind of stereotypic response. They are also aware that they are in a poor position to judge, since they hardly ever see female patients, and in any event, being male, can hardly expect too much accurate information on this subject, even from the few they do see. They are of the opinion that since an orgasm entails both a cerebral response and physiological responses involving muscle contractions, respiratory and vascular events, and so on, the physiological phenomenon is generally present but damaged or lessened in circumcised women. In compensation, they feel, the cerebral component may be heightened.

Shandall (1967) reports that some of the women he interviewed in Sudan had no idea of the existence of orgasm. He does not go on to report about the rest of them.

Western literature on the subject of sexual mutilation and orgasm has been sparse but convincing. In his study on hermaphroditism, Money (1955) comments that clitoridectomy (which is performed for cosmetic reasons when a serious genital anomaly exists in genetic women or girls) is the genital surgical procedure most likely to rouse psychologic debate among experts, particularly on the issue of loss of erotic sensation. He sought information about erotic sensation from the dozen nonjuvenile hyperadrenocortical virilized women he studied. There was no evidence of a deleterious effect of clitoridectomy. He further reports phantom orgasm in paraplegic and quadriplegic individuals, and found that in cases of penile amputations orgasm continued to occur. Paraplegics and quadriplegics may develop areas from which orgasm can be elicited when they have lost genital sensation.

Verkauf (1975) also reports on cases of clitoral pathology, such as tumors, that cannot be successfully treated by any other means than clitoridectomy. There seems to be no resulting impairment to sexual functioning in the cases reported.

Ladas, Whipple, and Perry (1982) claim to have found that stimulation of an area in the anterior wall of the vagina, called the Grafenberg spot, elicits ejaculation in females. They also found that uterine orgasm can occur when there is no vaginal response and no clitoral stimulation. Although they felt that most women experienced a "blended" orgasm, they also proposed that a "vulval" and "uterine" orgasm describe two ends of a continuum that represents the involvement of major muscles that participate in the different types.

Masters and Johnson (1966) report observing orgasmic response subsequent to breast manipulation.

There are women who have orgasm simply by being embraced. Other women who had their babies by natural childbirth gave glowing descriptions of orgasmic experience while giving birth, and could hardly wait to have another baby. Brain phenomena appear to be more important in producing or preventing orgasm than such questions as exactly what anatomical structures are stimulated or how they are stimulated. The purely anatomical aspects will usually take care of themselves. Although the female is capable of multiple orgasms in contrast to the male, the qualitative response in the female is related to the background, education, experience, degree of tenderness, and mutual participation in the sex act. The orgasm is a result of physiological, psychological, and sociological determinants.

Vaginal sensations are believed to be proprioceptive, which is to say they are sensations resulting from a stimulus *within* the body, not imposed from outside. The area in which the orgasm is experienced need not be the area of stimulation, and there is great variation in the area or areas stimulated, as well as the area or areas where orgasm is felt.

Among Western women the cervix has been identified by some of Kinsey's subjects, as well as many of the patients who go to gynecologists, as an area which must be stimulated by the penetrating male organ before they can achieve full and complete satisfaction in orgasm. Many females, perhaps a majority of them, find that when coitus involves deep vaginal penetrations, they secure a type of satisfaction which differs from that provided by the stimulation of the labia or clitoris alone (Kinsey, 1953). It is this type of satisfaction that women whose clitoris and labia have been excised apparently are able to retain.

While the clitoris tends to be reported as the most erotically sensitive organ in uncircumcised females, other sensitive parts of the body, such as the labia minora, the breasts, and the lips, are found to take over this erotic function in clitoridectomized females (Megafu, 1983).

For the sake of completeness, I also mention here two contributions from the popular literature: A survey by Seaman in 1972 reports on 103 contemporary American career women and students whom she describes as "models of the new woman who enjoys more than average sexual awareness and freedom." A group of women in this survey could not comment on the clitoral versus the vaginal orgasm at all, and said that to them the whole debate seemed meaningless. These women simply did not experience their orgasms in one place more than the other. Among the remainder were two extremes of women who stated a preference for or more frequent experience of one type or the other. Some women noted a difference in their response to vaginal stimulation after childbirth.

In her book *Don't Fall Off the Mountain* (1970), the actress Shirley MacLaine quotes her conversation with a Parisian prostitute:

> "Do you love your *mec?*" I asked.
> "Of course."
> "And he loves you, and doesn't mind that you are with 35 men a night?"
> "No," she shrugged. "Of course not. He got me this job and it is a good one. I get paid well, and I like my job."
> I asked her if she enjoyed physical love with her *mec*.
> "Oh yes," she said, "but not the way I used to."
> "What do you mean," I asked.
> She seemed pleased to explain, as though she were answering a question she knew intrigued everyone. "It's a question of your private place," she said. "My private place isn't here any more." She patted herself and shrugged. She reached up behind her back, touching the space between her shoulder blades. "When my *mec* caresses me here, that is all I need. But if a customer accidentally touches this place, I stop working immediately and give him his money back.
> I was overwhelmed to discover that so necessary was it for a woman to have a private place between herself and the man she loved that she actually transforms nature.

When asked to name the most sensitive parts of their bodies, circumcised women generally refer to their breasts, bellies, thighs, or necks. The genital region is almost never named spontaneously. This area is addressed only when the next question specifically asks about erotic sensation around the area of the circumcision scar or within the vagina. It is difficult to determine how much of this phenomenon is attributable to cultural factors, and how much to relocation of erogenous zones. It is most likely that both of these variables play a part, to a different extent in individual women.

In Sudan, where most marriages are arranged by the families, the relationship between men and women is far more often than not unusually loving and strongly supportive when the woman is allowed to marry a man of her own choice, or if she at least concurs with her family's choice on her behalf, and is unsuccessful when the marriage is arranged without her agreement. This distinction does not always hold true, however. Many such imposed marriages prove to be surprisingly successful. Even modern marriages are still arranged by the families, but generally with the agreement of bride and groom, or at their instigation. They appear to have a far better chance when both partners are from the same community, and where the bride is not relocated away from her own extended family to another community or her husband's extended family.

Men are not able to marry until they have raised the dowry that they must pay to the bride's family to obtain their bride. Hence, marriage is often delayed for them into the late 30s or even 40s and they tend to marry girls much younger than themselves. Many men have no heterosexual experiences whatsoever until that time. Premarital homosexual activity appears to be a widespread situational recourse, and is apparently an accepted part of the culture for all intents and purposes. Some men are willing to discuss this, others are not.

Whatever rare or isolated premarital heterosexual experience some men may have is generally with prostitutes. Prostitution in Sudan is relatively rare, and when it does exist, is very much an underground and usually urban phenomenon. In spite of the great demand for their services, prostitutes are generally not tolerated in the smaller communities, where the Islamic religion is the pervading force. Islam allows multiple marriages and concubinage, but severely disapproves of prostitution. Upon being questioned about their sexual histories, men will often say: "I was already sexually *experienced* (sic) when I married. My uncles (or other male relatives) took me to a prostitute when I reached manhood."

Female anatomy and function are generally a total mystery to men, and remain so even after marriage. The culture requires women to be extremely secretive about these matters, and so there is no sex education to be had for the young man, even from his married elders.

Doctors report that in an attempt to penetrate their wives vaginally, men often penetrate into the urinary system. Some men

create wounds (using knives, razor blades or any other cutting in-
strument) which they believe to be the vaginal orifice, and which
they then continue to use, with agonizing pain to the wife. Because
no sex education exists for women either, they are equally ignorant,
not only of male anatomy and function, but of their own anatomy
and function, and so both may continue in this fashion, believing
that things are entirely normal. Women are taught that they must
expect to suffer pain, and men that they must inflict it, and these
roles are not questioned.

The fact that most marriages are able to transcend the initial sexual trauma of penetration is nothing short of miraculous. Love and
trust play a significant role in this phenomenon. It is quite likely
that the successful overcoming of this mutually frightening, horrendous obstacle to normal sexual relations by mutual cooperation is
what cements relationships in a significant number of cases. In others, the trauma to the woman creates a permanent rift that is irreparable.

Penetration is remembered by all pharaonically infibulated
women with nightmarish clarity. The process lasts for weeks and
months and sometimes years, and every attempt — which creates
and must maintain an open wound that must not be allowed to
heal — results in more pain. There can be no question of sexual pleasure at this point. The experience is pure ordeal, and many girls run
away repeatedly from their husbands in order to escape it. It is only
some time after penetration has been accomplished, when the pain
begins to lessen and ultimately stops after the wound heals, that the
woman may begin to experience sexual pleasure and perhaps orgasm.

An important factor in this surprising ability to overcome the
protracted trauma of penetration is, again, the woman's acceptance
of the fact that this is the way things are for all women in the world
as she knows it, and that no other viable options exist for her. This
is trial by ordeal, and overcoming it successfully carries its built-in
reward — favor in the eyes of Allah, of her husband, and ultimately
attained pleasure and orgasm.

The anxieties and apprehensions of men when they marry are of a
different nature. Not only do men tend to get severe abrasions of the

penis in their attempts to penetrate, but they must also maintain the fiction that throughout this ordeal their potency never fails them. Unquestionably, under such conditions, it often does, though men will not discuss this. Failure to penetrate reflects negatively on the man's self-image, to the highest degree. A recurring story told particularly by psychiatrists concerns men who commit suicide when this happens. Some, or nearly all (Widstrand, 1965), in desperation employ "the little knife" with no anatomical knowledge to guide them, and all too often create yet more damage to the woman. In the end the midwife generally does the job, and is handsomely paid not only for her skill, but for her secrecy.

From men's personal inventories of sexual partners among intact, clitoridectomized, and pharaonically circumcised women, some comparative data are obtainable. Both Sudanese men and men from other African as well as European cultures are in general agreement that pharaonically circumcised women lose a lot. Information on the effects suffered by women who have been clitoridectomized or partially clitoridectomized but not infibulated tends to be a great deal more vague (see Appendix II).

One may only speculate as to which among the group of variables is cause and which is effect. Physical damage and trauma, psychic trauma, social values and prohibitions, cultural demands, and custom must all be considered. In any event, men generally report that pharaonically circumcised women tend as a rule to show no interest in sex, do not participate actively in the sex act, but do appear to have orgasm. They very rarely move during coitus, and when they do, it is in a characteristic rotational rather than up and down movement.

Orgasm is reported to be perceptible to the men by vaginal contractions and an increase in vaginal secretion. The orgasm, as it is thus perceived, appears weaker and less prevalent than in normal women. It also takes more time to elicit, as reported by most men who were interviewed.

Clitoridectomized and partially clitoridectomized women from Egypt and other African countries, where the lesser type of circumcision procedure is practiced, tend to be perceived as being a great deal closer to normal. Some men perceived no difference between these groups and normal women at all. Clitoridectomized and unmutilated women from bordering Ethiopia were much in demand by Sudanese men for sexual partners. Among the upper classes, European women were at a premium, unquestionably for their sexual intactness.

Shandall (1967) reports on 300 Sudanese husbands. All the men were married to two wives, one pharaonically circumcised and the other clitoridectomized or intact. All stated that they preferred the latter category sexually, because there were fewer sexual difficulties and the husband and wife shared a more equal level of sexual desire and feelings.

While the Western mind is as revolted by the contemplation of ritual clitoridectomy as it is by pharaonic circumcision and infibulation, one must nonetheless be clearly aware of the difference in medical consequences to the woman and the consequences to her marital adjustment. The more extreme procedures are unquestionably more damaging to all aspects of the woman's health and the couple's sexual adjustment. The findings of Bakr (1979), suggest that delayed sexual arousal in the pharaonically circumcised woman may be related to vulval nerve destruction. What is left out of the comparative data is the subjective experience of the woman herself. Such data are impossible to obtain, since girls are deprived of their outer genitalia long before their first heterosexual experience.

What about those women who describe themselves as being capable of very little or no sexual pleasure at all? It was obvious from the interviews that nearly all of the women who were anorgasmic were unable to experience pleasure and orgasm because sexual contact continued to be painful to their damaged bodies. In view of the repeated trauma to the sex organs in the course of their lives, this stage may be reached at any point in a woman's life, even among previously fulfilled women.

A grim, black humor has developed in women as a result of this. I was told the following "joke":

A man sets out to find a new pair of shoes, to replace his old ones, which have worn out. He is heard to mutter: "I wish I could find a pair of shoes that is made of the same material that women's sex organs are made of. They are indestructible: No matter how much you cut them and sew them back together, they are always as good as new!''

Without question there is among this group of women also a number who have been unable to process their traumata mentally, and who are, or who become at some stage in life, disinclined to participate in sexual activity as a result of this failure. Some doctors in Sudan observe, "there is no doubt that circumcision is a source of sexual and psychological shock to the girl, and leads to varying degrees of sexual aversion."

Nearly all of the women interviewed, whether at the insistence of their husbands, their own initiative, or as a result of family pressure, had themselves refibulated to pinhole size after each birth, ostensibly to enhance their desirability as sexual partners. Most women were multiparous, and went through these procedures with each birth, accumulating progressively massive scarring. A period of forcing the woman's vaginal tract open once more followed each of these resuturing procedures, which are called, rather ironically, "recircumcision" by the Sudanese. Again this process subjected women to prolonged periods of extreme pain.

Curiously, recircumcision is a "modern innovation," unlike pharaonic circumcision. It was unknown in Sudan only 50 years ago, and nearly all of the women over 60 that were interviewed had never had it performed on them. It is now practiced by a majority of women, and even more curiously, it is a phenomenon that begins with educated urban dwellers, and spreads to the uneducated in the villages.

In an extensive statistical study performed over a 5-year period by Asma El Dareer, a Sudanese doctor, for the Ministry of Health (1982a) — the first of its kind conducted there by a woman — among more than 3,000 women studied, it was found that 54% between the ages of 25 and 34 had been refibulated. This had been done to only 2% of those over the age of 64. Urban dwellers comprised 70% of refibulated women; 28% lived in rural areas. Among illiterates only 32% practiced this "repair." *All* of those who had graduated from high school or received some university training had at some time been resutured to pinhole size. Later that same year she reports that

80% of all married women in Khartoum Province undergo recir- cumcision (p. 58). She remarks that (p. 59):

> 4.2% of cases were done by doctors. One said that he talked to every woman who came to him for this purpose, explaining the consequences and saying that it was unneccessary, but found they insisted upon having it done, so he complies. His justification was that he did it in a hygienic way and lost noth- ing by it, on the contrary, he gained money. But he overlooked the fact that he is acting unethically, losing his reputation and respect instead of being a model of enlightenment for others; one can only assume that he is simply pursuing his own inter- ests. The negative effect of this is that when we try to convince women that this operation is not necessary, they immediately reply that doctors do it, therefore it must be a good thing.

The reasons for the recent, rapid popularization of this type of resuturing are difficult to pin down, although there are many ration- alizations. Men often say that women do it without consulting them. Yet it is men who pay the midwife — often a substantial amount. Women tend to say that they do it for the man's pleasure alone, and that it is done at the urging of the elder female members of the family, "so that you will be tight, and your husband will not be tempted to marry another wife" — in other words, for the wom- an's own good.

> Of the women respondents 88% (881 out of 1,100) said that their husbands agreed to it and 84% (423) of the men respon- dents wanted their wives to be recircumcised. The women in- sisted that their husbands wanted recircumcision, otherwise they would not have it done, neither would their husbands have given them money for it. Even if we told them that their husbands had said they did not want recircumcision and there- fore they had done it by themselves, they would say "They are liars, bring them here and you will see". The reason men want recircumcision for their wives is because they think that tight- ness will result in greater sexual pleasure. . . . Compliance with this operation really manifests the ignorance of women

and their acceptance of a position merely as instruments for men's pleasure. They deny their rights to equality and to have mutual feeling. What is really pitiful is that it is the younger, educated women who do it, when they should oppose, rather than popularize this practice. The most iniquitous aspect is that they set an example which is followed in the name of conformity with the mores of educated society. (Dareer, 1982a, p. 61)

(For a further discussion on this subject by an educated Sudanese woman who has this procedure done periodically, see the conversation with Eclas, pp. 111-123.)

Clearly, the intent of this practice is cosmetic, and it has developed in Sudan with its own characteristic, torturing twist. Women have themselves resutured to pinhole size in order to be "like virgins once more." The process of forcing them open once again is aimed at providing their men with a greater, special pleasure. Some men readily admit that it does this for them. Others say that they would prefer a more reasonable repair, and a more reasonably sized opening that can be penetrated easily. Such an admission is looked upon as "unmasculine," however, and a sign of weakness. In any event the matter, by their say-so, is generally taken out of their hands. "It is women's business. They do not allow you to interfere." By the time that they are able to resume intercourse, after the prescribed 40-day interval, their wives have already been sewn shut.

This concept of renewable virginity is characteristically Sudanese, and an anomaly to the Western world, where virginity is a physical condition that is absolutely and irrevocably changed by a specific behavior. By Sudanese definition, a virgin is a woman with an intact infibulation, no matter how often or for what reasons she is infibulated (Hayes, 1975, p. 622). (See also the conversation with Dr. Mohammed Abu, pp. 156-160.)

Both parties tell you that the arrangements are generally "taken care of by the grandmothers." (The old women tend to be cast as villainous scapegoats, of the evil mother-in-law variety.) They do in fact have a great deal of power over the lives of young women and girls. Women's matters are their only domain, and they may exercise this power to the fullest, in ways that peripherally also give them power over men. The young mother herself often has little say in what is done to her. There appears to be little or no communication about this crucial matter between marriage partners, and this is what puts the power so firmly into the hands of the grandmothers.

Further probing into the matter elicits the information that sexual pleasure is often enhanced for *both* partners by a tight repair. A tight fit makes the most of what is left after an extreme excision. Women are generally convinced that the remaining tissue will immediately go slack if the repair is not done very tightly. Again, the grandmothers are said to be the instigators of this. They reputedly tell the young woman that the more pain a woman experiences, the more her husband's manhood will be enhanced, and the greater will be his pleasure.

A study by Hussein et al. (1982) found, to the contrary, that 20% of Sudanese men who took a second wife said they did so only because they could no longer endure the ordeal of penetrating the progressively tightening circumcision scars of their first wives every time they had babies.

Whatever the real facts, one thing is quite clear: the midwives gain the most. Refibulations command an excellent fee, and so there is no dearth of midwives who tout and perform these procedures.

In educating young mothers in this matter, a productive tack may well be not to try to prevent them from what they apparently view as a necessary operation to keep their marriages intact, but to convince them that in an undamaged and uninfibulated female the whole vicious cycle would never have to be started at all, and therefore it behooves them to do as little damage to their daughters as is humanly possible within their own individual contexts.

There is a repeated theme of pain linked to eroticism — plainly admitted by some of my informants, and evasively denied by most. It is not surprising that many women eventually lose more and more of their desire for sex and their ability to have orgasm as they progress through these repeated traumata. Eventually many of them are defeated. It is not clear how many. It certainly is evident that among women who have had frequent cutting, resuturing, and forcible

penetrations, eventually no further repair is possible because no us-
able tissue is left for this. One can only conjecture what sinister
effects all of this pain and torture have on the mind in later years
when it is all over except, perhaps, the remaining chronic infections
and grandmotherhood.

4. Episodes and Conversations

THE HOTEL

It is nearly sundown. The train has pulled into Port Sudan, and a seemingly endless stream of dust-covered, travel-weary occupants are piling out of the densely crowded compartments and from off the roofs of the railroad cars. I have been told that there is a small hotel within perhaps a mile's walk, and so I wearily hoist my pack upon my back, grateful for the receding heat of the day, and begin my trudge up the dirt road that will lead me to it.

After perhaps three-quarters of a mile I see a fair-sized building ahead and at first assume that this will be the hotel. As I draw nearer, it becomes evident that this is some kind of medical installation, a clinic or small hospital. I continue to trek, and pretty soon I see a concrete two-story building, surrounded by a courtyard in which there are several flowering trees, an obvious relic of colonial days. This must be what I am searching for.

I enter the courtyard and walk to the entrance of the building, where there is a makeshift desk. Three men in Islamic garb are squatting on the ground against the outer wall, and as I come to a halt in front of the desk, one of them rises and walks over to me.

"Madam, what do you wish?" he asks me in English. A marked Cockney inflection suggests some past connection with London.

"I would like a room for the night."

There is a moment of reflective silence while he studies me closely.

Finally he speaks again, somewhat tentatively.

"Madam wishes a room for herself and her husband?"

"No," I answer, returning his gaze. "A room only for myself."

"But Madam," he says, apparently somehow agitated, "we have rooms for two people only."

"No matter," I say encouragingly. "I will pay for a room for two people."

As he appears to weigh this for a moment, I lower my heavy backpack to the ground, and add with some urgency, "I have been traveling for 3 days and nights. I am very tired."

Reluctantly he begins to rummage in a cardboard box, grunting and moaning to himself, and finally comes up with a key which he yields to me after a final moment of hesitation. "It is the very last room on the left on the second floor," he says finally.

I ascend the bare concrete stairs and go in search of my haven for the night. In the poorly lit hallway I pass a number of decrepit looking sinks, apparently the only facilities on the floor for washing. The room turns out to be small, musty, and starkly bare, containing only an ominously sagging bed, a battered enamel pan on the floor, and one dim, naked light bulb. The single small window is uncurtained and sports the tattered remains of a long defunct screen.

I pick up the enamel pan and retreat to the empty hall, in hopes of finding a faucet that will yield me some water. No water comes from the first one, and none from the second. At the third, I am vastly relieved to be rewarded by a thin trickle of rusty, brackish water. It will do for my needs.

I carry the pan of water back to the room, lock my door, turn off the light, take off my clothes and perform my ablutions in the dark. Then I drag the mattress off the bed and onto the floor, cover it with my sleeping bag, and lie down to sleep.

It must be some hours later. I am catapulted from a deep sleep into instant, bolt-upright wakefulness by a piercing shriek, followed by another and another and yet another, rising ever higher into a range seemingly impossible to the human voice, and yet unquestionably redolent with some horrendous human terror or human agony.

With shaking fingers I pull on my clothes, unlock the door and yank it open. The hall is empty. The screams have now given way to a shrill wail, and finally a howling of the same unintelligible phrase over and over again.

I run down the stairs with trembling legs, toward the door and out into the courtyard. The same three men are squatting against the wall. One of them is chanting in a high whining monotone: "Allah! Allah! Allah! Allah! Allah!"

I run over to them. "What is happening? What were those screams? They came from the room next to mine! Quickly, you must go to see what is going on!"

The English speaking one comes toward me and tries to soothe me in a voice that one would use with a frightened child. "It is nothing, Madam. Go back to sleep."

I am about to protest when yet another voice begins to wail, despairing, hopeless, from another part of the hotel.

I begin to lose control. "Someone is being hurt!" I shout at the man. "You must *do* something!" And when he does not move: "What kind of place *is* this?"

The third man rises to help calm me down. He too speaks English. "Madam," I hear him say in his gentle African voice, "did they not tell you? This is a honeymoon hotel. There is nothing to be done."

It is as if icy water has been dashed in my face. I take a deep breath and almost instantly stop trembling. I look at him and smile bitterly. "But of course. It is all so logical. The honeymoon hotel is right next to the hospital." My voice has returned to something akin to normal. I feel numb all over.

Slowly I walk up the stairs, back to my room, wrestle the mattress back onto the springs, gather my gear together, heave my pack onto my back and leave the honeymoon hotel without so much as a backward glance.

Back at the train station I see that a large number of people are already sleeping alongside the track, waiting for tomorrow's train. It is here that I spend the night.

SOFIA AND SIDAHAMED

Sofia has haunted, tragic eyes, set in a discontented face. The greatest source of her unhappiness is Sidahamed, her husband, who has two other wives. Sidahamed, an animated, charming, and slightly odd fellow, is a doctor. His house is frequented by a never-ending flow of all manner of friends. He does not own a vehicle, so a stream of these friends drives him wherever he needs to go.

Whenever I require some sort of permission from the authorities, Sidahamed provides me with letters of introduction, and I need only produce such a letter and the recipient immediately breaks into happy laughter. "Ah yes, Doctor Sidahamed! What a wonderful, funny man. I went to school with him." Or: "We were in the Army together!" And then there follow all kinds of Sidahamed anecdotes, illustrating what a clever, amusing chap he is, and what wonderful pranks he used to organize, and what splendid solutions he finds to all sorts of problems.

Anyone who is a friend of Sidahamed's immediately becomes a friend of theirs, and so do I. "You say you want a vehicle to take you to the medical installation? Of course. We can arrange it." "You would like to obtain transport to Juba? Certainly. It is no problem at all. A military plane will fly there next week sometime. It can all be arranged." Sidahamed, it appears, is definitely a good man to know.

Eventually all the good intentions and promises come to naught, as is customary in my dealings with the Sudanese bureaucracy, and it is found that after all nothing can be done, to everyone's great regret. But how charmingly one is informed of this! "What a shame. There is no petrol to be had." "It is really too bad. The transport plane is not going to Juba after all." (From my own sources I find out that it has already left, and that its mission is such that my presence on it would have proven to be embarrassing.) And so, as usual, I am left to find other arrangements, somewhat more devious, and without the blessings of officialdom—but far, far more effective.

Still, what a delightful, clever man Sidahamed is. Everyone seems to love him. His colleagues all say that he is a very intelligent man, if somewhat nervous. They do not approve of his many wives, and so they are never among the many friends that frequent Sidahamed's house. They tell me that polygamy is not at all acceptable to educated people nowadays, and think of his behavior as quite scandalous.

Sidahamed has installed his mother in a hut on the border of the most pestilent slum in Port Sudan, a fly-infested disease pit of cardboard and tin can shacks, populated by half-starved Erytrean refugees and other African displaced persons and migrants. In spite of the suffocating stench of garbage, she seems to be quite comfortable there, preferring the autonomy of this hut to sharing Sofia's quarters in what is at best an uneasy impasse.

Sofia thinks that what Sidahamed has done with his mother is disgraceful, and she says so often and with great vehemence behind his back. There is no love lost between her and the old woman, but Sofia's sense of what is right and what is wrong in this regard is outraged. "He would not have to put his mother into such a terrible place if he did not have three wives to support," she tells me bitterly. "He maintains four separate households, and every one of them is poor! Only Fahtma has decent furniture."

When I met Sofia on my first journey to Sudan, her only other rival was Fahtma, a heavy, jowled, chronically angry woman who lives in the apartment adjoining Sofia's. The two women hate one another openly, and never speak to each other. If communication becomes necessary, messages are relayed via the children, who move freely from one dwelling to the other and appear to get on quite well together. When by chance the wives pass each other in the passage way, they turn cold, haughty faces away and proceed in stony silence, cultivating their anger.

Sofia tells me that when Sidahamed first courted her they wrote poetry to one another. He promised her that if she would marry him, he would divorce Fahtma. But he broke his promise, she tells me bitterly. Fahtma's family was much too influential to allow the divorce, and she had already given birth to Sidahamed's three sons. And so, instead of divorcing her, Sidahamed told Fahtma that he was taking a second wife. He gave her his reasons: She was too demanding and domineering. He felt stifled by her.

He spent the first 4 weeks of his new marriage with Sofia, and then settled into a new routine of alternate days with each wife. Sofia has never been able to accept this bitter betrayal. She suffers acutely from jealousy whenever Sidahamed is with Fahtma. "He is a bad man," she tells me, "and a liar. I never would have married him if I had known he would do this."

Sofia is headmistress at the secondary high school for girls. Although she holds a very responsible position she earns only a small salary. Teachers in general are poorly paid in Sudan, and those that teach in girls' schools earn a fraction of what those teaching in boys' schools earn. She complains about this a great deal, and Sidahamed likes to tease her. "Sofia is going to learn how to be a midwife," he tells me. "She is going to learn how to do circumcisions. Then she will have all the money she needs, and many gifts besides." Sofia shakes her head emphatically. "Don't listen to him," she snaps. "He is teasing both of us. I would never even think of doing such a thing." She glares at Sidahamed openly, "Why do you say such things to her when you know it isn't true?" Obviously, however, the thought has more than just crossed her mind. Sofia's unhappiness expresses itself in greed. She tries constantly to wheedle from me my camera, my golden ring, my clothing, my shoes.

Sofia has three sons and four daughters. All but the youngest girl have already been pharaonically circumcised. Only the little one remains intact, she tells me.

I ask Sidahamed to describe the circumcision of his daughters to me. "It is all very primitive and barbaric," he tells me in a detached manner. "During the summer they are taken to a kind of resort by their grandmothers. The girls are taken by force and without anesthesia. A midwife performs the operation, while four or five women hold the girl down. Afterwards, the legs are tied together while the girl heals, and after 40 days, the grandmother returns home with her." If there are no complications the only difference that is apparent to him afterwards is that the girl appears to be "less hyperactive, more quiet and withdrawn."

Sofia's youngest is only 1-year-old. She toddles about happily, without a care in the world. "What will you do when her time comes?" I ask Sofia. "I will do *sunna*," she says. "I wanted to do *sunna* with the others, but Sidahamed's mother insisted on the pharaonic. When I told him that I felt it would be better to do *sunna*, he gave me no support and left the whole thing up to his mother. "She is wiser than we both are." That was his excuse. But I think that he is weak, and not the master of his own house. He is a grown man, and too old to have to listen to a mother who is an ignorant village woman. With the little one perhaps I will have a chance, because she no longer lives with us now." She sighs deeply. "Yes I must try. I want to do *sunna*, only a part of the clitoris. I do not dare leave her uncircumcised, because if I do, Sidahamed's relatives will surely take her and do the pharaonic."

Two years later I return to Sudan and visit Sofia once more. "I told you he was a bad man," she announces triumphantly as soon as I enter the house. "He has taken a third wife! He has married Muna. Now I see him only every *third* day, and the children hardly know their father. He is very bad and you will see, he will marry a *fourth* one. He will marry a fourth one because I myself will bring her to him!" she concludes with bitter anger.

Muna is a beautiful young Nigerian, formerly Sidahamed's medical technician. He is obviously much enthralled by her, and proud of the fact that she is relatively well educated. She lives serenely in a modest mud house, next to her sister in the nearby village of Suakin, with her newborn son Mohammed. Sidahamed spends every third night with her, in turn with his other two wives. He is scrupulously correct in 'this, no matter where his inclinations may pull him. However, Muna also accompanies him daily to the office, where she sits quietly playing with Mohammed in the anteroom while he is seeing his patients. He spends whatever free time he has with them. He is also openly affectionate with Muna, who accepts this with great pleasure.

"I knew it was going to happen," Sofia tells me. "He called the whole family together to give us all his reasons for marrying again. He told Fahtma that she is an ill-tempered old woman whom no one could please." She snorts with evident satisfaction. Then she tosses her head, "He told *me* I was jealous and greedy. He said he had no peace with either of us, and he was marrying Muna because she was always pleasant and easy to satisfy." She laughs bitterly. "Well, let us wait and see how satisfied she is in a few years' time, when he begins writing poetry to another woman, and he calls us all together again and tells us what is wrong with us!" She shakes her head sadly. "I am not angry at Muna," she says. "It is not her fault. She is a good girl. But he is a bad man, a very bad man."

Sofia's youngest is now 3 years old. She is a lively little imp, full of mischief. She loves to mimic my speech and dissolves into giggles at the garbled sounds she produces. She climbs everywhere, onto the furniture, along the stair railings and onto the stone abutments. She even stacks a teetering tower of boxes alongside the refrigerator, and attempts to scale its dizzying heights.

She loves to take off her underclothes in the manner of small girls everywhere, and her little hand often explores between her legs. Sofia sees my eyes on the child and guesses correctly that I'm trying to see whether she is still intact. "I did *sunna* on her," she tells me. "So very young?" I ask. She nods assent. "I could not bear to wait. She is the last one, and I wanted it over once and for all. I did it without telling the doctor or his mother beforehand. Only the tip of the clitoris, no more. Hardly anything at all. Just the part that protrudes; she does not miss it. There were no complications. It was all over in 3 days." She looks pleased.

Two years after this conversation I visit Sidahamed and his wives once more. Sofia is largely unchanged, as is Fahtma, except that they have both grown still more angry and contentious. Sofia's former beauty has all but disappeared under rolls of overlapping fat. She moves more and more slowly. Her voice has grown monotonous, her eyes hopeless.

In Muna's beautiful face, lines of anxiety have appeared where there were none before. She has just given birth to a second son, Sidahamed's 15th child. She never takes her eyes away from Sidahamed, chewing her tongue all the while. Her formerly radiant smile appears to be gone. I no longer see it light her face.

Sidahamed is once more writing poetry. He shows me a poem on which he is presently working. It is a love poem.

Sofia's smallest girl is now 5. There has been a considerable change in her. No trace of her former high spirits remains. The child clings to Sofia's skirts, constantly following her mother around the house. Whenever Sofia sits down, she crawls into her lap, and at night she sleeps curled up in the crook of Sofia's body like a small marsupial.

"She goes everywhere with me," Sofia tells me, staring into space, as if at some phantasm. "She only wants her mother. She is afraid I will leave her, and when I go to work at the school, she comes with me and sits in my office drawing pictures." She cuddles the child to her opulent body tenderly. "I think she is afraid of growing up," she says.

The child no longer plays her little teasing games with me. She helps her mother with the housework, meticulously washing the floor. She wraps her small body in her mother's garments. No longer does she climb furniture or explore her body.

It is not difficult to figure out the truth, and yet the truth comes as a shock, almost as a betrayal. The supposed *sunna* that Sofia claims to have done on her child was no more than wishful thinking. The child has in fact been subjected to a pharaonic circumcision only 4 months ago. A neighbor confirms this for me.

ECLAS

Eclas is a softly feminine woman of 43. She is a biology professor at the university, an intellectually liberated woman, and thereby something of a rarity in Sudan. Her assertiveness, her air of assurance and self-esteem, put her in a class by herself in this land where those qualities are only rarely seen in women.

In spite of her many friendships among colleagues, her large and closely knit extended family, and her outgoing personality, there is also an indefinable aura of loneliness about her. She is obviously unique at something of a price.

Among her male colleagues, she has become quite proficient in playing two roles. While being "one of the boys" with whom the men can discuss anything a Sudanese woman generally dares not discuss, she yet remains level-headed and altogether decorous in her interactions, as befits a woman's role.

I first meet Eclas due to some curious circumstances. At the beginning of my second journey to Khartoum, I find upon my arrival that my well planned and carefully arranged accommodations are nonexistent. A full afternoon's searching, carrying an impossibly heavy backpack in the blistering heat, reveals that there isn't a room to be had anywhere. I present myself, as evening falls, at the main police station, and ask to spend the night there, since I have long since learned that this is the way to solve such a problem in Sudan. There is the usual display of chagrin and shuffling around, the emphatic protestations that what I ask is completely impossible. I have also learned what I have to do next. I sit down and smile, and wait, and smile some more. Pretty soon things quiet down, there is some conferring in low voices, and then I am brought the usual glass of tea, and some pleasant conversation ensues. Since it is already well into the evening, it is agreed that I can spend the night sleeping on the station floor, among all sorts of other people who eventually also sleep there, and so I calmly pull out my sleeping bag, secure in the knowledge that I am going to be very well looked after.

In the morning there is more tea, and the usual letters of introduction are written. In the course of the day I am passed from person to person, and after a long, circuitous route eventually wind up at the house of Eclas, who serenely extends her hand, her hospitality, and accepts me into her household as if I were a lifelong and very dear friend.

Thereafter we have many long, searching conversations, and I am touched by her candor and the willingness with which she opens the book of her life to me. She lets me know that she strongly believes in the value of what I am doing, and explores the intimate facets of her life for me, while I record them.

"Those of us who have been circumcised, and who come in contact with books and information from the outside world, gradually develop the awareness of a right we did not know existed—the right to a complete body. You are deprived of it as a small child by an act that may even take place with your consent. It is a meaningless consent because you are too young to understand what you are consenting to. As far as my own daughter is concerned, I am not going to have her circumcised as is customary. If she decides that she wants a circumcision when she is grown, it can be performed then, when she understands what it is all about. In my mother's day, when Egyptian women married Sudanese men, it was a common occurrence that they had themselves circumcised at marriage or after the birth of the first child. It was always done with the woman's consent, to give more pleasure to her husband. Some of them did not agree to it and told their husbands, 'This is how I am; you knew it when you married me. I shall stay that way.' But then often the women of his family would talk to the bride and tell her that there would be more excitement for her husband if she were sewn tightly, and eventually she would give in and have it done, generally after the delivery of the first child. Some continued to refuse and lived on like that, whether the husband liked it or not.

"I did not have my daughter done because I feel that perhaps she would be able to get more out of her sex life. I wanted to give her that chance. Suppose she gets married to someone who wants her intact. She may feel deprived and on the outs with her peer group now, but she will get some understanding when she grows up. I hope with all my heart that when she gets to be a woman things will have changed here. I am very sure that had I not been circumcised at all, I would have a far happier sexual relationship with my husband.

"I have not had as severe a circumcision as most of the women here have had. Part of my clitoris and all of the outer labia are left. Compared to what most women here have undergone, I am most fortunate. My condition is not what you would call normal, but with me things are certainly better than with most. I was infibulated only partially, and therefore have never had trouble with my menstruation. For that matter, I have never had any gynecological problems at all. I did not suffer any pain when I first had relations with my husband. True, I was terrified, but I did not suffer. After the first child, they sewed me up. I told the nurse who was an Italian nun: 'What you have opened, close again. Do not leave a wound there.' She herself decided to put in an extra stitch. After my second child I did not have any sewing up. After my third child, I myself decided to have the loose tissue tightened. My deliveries have always been relatively quick and easy. I tell the nurse: 'Don't give me any injections, any analgesics. Just cut what has to be cut, and get the child out.'

"I was brought up in a convent and was taught nothing about life. If someone had told me that babies just pop out of your belly I would have believed it. If it had not been for my own mother's deliveries and we girls having to wash and change her afterwards, I would have believed them if they had told me babies come out of your ears. I had absolutely no idea of what goes on between a man and a woman until the age of 17. Then I began to read about it, and learn what it could or should be like.

"I do get orgasms in my relations with my husband, but when I read books I realize that it is probably different with women who are not circumcised. I really have no way of knowing. If I had a husband who is not as sensitive a man as my present husband is, I don't think I could be as happy or satisfied as I am. If he did not know the art of making me part of the excitement, I think I would have become a very miserable person. I don't believe I would have stayed with him. I feel that I have been very lucky in this. It would have been terrible to have been deprived not only of something nature had endowed me with, but had I been married to a man who did not make an effort to give me pleasure, I don't think I would have been able to speak about my feelings. My husband and I talk about a lot of things together. I think he would have hated me if I had circumcised our daughter, but he never would have interfered. Things concerning her are left to me. He approved fully of my decision, but it was I who had to make it.

"My uncle was very much against having his daughters circumcised, but his wishes were not respected. His wife was with him when he worked in Saudi Arabia, where there is no circumcision. When the girls were of the customary age, she returned with them to Sudan. Her mother and aunt arranged for them to have a modified pharaonic. My uncle wrote letters, pleading that his daughters not be touched. After his return here, he would not speak to any of them for a full year. Then he accepted the situation as irreparable. What was done, was already done. He still hates all of them—all of them who participated in the crime. Yet in a way, his daughters were lucky. If his mother had made the arrangements, they surely would have had a complete pharaonic.

"I have many beautiful memories of my childhood. My father did not have any sons until much later in life, and everyone else in the family already did. Now that I think about it, he may have felt a bit deprived because he used to let us girls wear trousers and boys' shoes and to act like boys for many years. I was sent to boarding school when I was 4, and my three sisters and I used to spend our entire 3 months' summer vacation with our parents.

"The school was a Catholic mission, and I loved it there. I was so young when I came there that it was easy for me to adjust to the system. Sometimes it still surges up in me that I should have learned something about the facts of life there, but I also realize that the Catholic nuns were personally unable to teach it. I left them when I was 13 years old, and I feel now that to allow a child to enter puberty knowing nothing about her own body is very unfair.

"I cannot tell you when I was circumcised. Perhaps I was 4 or 5 years old. I don't remember anything except that I was lying in a bed with my three older sisters. We were all done on the same day, and I was the youngest. Perhaps it was done before I was sent off to school. It was in somebody's home, and this is truly all I can recall. I don't remember the operation at all. Only this large bed, and then there was something about eating boiled eggs. That is all. Nothing, nothing else comes to my mind. There was no such thing as analgesic at that time, but I remember no pain. My grandmother was a very progressive woman, and compared to what was done to others, she barely had us touched. Her granddaughters were not done, as they say, "properly." "Properly" means to cut everything off so that it looks clean, as if nothing had ever been there. A lot of my cousins, more than half of them, when it was time to get married had the whole thing done over. This was particularly true of the older cousins, who married into families where they would have been looked down upon if they had not been sewn up and closed before marriage. They would not have been considered to be the right quality without that. It made me realize how different the girls in my family were.

"When I was at boarding school there were just six of us. Two Egyptian girls and we four sisters. No one talked about circumcision. I naturally assumed that the Egyptian girls were circumcised, same as we. I don't know if they were or not. Later, my closest friend was a Syrian girl, and she was uncircumcised. The only time I heard the topic mentioned was still later, when I was at the American Mission School. All the girls there were Sudanese, and we would ask one another if we were circumcised. The conversation never went beyond that.

"The first time I heard a discussion of circumcision and its effect on women's subsequent lives was at the university, when I met some 3rd-year students. They talked quite freely about it among themselves, and for the first time in my life I realized we were different from women in other parts of the world. Until then I had not been aware of the fact that circumcision has an effect on your health and on your sexual life. Truthfully, my first reaction was one of relief, upon realizing that my circumcision was not as severe as theirs, and that the damage done to me and my whole life was correspondingly less.

"I have never before spoken to anyone about how grateful I am to my grandmother for not scraping me clean. She left me to be at least partially a normal woman, even if she did cut off some parts of me. She let me keep part of what is natural. Very primitive people who live close to the animals are untouched, yet they live as human beings. When you begin to cut parts of a human being away, you remove part of their humanity and part of their natural state. You reduce them. A child of 5 or 6 is not capable of giving her consent to this. If everyone in her family is circumcised and expects her to be circumcised, how can she say no, even if they ask her?

"It is different now with the tribal scars. When they ask children nowadays if they want the tribal markings, they say no, and when the woman who does them comes, they run away. So that practice is beginning to stop, and many teenagers have unmarked faces. But we are brought up to believe that all sorts of evil things will happen to us if we are not circumcised. The only thing they say to you if you do not consent to the tribal mark is: "If you refuse to do it, you will not be beautiful." That is all. It is not shameful to go without tribal scars, but it is very shameful not to be circumcised. Only the daughters of prostitutes, slaves, and idiots are not circumcised. Nobody wants to be categorized along with those.

"I got married when I was 25. I was afraid my first sexual experience would be cruel and painful. I had heard many terrible stories from my friends. I had known my husband as such a loving person before our marriage. I could not help but think of what might happen to my feelings toward him if my first experiences were as terrible as some I had heard about. What helped a lot was that we got married outside the country, and there was no one to poison my mind. It is customary for the older women of the family to indoctrinate the bride on how she is to behave sexually toward her husband, and what she can expect. My husband never allowed this.

"My own sister tried to talk to me, and even though she meant well and was trying to prepare me for the worst, I would not listen to her. She tried to tell me not to give myself to my husband immediately, to tease and tantalize him, to excite him, but I told her not to waste her energy. I wanted things to happen as they would happen, just between the two of us. She told me I would regret my stubborn attitude, but I never did. My father had brought me up to be myself, so I was able to have my own way.

"I suppose I also learned to be strong when I had to look out for myself at a very early age. In a boarding school you learn to fend for yourself early. I managed to survive that way and I learned to fight.

"My happiest times were with my father. He worked with the engineering department, which meant that he spent most of his time in the field, in the vicinity of some small village or other. We used to be able to go with him and live a lot of the time in nature as free as birds. After all year in a strict boarding school it was heaven.

"My father was very proud of us. He always said: 'One of my daughters is better than 10 men.' It really made us feel great. Our chins were always up in the air. We must have been the only Sudanese females then who were free to roam around instead of being cooped up and overprotected. We had 100 times more freedom than even the European girls we knew. When we went back to the strictness of school, we fitted ourselves right back into the system without any difficulties. One was vacation, and the other was school, and we knew the difference between the two. Then, whenever we came to the capital, he took us out and showed us a really good time. I loved him very much. I loved both of them very much. I never had any bad feelings toward them. I don't think my circumcision made any difference in that. I probably screamed and carried on a lot. Most girls do. But if it had been a prolonged, agonizing experience I would have remembered it. I think that if something like that happens to you, you remember it no matter how young you were when it happened. Perhaps it was painful at the time that it was done, but it was not something that created continuous pain and difficulties for me later. I think what made the difference was that my grandmother left me partially opened. She did not sew me shut all the way.

"Whenever I have a delivery, and I have some stitches where I'd been cut, for the first week or two it is painful to urinate. The urine burns on the wounded places. If I had had this experience in childhood, I do not think I would have forgotten it. There may be some other explanation, but I have no idea what it could be.

"Suppose I had been pharaonically circumcised. This is how I would probably feel: 'I have survived; it is done. I don't know anything else about life and women and sex except that this is the way things are, and this is the way things should be. It is done to all women in the world as far as I know about it. The world in which it is not done, as far as I perceive, does not exist. I live my life in a community where every other woman is like me.'

"Then, suppose one day I see one of those films that shows what a circumcision is like, and I see the horrible operation that has been done to me in this film. Not only I, but all of us to whom this had been done would be shocked and disgusted by the cutting and gushing of blood and the stitching. Then we would think of it as a horrible crime. Then we would understand what we have suffered. But the women who have experienced these things as a temporary pain, lasting perhaps 4 days or a week, normally don't think about them. It is not something that stays in their minds.

"It is done at such a young age, and in no time at all they are well again and go back to playing their games. It doesn't really sink in, what has been done, and the problems later, when you are a woman, seem to have no connection to it. If you were to show this film to little girls who want to be circumcised and tell them that this will be done to them, you wouldn't be able to catch them, they would run away so fast. They would not be able to sleep, knowing what was in store for them. Ignorance is what we must fight against if we are to stop this custom.

"I never felt that my parents let me down or that they did not love me. All my life I have boasted about how well they treated me and all they have done for me. I trusted them completely, and they never once betrayed that trust. It was not my mother and father who did this thing to me. It was my grandmother. It is àlways someone outside of the nuclear family. It is the job of the midwife, the *bahara*. When a girl does not obey her parents, they will say: 'I am going to get the *bahara* with her razor blade.'

"I was a particularly lucky child, especially in the father I had. He must have loved us a lot to put us in that boarding school. I know he had to sacrifice a great deal to be able to do it. I married a man who is very much like him. He was my university professor and quite a few years older than I was. I don't think I would have been happy with a contemporary.

"I want to tell you something about my grandmother. She was left with a big family when her husband died suddenly in the prime of life. She had a very strong character. She brought up her children alone, and everyone had deep respect for her. She was one of the first medically trained midwives, and was highly thought of by everyone.

"No one in the entire family dared oppose her. All the kids, my sisters and cousins, were terrified of her. If one of us did something wrong and she could not find out which one of us had done it, she would put us all in a row, perhaps 20 of us, and she would whip us all, one right after the other. She used to come and stay with us once in a while, and she was the best of all grandmothers. She would tell us stories in the evenings, and she had a wonderful sense of humor. Those were the best times of all. Later, when I was at university, she became partially paralyzed. It did not stop her from telling her stories about the old days, and she made us live the wonderfully vivid experiences she related to us. She was much respected and loved by everyone who had contact with her, and I remember her with a great deal of happiness and love.

"Some in the family did not feel the gratitude I felt that she did not scrape us clean. It happened several times; when one of my cousins was getting married it was said: 'If grandmother had circumcised her properly, she would not have to be done over now.' There were quite a few of us who were afraid we would be looked down upon by our future husbands' families because of this. It was of course common knowledge that we were circumcised in this fashion. Generally it would be resolved with the mothers getting together and having the girl done 'properly.'

"My own husband had lived abroad a lot and he was happy to find out that I was only 'half done.' I keep joking with him and telling him half done is better than nothing.

"A cousin of mine has a repair operation every time she delivers. She is one of the ones who got herself done 'properly.' After the last delivery she was told not to come again for a repair. There was no tissue left with which to repair her. This kind of thing happens to a lot of pharaonically circumcised women sooner or later. This one had repairs done sometimes even when she had not had a baby. A lot of women do this, as a kind of a gift to their husbands.

"Suppose your husband has to go abroad for 3 or 4 months. And suppose your youngest child is 3 or 4 years old. And suppose you feel you will give and receive more pleasure if you have a few stitches to tighten your vagina — well, you do it and you have a nice surprise for your husband when he returns. A lot of women don't wait to have a child to do it.

"With all respect to my husband, I would not cut myself up for anybody else. But if I myself am going to get pleasure out of it, I'll do it. I think most women feel this way. If a woman has to compete with another wife, she might do it for her husband's pleasure in order to hold him. But in most cases women accept the pain because the result will bring them more pleasure.

"This is how I see it: Most of your sensitive parts have been cut off. All you have left is a hole, and this hole at a certain degree of tightness gives pleasure to a woman by her husband's penis rubbing against the sensitive area inside. He gets pleasure from the tightness. With use, this tightness of damaged tissue begins to give, and his pleasure is diminished when he goes in and out of a loose opening, not touching anything. It must be very frustrating to the man when this happens. At the same time, he is not placing any friction on her sensitive inner areas. You must remember that she is completely dependent on those areas for her pleasure, and when these are not sufficiently stimulated, she feels nothing.

"When things reach this state of affairs, where neither of them is getting pleasure, he might not directly say anything to her, but she will perceive that he is progressively exhausting himself without either of them reaching a climax. They will both become increasingly frustrated and irritable and she will reach a point where she decides to go and have this stitching operation done on herself, not only for his pleasure, but for her own as well.

"People are by nature selfish, and a person, especially a modern, educated woman, would not have an operation done on her own body just to please someone else. It has to be because she herself is no longer getting pleasure.

"It is sad that the most sensitive parts of a woman are cut away, so that in order to have any pleasure at all, a woman has to keep having these operations. If they had left her intact to begin with, she would not have to go through all this. She would not have to be cut and repaired every time she gives birth.

"It must be even more frustrating in the later years of a woman's life, when you are at an age at which people feel you should no longer have any interest in sex. You would like to continue having an active sex life, and yet you may not have the courage to have another tightening operation for fear of what people will say about you. 'Look at her,' they will say, 'At her age she is doing that.'

"Everybody knows everybody's business, and when you have that operation you have to be in bed for a few days. When a woman has a child at the same time as her daughter, they talk about her behind her back. She may yet be a young woman if she had her daughter at a very young age, and if her daughter married young as well. She will not have the courage to have the operation, so her married life suffers, and she suffers. A lot of women want to continue to have a healthy, normal sex life, say, after the age of 40 or 45, but they can't have that. Perhaps this is why some men take a young second wife at that period. Believe me, they love their first wife and they feel a great deal of sadness about it. If they could hide that aspect of their lives, they'd do so. If they could have their sexual needs satisfied, without anyone finding out, they would, if only for their children, who by this time are old enough to know what is going on.

"Women tend to age faster here than men do. When they get to be a certain age, they resign themselves to being grandmothers, and to want nothing else from life for themselves. I am almost at that age, but I want more than that from life, believe me.

"I sometimes wonder if my husband would not be happier if he had married a European woman. I think perhaps our relations would be different if I had not been circumcised. I'm sure he had had experience with women in Europe before he married me. Even if I am not circumcised in the pharaonic way, I am still circumcised, and I must be different from other women to whom this has not been done.

"He never says to me that he is not satisfied. In fact, all I ever hear from him is the exact opposite. He tells me very often that he is very pleased with our relations. One does not generally say these things, but he has never given me reason to believe that he feels we are not extremely good together. He is sexually very happy with me, and I am very happy with him.

"Before I married I used to be afraid I would never have an

orgasm. There was no way I could find out before marriage if I would or would not, and so this anxiety stayed with me for some time since I married rather late. I think every unmarried woman in Sudan has that fear.

"You have asked me how the pharaonic affects women psychologically. Well, I think in order to get an answer to that question you would have to get a well-educated girl who has had considerable life experience—far more than most women have the chance to have here. She will have been circumcised in the pharaonic way, and she has been so scarred pyschologically that she is full of repressed rage. I think that you would find that she is unable to feel any pleasure at all, that she accepts intercourse without any desire or any feeling. She goes to bed with her husband out of a sense of duty, and tries to keep from him the fact that she really hates the whole business and gets nothing out of it.

"She would look for a platonic relationship and she would love a man to the point of madness—but never in a physical way. Her relationship would be extremely fragile, easily shattered. She would be so sensitive that the least little thing could upset her state of balance. She would have such an enormous feeling of deprivation inside of her, that she could hardly handle her feelings of rage. She could be beautiful, educated, economically secure, and sought after. She would still feel monstrously deprived and cheated and nothing would satisfy her.

"Her rage would be felt toward society in general, but it would be directed largely at her husband. Oh, he might be good to her, and she would say how very good to her he is, but the rest of it she would not say, and that would be, 'But I cannot love him or any man.'

"This was true of me in a way when I first married my husband. If it had not been for somebody who told me to be patient, I would have left him.

"Some women who are very, very strong live with their feelings of deprivation and their rage and their inability to love, and no one will know how they really feel. They will be dead inside, only nobody else will know this. They will simply live a lie.

"Do you want to know what happens to the rage? Perhaps when they get to be older they exercise power over young people's lives.

They deprive their daughters and their granddaughters of what they themselves have been deprived of. When they inflict these things on their children, they make another man suffer for what they have suffered with their own husbands."

AHMED

Ahmed, a 32-year-old veterinarian, is the half-brother of Eclas, born to their father by a later marriage. His young wife, a doe-eyed, flowerlike girl, openly adores him. When Ahmed and Eclas speak of their father, it is as if they were speaking of two entirely different men. Ahmed, so soft and protective toward the two women, bristles with resentment as he speaks of him.

"My mother had 10 children, and my father, in his life-time, had 5 wives. Two he divorced because they were sterile. Altogether, he had 25 children. My mother was the third wife.

"I've always had a fairly good chance in life because my father was an engineer, a very unusual thing at the time, and very well paid by Sudanese standards. We lived and dressed well, and had the opportunity to receive an education. Our circumstances were certainly well above the average.

"I was always close to my brothers. We did everything together. The relationship to our father was hard. Fathers by tradition are very tough on their sons here. I don't remember my father ever smiling at me. He simply gave orders and I had to obey them. I was very much afraid of him. I am still afraid of him. Most people of my age here cannot even smoke in front of their fathers. This is true even when they are 40 or 50 years old. Things are changing now, and I am not treating my children the same way. I am going to give them all the love I possibly can.

"My father beat me a lot, for everything and anything, for the slightest mistake. It was just his way, the way he himself had been brought up. Things were rough at that time. There were so many of us children.

"My mother received orders from my father, and she also had to carry them out exactly as he wanted. Women here usually have very little to say. When my father died, she brought us up alone. She sacrificed a lot for our education. I actually know very little about my father. He was with us so rarely, he had so many wives. I was always with my mother. She worked very hard, keeping house. She was a very gentle woman. I don't remember ever being afraid of her.

"My first sexual experience was with a prostitute. It was very quick because I was so afraid and I wanted to get it over with as fast as possible. She was a Sudanese woman, and of course was pharaonically circumcised. At that time I did not know that there was anything other than women being circumcised. As a matter of fact, until recently it never occurred to me that there was anything *strange* about women's circumcision. In my mind it was a normal thing. I had grown up with it, and I had known about it far earlier than I had found out about the 'facts of life.' I did not become aware of the fact that there is anything wrong with it until I studied at the university and learned the function of these external genitalia that are removed, and how a woman's whole life is affected by their removal. Then I realized how awful it is for her. Before then, I had simply accepted it without question.

"I did not have any experience with European women when I attended the university there. I was too involved in my studies. But I was experienced in sexual matters when I married my wife. The first experiences were very painful for her. For a very long time we could not enjoy sex together, because it was a unilateral thing. It was I who had the orgasm. She only had fear and pain. I had had some experience, and I knew either I would ruin the whole relationship, or with gentleness and patience I would eventually solve the problem. I loved her very much, and for a long time, for several months, we both tried very hard to make it work. It was a nightmare. Of course I wanted sex. Every time I approached her sexually, she bled. The wound I had caused was never able to heal. I felt horribly guilty. The whole thing was so abnormal. The thought that I was hurting someone I loved so dearly troubled me greatly. I felt like an animal. It is an experience that I would rather not remember. It was bad for both of us. It was not until after our first child was born that she could have relations without pain, and then she was able to enjoy sex for the first time. The child was born in England, and she was not resutured. I don't think I would permit that to be done to her again. Things are very good the way they are now, and we both enjoy sex together very much, now that nobody is suffering any pain.

"Most men, when they talk among themselves, try to create the impression that they were able to penetrate their wives in the first night. I have had medical training as a veterinarian, and I know for a fact that this is virtually impossible. You are dealing with heavy scar tissue that is overgrown, and you are using flesh to penetrate it, and not iron. You could not penetrate a wall with flesh, and this is like a wall. Actually most men are afraid. Perhaps not as much as women are, because women suffer most of the pain, but nonetheless they too are afraid. I have two very good friends that are doctors. They used some local anesthetic on their wives, and opened them with surgical scissors. Then they gave them time to heal, and that was it. No problems.

"Other men use razors or knives. Or they take her to the midwife, secretly, and have the midwife cut her. A man who does not do this tends to get a lot of abrasions. Among the populace, there is a big celebration on the day the girl is penetrated. The couple is put in a room together, and everybody sits outside, chatting and laughing, waiting for the groom to do the job. The girl can be heard shrieking and crying. When the man finally comes out, he very often has to go to the hospital himself, along with his wife. He will have injured himself as well. A friend of mine got abrasions all over his penis—for being such a fool. Most of the men who try to get through the first day get very drunk so they will not feel what they are doing, because they know they are doing something wrong. When they are drunk, they do not care what their partners are suffering.

"Most men do not want their wives closed up again after they have had children—at least not as tightly as they sew them here. That bit of business is generally the doing of the girl's mother, most likely. That is the way they were brought up. They believe that this is the way men want it, and it is not a matter that men and women have ever talked about. Now they discuss it more and more. I know so many people where the wives had this done, and the husbands told them to go back to the *daya* who did it and to have it partially opened again. They want to make it easier for themselves."

DR. SAIDA

Dr. Saida is plainly a much overworked doctor. She is one of a mere handful of women in this profession in Sudan, and as a gynecologist, she is tremendously in demand. Unlike most of her colleagues in other specialities, who, in an underused socialized medicine system seem to have a great deal of time on their hands, she gives the impression of being very harried. My conversation with her takes place at the Khartoum Teaching Hospital, simultaneous to her examining and treating patients. She explains in a gracious but matter-of-fact way that although she is very happy to talk with me, this is the only way that it is possible. There simply is not enough time.

"In childhood children do not understand the implications of things that happen to them. They become aware of circumcision as a fact of their lives at a very early age. They are aware that being circumcised makes them important — it carries with it the status of adulthood. At the same time they realize it is connected with pain, with being bound, with difficulty in passing urine. They see the ceremony many times before their turn comes, and look forward to the event, but when the time actually comes, they are apprehensive and anxious. They may actually be screaming hysterically with fear.

"So it is done. In most parts of Sudan it is done by untrained women who do not know how to administer a local anesthetic, and so it is done without any analgesic. This is a tremendous trauma to the child and to the family as well. You will find the mother and other relatives crying hysterically as they hear the screams from the next room. They understand the suffering that the child is going through, because they have all gone through it themselves. I have seen girls not passing urine for 4 or 5 days, they are so fearful of the agonizing pain. This of course compounds the problem when they finally do pass urine, since by then the urine has become so concentrated that it only burns more. They hold it in because they have heard other girls screaming when they first attempt to urinate.

"In the primitive areas, where no education exists, the girl accepts her lot without question. However, if she is a member of the educated class, she will come to realize in her own mind that what has been done to her is not right. Her parents also know that it is not right, and they are in conflict with the deeply rooted customs of this society.

"Take the example of an enlightened young mother whose girl comes of age. She does not want to circumcise her daughter, but she is afraid of the consequences if she does not do so. She is afraid she will be shamed by her friends and associates. People talk a great deal about other people here, and if a girl is not circumcised, she will be ridiculed at school and in the neighborhood where she lives. This mother would have to have enormous personal courage, and the ability to give her daughter the strength to withstand all of the social pressure. I will be very happy when some woman can actually stand up to everyone and say: 'I will not do it,' rather than, as some of them do, have a mock ceremony where no actual cutting takes place in the next room.

"The time is almost ripe for this to happen. There is continuous talk about it now in the media. Before now, there used to be something about circumcision in the media every 3 or 4 years. This is not enough. There has to be constant pressure. The subject has to be constantly brought before the public. The physical and psychological consequences have to be stressed again and again, otherwise people just forget it, especially when you are dealing with totally uneducated people. If this is not done you very quickly move backwards. Pressure has to be maintained until the younger generation takes over, until the children of today are grown. The younger generation in general is being exposed to a lot of information about the ill effects of circumcision. They see how many complications and problems result. They want the custom over and done with. But they are still economically bound by the older generation so they have to submit and accept. As they become economically independent, they are able to make their own decisions. With the older women there is often the element of: 'If it was done to me, why should it not be done to the young girls?' It is their way of exercising power. If you study this society, you can see that women in general have very little say in anything. They certainly have nothing to say when it comes to their sons. So their exertion of power is all directed toward the girls. If a women has suffered a great deal herself, subconsciously she wants to retaliate, and she can retaliate only through her daughters. She has mixed feelings of course, and she feels love for them as well. Also she is in a dilemma. These things have never been questioned before. She really does not know what is right or wrong, or what she should do.

"She is subject to great pressure from the grandmothers, who are uneducated, and who have been brought up to preserve virginity at all cost. In their day, a girl did not see any men. She'd hardly even seen her husband before the wedding. The grandmothers still live in that age. The concepts of mixed schools, dating, and friendships between boys and girls are totally strange to them. They resist all change, especially where domestic issues are concerned, and they exert a great deal of power in the family. Customs in general are in a period of transition here. The grandmothers are afraid that if they allow any part of custom to change, the whole fabric of society will come apart, and they will lose the power they now have, so they tenaciously resist change.

"Our religion does not allow premarital relations. Even *my* generation will insist on this. I personally am strong enough to know that I can bring up my daughters to respect and accept this rule by other means than circumcising them. Most grandmothers believe that the pharaonic is the only way to insure premarital virginity. The two of them are inseparable.

"So we must realize that the grandmothers are not evil people. They are generally devout women who are persuaded that the pharaonic is completely necessary to keep girls modest and chaste. They will never come over to our side. They will never change their minds. The only way that change will come about is if we address young girls, and young mothers who have girls.

"It is extremely difficult to deal medically with a circumcised girl and sometimes I am at a loss, as a doctor, to sort out her difficulties. To begin with, it is impossible to do an internal examination. You cannot do a vaginal smear. You cannot even insert a catheter. Even if you could get a look, the whole thing is so abnormal that you very often arrive at a wrong diagnosis. Even after a woman is married, it is sometimes impossible to arrive at a diagnosis.

"Women know that if they have internal problems, they may

have to have an unnecessary operation, just so they can be treated. It is painful, expensive and traumatic for them, and fraught with risk. From the point of view of an overworked doctor, it is an unnecessary waste of precious time. Without exception these women will tell you: 'I will never do this to my children.' Yet as soon as they have had the operation done, as soon as the moment of distress is past, they do it to their children. It is the path of least resistance, and they follow it every time.

"Again, on the delivery table, when the baby is ready to be born, they know they are going to be cut. They may have a local anesthetic, which might or might not work. They know the scissors are coming. There is no way to avoid them. Their whole pleasure at having a child is blighted by fear of the scissors. Then, after they give birth they have to be resutured. Again, the suturing is going to be painful, and again there will be the anxiety: 'Am I going to bleed; am I going to have trouble; is it going to hurt; am I going to be infected; am I going to be able to pass urine?' They know that with each child they will have to go through all this again.

"As a doctor I'm under constant stress. So many things can go wrong medically. It has caused me a great deal of unhappiness not being able to diagnose or treat patients properly, as I want to do. It makes me feel incompetent. It frustrates me terribly.

"Women are constantly under stress and anxiety. This is particularly true when a girl marries. If she has been sewn tightly she knows this must be undone by her husband, and this is not something which is done with anesthesia. She is completely powerless. If she were to have it undone surgically—and it is a very simple operation—the man would never believe she is a virgin. So she cannot do this. As a consequence, brides are terrified and subject to a prolonged period of pain, and it is an awfully long time before they are able to enjoy sex. Until she is penetrated completely, every time the couple practices sex, she will be hurt. Sometimes I have brides come to see me who are as they were, untouched, after 3 months or more. They are hysterical with fear, finding excuses, manufacturing symptoms, just to put off the pain a bit longer. A Sudanese women is in constant pain, at all stages in life.

"Women here in general are very passive. From very early in life they learn that they have no say over anything, especially their own bodies. Their circumcision takes place when they have no say at all. Their consent at that age is meaningless. Not only are they too young to understand, but what 4 or 6-year-old can stand up to her parents and say: 'Don't do this thing to me. I do not want it!' If the circumcision took place when they were 13 or 14, they would have some understanding, and perhaps some say in the matter. But not at 4 or 6. At that age she still has to be told to wash up in the morning. She cannot make a decision or contradict her parents.

"Then one thing follows another, and in everything from then on, she does only what she is told. Women get used to accepting what happens to them. If she comes into the hospital and her husband says that she will not be seen by a male doctor, she will not be seen by a male doctor no matter how sick she is. And how many female doctors are there to look after this man's wife? She is going to take risks with her life because her husband says so. Even in the matter of life or death she will do this. When it comes to blood transfusions she will tell you she does not want blood, and it's because if she is to get blood her husband must donate. She will tell me it is because he has to look after the family; he has responsibilities. She herself feels completely unimportant and expendable. She places no value on herself. This is true of practically every women here.

"Of course there are a few educated ones who are self-supporting, who know their own value and act on this knowledge. I am hoping that all women will do so in the near future. So far they are exceedingly few in number. It is extremely difficult for women to work, because of the problems they have with menstruation. Because the vaginal opening is so narrow in circumcised women the blood cannot be passed normally. It is retained for a long time and results in a great deal of pain. It can only be passed gradually, so menstruation goes on for several more days than is normal. The blood is black by the time it is passed, and there is much clotting. Women are very ashamed and embarrassed about their periods, which trickle on for many days each month, and which are quite malodorous due to retention. They tend to be withdrawn and depressed during that time. They are very afraid they will get soiled, and that people will know they have the 'curse,' as it is called here for very good reasons. They cannot use tampons either, obviously.

They never feel they can become equal in importance to men. It is a constant problem at school, at university, and on the job.

"A lot of women have sexual problems. When I interview patients, this is the last thing they will talk about. They may very well have feelings of sexual inadequacy, but they are too embarrassed to talk about such feelings. They come with all sorts of complaints, and I very frequently have the feeling when I am interviewing a patient that she is not telling me the real reason why she has come to see me. Even if you ask a direct question, very few will admit to sexual difficulties. Even if they tell you about their many orgasms, they really have no basis for comparison. None of them has had a sexual experience before circumcision, because it occurred when they were so little. So they don't know if they are missing anything, or even what it is. They are in a constant state of uncertainty toward their husbands. They may think they are responding and giving enough, but many are told by their husbands that they are not, and then the guilt and the fear that their husband will take another wife begins. This is the worst possible thing that can happen to a woman in marriage. Her anxiety keeps growing. She loses all measure of security when this happens."

Q: *Why do women have themselves circumcised to pinhole size after they have given birth? Is this because men want it or do the women do it of their own initiative and for their own reasons?*

A: "If you were to talk to men and women on this subject, you would get some totally different answers. There would be a lot of discrepancies between what the men and women say. The truth will be lost somewhere in between. When women tell you that they have themselves resutured tightly as before marriage to please their men after they have had babies, and men tell you they do not want women to do it, but they do it anyway, there is something hidden.

"The entire thing in this society is to please men. This is very much related to the fact that a woman is entirely dependent on men for her living. She is dependent on her father when she is a child, her brother, when the father is no longer able to make a living, and later on her husband. A woman in this country who does not marry has no recourse. She cannot support herself. Even if she has the money, she cannot go into business for herself. She cannot go out into society. Her money is dead, unless she has her father or brother to look after it. If she is not married, she has no social life whatsoever. What she gets out of marriage in terms of enjoyment is not considered. She can have 10 daughters, and still not be considered as having produced a family. She must have a son first.

"Female education is on the increase in this country, but only 2 to 3% of women are educated at all. Until we get 50%, nothing will change. As long as woman is behind man in education she will always be dependent on him. It is largely an economic problem that we have to deal with as women. If we can change that, if women can have a say in their lives, they will be able to decide for themselves. As soon as women will be able to be as useful as men, to earn as much as men, they will automatically be given a say in their lives the day they are born. They will have equal importance."

FAHTMA

Fahtma and her family have recently returned from a 6 year stay in the United States. Her husband, now a high official in one of the Sudanese ministries, studied at a midwestern university during that time, and has completed a doctoral degree there. They now live once more in El Fasher, a governmental center in Western Sudan. Fahtma has three sons and a daughter. Her last two children were born in the United States. At the time of this conversation, she is in the last month of her fifth pregnancy. This child will be born in El Fasher, a place not noted for the quality of its medical facilities.

Fahtma: "They asked me at the hospital if they could take pictures," she says. "They had never seen anything like it before." I said, "Sure, why not." It didn't make any difference to me. They weren't going to photograph my face, after all. So they took pictures of the whole birth. I have copies here somewhere. You may have them if they will be any help to you." She rummages through a briefcase full of photographs she has brought back from the United States with her.

"It was very funny," she says, and laughs ruefully at the recollection. "The nurse came in with a tray, carrying a razor, soap, and a bowl of water. She was going to shave me. She pulled down the covers and then pulled up my hospital gown. When she looked at the place she was going to shave, she screamed and dropped the tray. The whole bed was full of water, and they had to change the sheets and the blankets and give me a fresh gown. The nurse was so upset. She kept apologizing. They must have asked her why she screamed like that, and she must have told them, because they all looked so stricken and embarrassed, and I could tell they all wanted to see it, but they did not want to ask because they were afraid that they would hurt my feelings. I kept telling them that it was all right. I wanted them to feel better. They all knew me, because I had been working at the hospital as a practical nurse. It did not bother me to let them see. They had all been so kind to me, and after that they were still more kind. They could hardly do enough for me, it seemed.

"I came from a bad, bad village in the west, where they scrape off everything. There is not even skin left to sew up and they tie your legs together for 40 days, until a scar forms. There is nothing left with which to feel. When your husband comes to you, it is the same as if he came with a stick to a piece of leather.

"I will not do this to my daughter. I have told my family that even if I have 10 daughters, I will not do it to one of them. I see no sense in it. I have seen how other women give birth, both here and in the United States. It is terrible here, especially in the villages.

"My daughter is 9 years old now, and all the girls her age are already circumcised. Here they usually do them at the age of 5. I gave birth to two of my children in the United States and I know it would be cruel and pointless to do that to her. There isn't one single good reason for it, no matter what they try to tell you here. Everyone tries to persuade me that it must be done to my daughter, saying that no one will marry her, but I tell them I don't care. Let her get old enough to decide what she wants for herself. In a year or so I will have a party for her and pretend that I am going to circumcise her. I will buy her new clothes, paint her hands with henna, and call in the midwife, exactly as I would if I were to have her circumcised. Then I will pay the midwife to do nothing, and tell everyone that it has been done. Then everyone will be satisfied, and leave me alone. No one is going to take her clothes off and look.

"I have suffered a lot after having my children. For 40 days with the first two I could do nothing but lie in bed. I could not walk or do my house work, because they had sewn me so tightly again. When I had my children in the United States they sewed only what they had to, only what had been cut, and after 7 days I was as good as new. I had no problems at all."

Q: *One woman I spoke to told me that she likes to be sewn tightly, because in this way she is able to have more sexual pleasure. Can you explain that?*

A: "No. Because it must be different for her. For me it only creates problems. I have no sexual pleasure at all. It is only for my husband. When they had scraped everything away, as they did with me, I could feel nothing. I just lie there, and that is all. Perhaps I felt a little when I first married, but now I don't feel anything. I have had a very severe circumcision, the worst. They have left me nothing at all."

Q: *Do you suffer from feelings of sexual frustrations?*

A: "Not very much. I have no desire, and I feel nothing, so I do what I have to do, and I do not feel frustrated. I have some friends in the United States who told me they always let their husbands know when they want sex. A Sudanese woman hardly ever asks her husband. I don't think she has any interest. Before you marry, you really want it. You are very much interested, and you are very curious what it is all about. The girls in America used to talk to me about how they enjoy it, but all of them were intact."

Q: *Do you ever feel angry when you talk to such women and realize how you have been deprived?*

A: No, because that is the culture here. They do it to everybody without exception. It's not just me; it's my whole family, everybody. But if I have 10 daughters I will not touch one of them. I decided this as far back as my wedding. I told my family and my husband that if I had daughters they would not be circumcised. My husband said to wait until I had daughters. Then when I went to the United States, I saw the difference in the lives of women there, and it made me even stronger in my resolution. My husband leaves the decision to me, so it is all right."

Q: *Do you know any other women who feel the way you do?*

A: "No. I have spoken to a number of them, and tried to win them over to my way of thinking, but they have all told me that they feel they have to follow custom."

Q: *Do you think your girls will have any difficulties in this society if they are not circumcised?*

A: "I don't think so, because there are some people in Khartoum now who are not doing it. Times are changing a little. In 200 years, people will not do it any more."

Q: *Do you feel that it will take that long?*

A: "Yes, maybe even more. Maybe 300. Even educated people still do it as before. If they had strong laws and enforced them, it could be over much sooner. If they took all the midwives who do it and put them in jail, it would stop. If you killed a few publicly, it would stop."

Q: *If you got rid of the midwives and nurses who do it, wouldn't there be other, untrained women who would take their place?*

A: "No, I don't think so. It would stop altogether if you made an example of some of them. Then they would be afraid to do it."

Q: *It is known that China used to have a tremendous drug problem. In recent years they got rid of it totally. I asked one Chinese official how this was accomplished. He told me: "We dealt harshly with all the drug dealers." When I asked him what he meant by "harshly," he told me, "We dealt with them very harshly!" One hates to believe that a very harsh solution is the only one for this problem.*

A: "There are so many people without jobs here. If you train some of the young ones to be nurses or midwives, you could get rid of all the old ones who do circumcision. And you would have to show a film of a normal birth, the way birth is in the United States, and one of the way it is here. That would be much more effective than telling people to stop doing it. If you show it to a woman who is in pain, after she has given birth, she will believe it. She will remember it.

"I wish I were back in the United States—any place but here. I am so afraid of what will happen to me in the hospital here. I have been through it twice before, and I know how much I will suffer.

They can do anything they want to you, and there is no way you can defend yourself against it. I am so terribly afraid!''

DR. YAHIA OUN ALLA

Dr. Yahia Oun Alla is an intensely serious psychiatrist who has spent his youth and part of his professional life in the more remote areas of Sudan. He speaks with authority on the techniques of native healing practitioners and on tribal practices that are gradually disappearing.

Q: *Would you say that any changes have been taking place in this country in regard to female circumcision in recent years?*

A: ''As someone who has been living in this society since birth, I believe that some sort of change has taken place. I do believe that education has done a great deal to enlighten women as to the consequences of the pharaonic type of circumcision.''

Q: *How do you mean?*

A: ''It is women who make the decisions about female circumcision. For men, although we may be in conflict about it, tradition is very strong in our lives. We still find it difficult to depart from our social customs. As far as female circumcision goes, the educated person leaves this to women.''

Q: *Women say it is performed for men, that men will not marry an uncircumcised woman.*

A: ''This is not so among the educated. There's a definite change there. Among the uneducated, if a man found his wife to be uncircumcised, he would divorce her. He has been taught circumcision is associated with virginity. If she is not tightly infibulated he would not be sure she has not been with other men. If she is tightly sewn, then he is definitely sure she is chaste.''

Q: *I have talked to quite a few educated men and women who say they do not intend to circumcise their child, and then, when the times comes, they do. They yield to their own anxieties about their child. According to all my sources of information, this happens rather consistently.*

A: "Not every family would yield to such pressure. I know a couple, both of whom are educated, he more than she, and they are not living within an extended family. This gives them a lot more freedom to exercise their own ideas, and they have been successful in not circumcising their daughters. Under ideal conditions it is possible."

Q: *This type of situation is exceedingly rare, far more rare than one is led to believe, however, isn't it?*

A: "Of course. It is a very slow process. The pressures are all still there. Even educated people still live within a family and a society that disagrees with them strongly, and which they cannot choose to ignore. They still face a great deal of ridicule from their peers."

Q: *It is still the greatest insult to be called the son of an uncircumcised woman, isn't it?*

A: "In my opinion, this insult does not refer to circumcision directly. It has to do with the fact that uncircumcised women traditionally have been slaves in this society. To call a man the son of a uncircumcised woman is to imply that he is not of Arab origin."

Q: *In other words circumcision is a sign of status?*

A: "It seems to be."

Q: *Do you see a lot of cases of emotional disturbance that can be traced to circumcision in your practice?*

A: "I do see a few cases, but when you compare their number to that of the number of women that are circumcised, they are very trivial indeed."

Q: *Do most cases of emotional disturbances here reach doctors, or is the problem dealt with in some other way?*

A: "Those that are related to sexual problems are rarely seen. When we do see them, the presenting problem is of a different nature. For example, a man may complain of a sleeping problem, loss of appetite, depression. If you probe into the situation, you will probably find that the reason for this is impotence, but he will not talk about this unless you confront him directly."

Q: *What about women? What kind of problems do they present?*

A: "If they are brought to a psychiatrist at all, and very few are, it would be because of infertility, pain in the lower abdomen, this type of complaint. When they are examined, this is usually the result of a very tight infibulation."

Q: *What happens to the psychological trauma that women experience as a result of circumcision? How is this handled emotionally?*

A: "Perhaps you have heard of the *Zhar* cult. These are healing practitioners that are women. It is exclusively women's concern. Let us say a woman has some form of emotional problem. Perhaps she has been going to doctors for some time without any result. She may then resort to the *Zhar* healer. The *Zhar* are spirits that inhabit women. Some are good spirits, and some are evil. The healers will perform some sort of preliminary ritual to diagnose the nature of the spirit that inhabits the woman, and then will call a gathering. They will then communicate with the spirit, which speaks through the woman, and they will ask it what it wants. The spirit may ask for a certain kind of dress or a man's clothes, or perhaps alcohol, which women are not allowed to have here, that type of thing. These are most likely repressed desires that the woman is expressing, and her desires are then satisfied in this gathering."

Q: *What if she wants something different? What if she wants to beat her husband?*

A: "I have known of cases where she beat him quite severely."

Q: *What if she wants to sleep with another man?*

A: "No."

Q: *So it has definite limits.*

A: "Yes."

Q: *Does the ceremony have some sort of curative effect?*

A: "In some cases, yes. If she can say what it is she wants, and is able to get it, it often helps. If the diagnosis the *Zhar* healer makes is incorrect, of course she is not helped. If it is correct, then that is it. Of course, the *Zhar* cannot deal with a genuinely organic problem. Then the result of the ritual is that the woman gets worse, due to exhaustion. Actually, it works only in cases of hysteria."

Q: *What about other forms of emotional disturbance?*

A: "Anything of an erotic origin. There may not be a cure, but often there is a lessening of the problem."

Q: *Under a system where it can be said that a woman does not possess her own body, and where she feels that parts of her body must be given up to someone who owns her, what happens to the self-image of women?*

A: "I don't think that women here feel that they do not own their bodies. We sometimes try to extrapolate from one culture to another, and it cannot be done. To the girls here circumcision does not mean taking away part of their bodies. It is a normal occurrence that happens to everyone. When you consider the ceremony, the festivity, the drumming, the gifts, the new clothes, the feasts that go with a circumcision ceremony, you realize that it is a pleasing psychological experience to the girl. Some of them, if they have seen another circumcision where there was a lot of blood, might be affected. A great majority of them take it for granted that this is something any woman should have. Of course, some of them have had serious medical problems, and if they are educated, know these problems are a result of their circumcision. Those that are uneducated have no notion of cause and effect when it comes to problems later on in life, and so they all accept circumcision without question."

Q: *What do you think the result of more education for women will be?*

A: "There will be a very slow change in which circumcision over a prolonged period of time will become progressively less drastic, and eventually the practice will disappear."

Q: *How long do you think that will take?*

A: "It depends on the rate at which we work on it. The higher the rate of education, the quicker it will proceed. Circumcision is not the only custom that is undergoing transition. Mourning practices, tribal scarring, and health practices in general are being revised. Many of the rituals connected with these are disabling, unhygienic, and time-wasting practices."

Q: *Do you think that these changes are all for the better?*

A: "Definitely so."

Q: *What are some other practices that are dying out?*

A: "Some of the rituals at marriage. There was, for instance, body lashing. The young men of the village would be lashed by the bridegroom. The object was for the young men to show how stoically they could tolerate pain. It was done to impress the young women. There would be a procession to the place of marriage. Everyone would form a circle. Then the young men would take off their outer garments and offer their shoulders to be lashed. They had to take the lashing without flickering an eyelash, without moving a muscle. They still do this in some villages, but it has disappeared from the larger towns and cities."

Q: *It seems that the people in this country stand in a totally different relationship to pain than people in the Western countries. Westerners in general do not court pain, nor are they able to tolerate much of it. Here, I am told, there may be a much higher tolerance of pain, and it appears, in many circumstances, to be considered to have positive value.*

A: "You could see this on occasions when a limb had to be amputated. This would be done with a sword. They would have the most beautiful women singing around the patient, and he would have to show bravery in front of the women, much as during the marriage ceremony."

Q: *In speaking to women about their circumcision, I have come across some every now and then who would tell me that there had been very little pain associated with the surgery, even though it was performed without any anesthesia or analgesic. I find this hard to believe. How would you say they arrive at this point psychologically? Do they successfully repress the pain? Do they simply deny it to me, an outsider? Or have they actually been able to process it in such a way—perhaps through self-hypnosis—so that they literally don't feel it?*

A: "The latter is most likely. The ceremony itself facilitates it. The preparation for festivities goes on for several days. The girl is the focus of attention. She is given many gifts. Also, she is never alone. Relatives and neighbors are with her constantly, supporting her. Her fears are minimized by this. When she is actually circumcised, she is again accompanied by relatives. She sees other girls who are going through the same experience, and she knows she is not alone."

Q: *It is generally done in groups then?*

A: "Yes, now it is done by appointment, in a setting that is much like a clinic. The girl will see two or three girls go in before her, and there may be some that are waiting their turn after hers. This tends to very much lessen the fear."

Q: *The fear, yes. What I am asking about is the actual physical pain. It must be enormous. How does she handle that?*

A: "It is all done very quickly. Even during the operation itself, she is encouraged and distracted from what is going on. That is what does the trick."

Q: *I have talked to a great number of women who have described the experience as something totally horrible, something that was so agonizing that the memory of it will haunt them all their lives. There is also a far smaller number who say with absolute finality, "It did not hurt. It was nothing." Are they showing the same kind of bravery that men show under the circumstances you described?*

A: "Women here are very much allowed to show their feelings. It is also a positive value for women to show themselves weaker than men. Quite possibly her expectation of the pain is so tremendous that the actual experience is lessened by comparison."

Q: *This still does not answer my question. Those same women who claimed there was no pain connected with the circumcision, will tell me about other operations or accidents of a relatively lesser nature occurring in their lives, and will go on in vivid detail and at great length about how painful those were. Also I have rarely spoken to a woman who did not recall her penetration as having been anything but traumatic to the extreme. It is very difficult for me, as a Western woman, to believe that pharaonic circumcision is on occasion painless. I can only accept that the girl is able in some instances to brainwash herself to later believe this to have been true – for whatever reason.*

A: "Perhaps this is true."

Q: *Have you had much experience with other cultures?*

A: "Yes, I spent a number of years in England and visited a number of Western countries."

Q: *What differences were evident in the psychological and social disorganization patterns in these places relative to this culture as far as you can determine?*

A: "As far as the major psychiatric problems were concerned the incidence and types seen were by and large the same. The significant difference, which is now being investigated, is that the rate of social recovery is somehow far better here than one would see in the Western countries."

Q: *How do you explain this?*

A: "The answer may lie in the extended family, which is more likely to continue in its support of a family member that is not able to function productively. Also the demands of life here are generally not as complicated as in the Western countries. Even in a capital like Khartoum, people always manage. When there is a scarcity of commodities, such as petrol, in a city like New York or London, there is chaos. If the power goes off for 24 hours, the whole city grinds to a halt. Here it can and does go on for quite a while. Sometimes whole sectors of the city will be without water for days or even weeks. Power failures occur almost daily."

Q: *"How do people deal with that"*?

A: "If they run out of water here, they will walk to another place, which may be miles away, to obtain it and carry it home. They do without electric lights. The ability to endure hardship, as the Westerner defines it, is considerably greater here. We still do not depend much on automation. We have the foresight to store water in large jugs, and when there is no petrol, we walk. We have learned at a very early age to accept things exactly as they are and we know that everyone else has to do the same. There are no other options. This is one of the primary facts of life here.''

DR. HASSABO

Dr. Hassabo, a psychiatrist, is a cheerful, charismatic man of about 40. He has spent a number of years in England, and is quite Westernized in his appearance and his attitudes. When he tells me that he would not tolerate the circumcision of his daughters under any circumstances whatsoever, it is not difficult to believe what he says, since he is also married to a European woman.

I drop by his hospital frequently to talk with him, always taking the chance that he might not have time for me. Telephones, although they exist in Khartoum, are nearly always out of order, and trying to announce myself through the mails is no better, since letters only very rarely reach their destination within the month, if at all. So I arrive unannounced, and to my great surprise, he is always pleased to see me, and we converse.

The hospital itself is a most curious place. Although there is a considerable number of staff doctors and nurses in evidence, I am made aware of only a rare and occasional patient.

In contrast to Dr. Hassabo, who strikes me as intelligent and competent, his staff physicians are neither very impressive nor particularly distinguishable from other untold numbers of relatively well paid but underemployed civil servants in Khartoum.

Q: *Can you tell me something about what pharaonic circumcision does to a woman psychologically?*

A: "Unless you go very deeply into the history of the patient, you don't get an answer to this, because talking about it is taboo. It is very difficult for a doctor to get any information about circumcision and sex. . . . When the girl reaches adulthood, she must marry, and the marriage is usually an arranged one. Even if the two have seen each other before marriage, they do not know one another, because there has been no opportunity for this. So they are virtually strangers when they are married. Neither of them has had any sex education. Hearing from other girls what the first night of marriage is like and recalling the screaming, the pleading accompanying the marriage of other family members, is tremendously fear producing. She also knows that there is no way out. She is cornered. This may produce neurotic or psychotic reactions, and in many cases, a psychosomatic disorder.

"After the marriage has been consummated, after 6 months or so, it is a very common occurrence for the girl to come into my office and tell me that she wants out, that she cannot live with this man. She does not want him. If the girl is strong enough to speak up for herself, she can get a divorce. If her father sees that this marriage is not working out, he will obtain the divorce for her. She then has to return to her parental home."

Q: *Are women in general strong enough to stand up for themselves when the marriage proves to be intolerable to them?*

A: "They often are after marriage. Before marriage, the girl is under the domination of her father, and she has to obey him without question. She does not even own her own body. Sometimes girls would marry any man at all, just to get it done with, just to leave the parental home. They are usually not dominated in marriage. The husband generally tries to understand the girl, and to be loving in his relation with her. Sometimes the marriage works, sometimes it doesn't. The likelihood of failure is fairly high among the educated, which is what I deal with here predominantly. The boy is equally dominated by his parents. He also has to marry the girl his parents want him to marry."

Q: *So the girl is property, but the boy is also property.*

A: "Yes, but the boy is generally more difficult to control. Very often if he has made up his mind to marry a particular girl, he can get his way. The girl has to accept without question, and on the surface she does accept. Inwardly, however, things might be quite different, and after a period, the marriage may not continue."

Q: *When it does continue, how does the girl handle those feelings of rebellion?*

A: "I doubt very much whether a deeper relationship becomes established after that. A sort of superficial relationship develops, and this is constantly reinforced by the husband's kind behavior to her. A child may cement the relationship even more. Or nowadays more and more often he may permit her to take a job. This often eases the strain.''

Q: *I have talked to a great number of women about their circumcision and their penetration. A number of them have totally repressed any pain connected to the circumcision and claim that there was little or no pain. With no exception, however, they remember quite vividly the pain of penetration. This to them was always terrible, even when the husband was described as being loving, considerate, and trying his utmost to get them both through the experience still sane.*

A: "The problem is very simply mechanical. You have to tear tissue apart. Pushing into tissues, tearing them apart, stretching nerve endings cannot help but result in a very painful procedure. In the old days, if you did not penetrate completely in the first night, you were not really a man. Even now, a doctor sees all sorts of surgical tears, perineal tears, or circumcision scars that have been cut with a dirty knife, and in the wrong direction. And of course, when the young man is sexually aroused, and perhaps full of false courage from strong drink, and he is egged on and taunted by his friends, he can do anything in that situation. It is often physically and mentally painful, not only for her, but for him as well. If a man does not succeed, he has to face his friends the next day. Sometimes there are circumcision scars that are frightfully difficult to cut through even with a surgical blade. I remember when as a young doctor I was working in a district about 200 miles north of Khartoum. A young man came to see me with his wife. They had been married for 7 years, and she was still a virgin. I tried to open her surgically while she was under general anesthesia. I found it impossible to cut into the fibrous mat that had formed under what remained of the labia majora. My scalpel broke. I'll never forget that. I lost three blades before I could finally cut it with a very strong pair of scissors.

"After I had repaired the girl, the husband pulled her out of the hospital immediately. He simply could not wait. People were still taunting him after 7 years.''

Q: *What do men resort to when this happens? Anal intercourse?*

A: "Yes, it is quite common. This, when girls are subjected to it, is often the reason why they want to leave their husbands. I have recently had two patients under 20 with this situation. Both told me that their husbands would approach them in a drunken state and demand anal intercourse, preferring this to the normal passage. Most women will not accept this. It is very unhealthy and makes for a bad relationship.

"Another crisis for women is when they give birth, particularly when it happens for the first time."

Q: *Why do they always have themselves resutured to pinhole size? I cannot seem to get a conclusive answer to this.*

A: "To please the man. At least that is what they think."

Q: *Then why do so many men say that they really do not want it?*

A: "He does not have a chance to say anything, because when the woman has given birth, he must according to custom and religious precepts stay away from her for 40 days. During this time there is the resewing by either the mother, the grandmother, or the midwife, and she has to accept it. She has no choice."

Q: *But what is really behind it? Why do women say men really want it? Why should they often insist on it even if they know it means more pain for them?*

A: "I don't think the man wants a pinhole closure. I think most men would prefer a more reasonable opening which would ensure an easier penetration. But women seem to think that if they are not closed to a pinhole, the whole thing will go slack with the first pressure."

Q: *How much truth is there in that?*

A: "There is no truth at all. However, there is normally a fibrous band where the girl has been circumcised, and due to the cutting away of tissue, this fibrous band is very weak when it is redone. In an uncircumcised girl, after parturition the anatomy goes back to normal, so that the man does not feel this emptiness, this slackness that exists in circumcised women when the musculature of the perineum is cut away along with the labia and the clitoris. They have this closure performed because it brings the perineum together, at least temporarily. This gives the man a feeling that penetration is not into emptiness. There actually is nothing there. This fibrous band is the last remains of the labia. Beyond that there is only a hole. When you examine the girls, you can really see that nothing remains of their genitalia except skin and bone.

"We did a bit of a study some time ago, and in the course of it I spoke to some young lads. They seemed very much to prefer uncircumcised women. It is very common for married men in this country to have Ethiopian girlfriends. They all seem to prefer these girlfriends to their wives, because their anatomies are normal. The poor wife does not really have a chance. Her psychosexual response has to be pure fake. Sexual response as a whole is neither psychic nor physical. Sex is a psychophysical activity. You cannot trigger off a sexual response without the necessary physical components unless it is purely emotional, in which case it becomes a purely conditioned reflex. Even with that, it takes a long time before it is finally established, and has to be reinforced all the time. I doubt very much that with pharaonic circumcision, the girl is ever able to get the true feeling of sexual response."

Q: *There is no way of determining, really. I have spoken to quite a few men who have had sexual experiences with pharaonically circumcised, clitoridectomized, and intact women, and they all pretty much agree that orgasm is generally much weaker, less frequent, and more delayed in pharaonically circumcised women.*

A: "And I rather doubt that this is not simulated in most cases."

Q: *The only thing that gives me any confidence that sexual pleasure and orgasm exist in pharaonically circumcised women at all is a sampling of twice married women among those I interviewed. Among each of these women the description of the two sexual relationships differed markedly. When the marriage had been forced on them and they were not happy in it, they told me that they had never shown themselves as sexually receptive, avoided sex whenever possible, and rarely, if ever, had pleasure or orgasm. When they had been able to marry a man they loved, they glowingly reported that they had sex with him as often as was possible, that they were very happy in all aspects of the relationship, and had frequent and in-*

tense orgasms. This appears to be evidence for the existence of true sexual response even in seriously mutilated women.

A: "I suppose you are getting the true facts in your interviews, because women speak freely in a girl-to-girl situation, when they would only give answers that they feel are expected of them in dealing with a male doctor."

Q: *Yes, I feel I have gotten a great deal of valid information. The tragedy is that so very many of them express the feeling that they are missing something out of life, but they have absolutely no idea what it is.*

A: "This is it. This is true. They are always insecure in their marriages as a result."

Q: *And always, very close to the surface there is a feeling of terror of not being adequate and of the husband taking another wife, because they are not able to give him what he wants. They feel they are not adequate, and there is no cure for this.*

A: "This is true. It is very common for the man to have a mistress. Whether this is caused by the situation or occurs simply because it is fashionable, nobody knows."

Q: *Well, it is often thought to be a measure of a man's virility in this or any other culture isn't it?*

A: "The point is this: If women know that they have missed a large part of their sex lives as a result of this mutilation, will they do it to their daughters?"

Q: *From what I know about it, they will consistently tell you that they won't—and then they will. What do you think some of the deeper reasons for this are, once you get beyond the obvious ones, such as: "I must do it to please my mother or grandmother"?*

A: "The social and familial pressures are very great, of course. Within the mother herself, there might be two conflicting reactions. On the one side is this: the devil she knows is better than the devil she doesn't know. She believes that the girl can get along with her husband if she is circumcised, as she herself has with the girl's father. On the less conscious level she may feel that because she herself did not have an intact body, the girl should also not have it. It is a kind of acting out, a form of revenge. She cannot get even for all her pain with those who inflicted it on her, because she perceives them as too powerful. So it turns on someone weaker, her daughter.''

Q: *What surprised me most in the women here is not the degree of mental pathology they manifest, but the general aura of serenity and balance they far more commonly exude, especially in the outlying areas. They appear to be far more balanced and emotionally healthy than a lot of Western women. How do you account for this?*

A: "Most of the girls here have a very high level of adaptation, because they have not been exposed to any conflicting choices. Very early in life they must tell themselves: 'This is the way life is for a woman.' They learn to live with that. In an Islamic society a woman is there for the pleasure and convenience of a man, and she accepts that.''

Q: *She accepts that she is property?*

A: "Yes, she accepts that she is there to fill the needs of the man, that she is property, same as the house, or the car, or the camel.''

Q: *You feel that in accepting this, women are quite able to be content?*

A: "Yes, they accept it from childhood on. They are not aware of any other options.''

Q: *In other words if circumcision is done away with completely, there is going to be at least one generation in which all of this is challenged, and in which a great deal of instability will occur before matters can be stabilized?*

A: "This is true. That generation is going to have to be sacrificed. There are going to be a lot of unstructured relationships. Girls will be unlike their mothers and they will have no role models to follow.''

Q: *In other words, a second-class citizen status has its compensations, in that no demands to make choices exist. She always knows exactly what is expected of her. So there are few uncertainties.*

A: "Exactly. With all the foreign influences, and with a raised level of education, there are going to be a lot of social changes within the next years, some good and some not so good. In any event, there is bound to be a period of social instability. Pharaonic circumcision is essentially something that is meant to control something that people feel they will not be able to stop otherwise, and that is women's free expression of sex. It will hang on for a long time as a social custom, because it keeps wives and daughters under control. I very seriously doubt whether the girls of today would hesitate to circumcise their granddaughters when they become grandmothers. Men will have to change first, I would think. This obsession with virginity will have to change. What is basically lacking for all the people in general is sex education. If you really give that to boys and girls at an early age, this would probably cause a breakthrough."

Q: *Most men when they marry here are sexually rather inexperienced, aren't they?*

A: "Absolutely. I think if you compare our boys here with boys in other societies, you would probably find ours are the least informed. If they have had any experience before marriage they have generally been few and far between, and generally with some poor girl who must do this to live."

Q: *And sex is frightening to the bridegroom as well as the bride then?*

A: "In my own age group that was certainly true. I was into my third year of medical school before I ever saw the naked body of a woman. I was then in my 20s. I have known any number of men who have had no sexual experiences of any kind until they were married, sometimes in their 30s and 40s. It is quite common, and emotionally quite demanding. It requires continuous suppression and often this takes the form of religious fanaticism. Doing the rituals connected with praying six times a day feeds the emotional emptiness, and it becomes a preoccupation."

Q: *Of what nature are the relationships of men to their mothers here?*

A: "Generally very good. Especially the eldest son is very much the favorite child of the mother. She intercedes for him with the father, who tends to be authoritarian with his sons. The mother tends to be the family stabilizer, the mediator, the source of affection and love. This early relationship enables the young man to be sensitive to his bride later on. There is no emotional poverty between young couples. When they are on their own, they are quite loving with one another. When they are with the families, however, they must hide their feelings, and make no outward show of them. A man here would never under any circumstances kiss his wife in front of others. Even when they are married and someone of the family comes to stay with them, the wife cannot go to the bedroom of her husband as long as they are there. She must sleep somewhere else, as if sex between them were some sort of shameful practice. You have to pretend you do not sleep together, even when you have five children.''

Q: *Do girls receive much love when they are children?*

A: ''Oh yes. The emotional life of a Sudanese family, by and large, is quite rich.''

Q: *The emotional life is rich, and the sexual life is poor?*

A: ''True. Children love one another, and parents love the children. There is a lot of warmth, gentleness, and feelings of being wanted and cared for.''

Q: *This seems to be the opposite of many families in America, where the sexual life can be very rich, and the emotional life is often impoverished.*

A: ''I think on the whole our kids here are more stable. Even with this kind of sexual deprivation, they are not emotionally deprived. You can see the happiness and serenity in the faces of our girls and boys. I think with this current younger generation, there will be a lot of changes, especially where pharaonic circumcision is concerned, and I believe they will have the emotional strength to weather this period of transition. It will have to proceed in stages before it is finally abandoned, with progressively less drastic operations.

''A girl came to see me recently. She was going to marry a man from a rural area, and she was worried about how he would react to her being circumcised in the modified way. I told her to bring the man in, and I would talk to him. When he came, I asked him if he knew anything about women's circumcision. He said no, he only knew that the woman should be closed, and that he would have to open her. I said: 'But you are a university graduate. This is a very poor answer.' And he said: 'But this is all I know!' So we had three or four sessions together, which were nothing more than sex education. They got married, and he came back to see me after a few months of marriage. 'I am very happy that I came to see you,' he told me. 'If I hadn't, I would have divorced my wife in no time, because if I had listened to my friends, they would have persuaded me that she was not a virgin, if she had been easy to penetrate.'"

Q: *Isn't that rather faulty reasoning? It would be easy enough for a woman to have herself reclosed before marriage if she has had premarital intercourse.*

A: "Of course. It would be no problem at all for a girl to have herself repaired. She could have had 100 affairs, and it does happen, you know. It is quite common when the young man wants a sealed-off woman. Just 2 months before marriage, the girls have themselves stitched up."

Q: *It's really an educational problem, isn't it?*

A: "There are so many dimensions to this whole business. There is the society, the religion, the family, the educational, and the sexual aspects and quite frankly, the medical aspect is a very big one. Such a multidimensional problem cannot possibly be solved at one go. It has to be worked on in stages."

Q: *What I find most challenging in this entire complex is the fact that women, in spite of what is done to them physically, in spite of the fact they can expect to and do suffer physically in an acute way at nearly every point in their lives, are able to survive and to remain emotionally relatively intact, apparently due to love and security they experience as children, and generally in their marriages as well.*

A: "Women also tend to be more tolerant of pain."

Q: *Well here they certainly had better be!*

A: "Yes. But it is also true that the pain threshold in women is higher than in men. Either that, or they cultivate the ability to forget pain.''

Q: *Emotional trauma then is far more destructive to the individual than physical trauma. But we are dealing with emotional trauma too, aren't we?*

A: ''The point is that when the circumcision has been done, as the girl matures she usually comes to terms with what has happened. She knows that it has been done by her family because they want her to be accepted by society and by her future husband. They do not want her to suffer the stigma of being different from other girls. She goes through a stage of reappraisal of the situation, and comes to accept that what has been done is in her best interest. She is given a lot of love and emotional support and this becomes the reward that reinforces her acceptance. She is taught to believe that her future husband will be pleased if she is tightly sewn, that he will not doubt her virginity, that she will be more interesting to him sexually, and she believes this. Especially uneducated girls tend to feel very secure in having lived up to what has been expected of them. It is true of course, that men, unless they are extremely well educated, will not accept them otherwise.''

Q: *In your practice as a psychiatrist, you obviously see some girls who have not been able to process the physical and emotional trauma. What in your opinion makes the difference?*

A: ''Some girls are basically emotionally unstable. The ones with hysteria are brought to the clinic most frequently. They are usually frigid, and every attempt at sexual contact does no more than reinforce this response in them. Sex is totally unrewarding to them, and this is why they wind up in my office. Their lack of gratification brings about a very unpleasant psychological reaction. They suffer from nervous tension, irritability, literally 'hysteria'.''

Q: *What is it in their home lives as children that makes the difference?*

A: ''It is not different in this culture than anywhere else. Some factors might be frequent conflicts between members of the family, early separation from one of the parents, a difficult father, a domineering mother, a broken home. If the mother and father are there to give them loving support they will, by and large, grow up emotionally stable. Sometimes there are genetic factors that figure into it, and of course there may be an unusually difficult set of physical complications that the girl has had to undergo. By and large we find mostly stable couples. If the boy and girl are brought up in a good home and have had very little difficulty growing up there, they will generally make it together. If they are brought up in a problem home without the necessary stabilities, this will reflect on their later relationships. It is only natural that they will carry this pathology into their married lives.''

Q: *Is there much wife beating or child abuse here?*

A: ''Not really. Not to any great degree.''

Q: *In America there is a great deal of that.*

A: ''Yes, the battered child syndrome. It is worldwide. I have observed it in Britain as well. Here when you hit your son, it is because he has done wrong, and he knows this as well as you do. You take him aside and say: 'Look, I told you if you did wrong I would punish you, and you did wrong.' Your punishment is reasonable, and you accept it. Very few parents act upon provocation, unless the child gets really abusive. Such things are rare here. The mother, as a matter of fact, disciplines more often than the father.''

Q: *In the town of El Obeid I stayed in the house of a woman who had scars that were obviously the result of a brutal whipping all over her shoulders and back. When I asked her about them, she laughed quite lightly and said that they used to horse-whip children in her village if they did not obey.*

A: ''It could be true. There are of course exceptions, especially in the outlying areas. But it is not common at all. No, not at all.''

MATERNITY HOSPITAL RESIDENT

This 28-year-old woman is one of a handful of female doctors who practice medicine in Sudan. She was pharaonically circumcised at the age of 8 and is presently as yet unmarried. She remarks, ''Part of the problem in general is that women do not feel any sense of loss, because they are small children when this is done to them. The concentration at that age is on the festivities and gifts. It is only when they get older that problems develop."

Q: *When did you personally realize the implications of what had ben done to you?*

A: "At 15 or so."

Q: *What brought the realization home to you?*

A: "I read books that told me how the body should be."

Q: *How did you feel then?*

A: "We don't know here what is normal, so it is hard to feel anything about this abnormal thing, but from my own experience and from the girls I have talked to, it doesn't feel right physically. Something feels tight there, and not as it should feel. During my menstrual time I feel this even more."

Q: *What about your emotions? What is it that you felt there?*

A: "Do you mean anger?"

Q: *Yes, I think I would have some very strong feelings of that order had this been done to me.*

A: "Of course none of us are happy about it, but we can live with it, as long as there are no serious medical complications."

Q: *How do you feel about being a woman in a society such as this one, where there is such an obsession with virginity?*

A: "There are problems of such tremendous magnitude in our society and in our lives, that it is not a primary problem to us. Survival is primary. Sexual matters are not as important here as in the Western world."

Q: *Is this true for men as well?*

A: "No, only for women."

Q: *Is that a result of the circumcision?*

A: "Yes, definitely."

Q: *Do you plan to marry?*

A: Yes, next year.

Q: *If you have daughters, what do you plan to do in regard to circumcision?*

A: "I will do nothing. I expect some opposition from my family, but they are far more flexible than they used to be. At least they are willing to listen. Given a few more years, they can be persuaded. Times are changing, but it will take time. Eight or ten years can make a perceptible difference in the city, because of television and other media. Wherever there is electricity, there will be change. But in the villages it will take a very long time. There are so many medical priorities and there is so little help. Doctor Bakr, our main opponent to this practice, is getting no help from the government. The authorities are the main problem."

DR. MOHAMMED ABU

Dr. Abu is the pediatrics resident of Omdurman Hospital.

Q: *Some people have told me that the incidence of pharaonic circumcision is decreasing in the city, and is being replaced by less drastic circumcision, or not performed at all on girls at the present time. What kinds of circumcision do you see on children brought to the hospital, whom you personally examine?*

A: Pharaonic circumcision.

Q: *Still the pharaonic?*

A: "With almost no exceptions."

Q: *What type of problems do you encounter on the pediatric ward?*

A: "I saw two cases of girls recently, 5 and 6 years old, respectively. They had been raped. There were horrible tear wounds because of the infibulation."

Q: *Who brings the children in when they have been raped?*

A: "The mother, sometimes the police."

Q: *They do report the rapes then?*

A: "Yes, sometimes. We could not treat them otherwise. They have to have a form from the police."

Q: *Do you think that most child rape cases that occur are brought to the hospital, or do most of them go unreported?*

A: "Very few of them are brought here."

Q: *Is there much child rape, then?*

A: "Yes."

Q: *Who is generally the perpetrator, a stranger or a member of the family?*

A: "Sometimes it is a member of the family. There has been a great migration to the city here, and life is getting difficult. So many people are crowded into one dwelling. When you find so many people sharing the same facilities, the same toilets, these things happen. Also, things are very difficult for youth here. There is no employment for them."

Q: *What do you think it is about this society, that brings on the rape of so many children?*

A: "Young men here are not allowed to have girlfriends, so there is a tremendous amount of sexual frustration. That is the crux of the whole matter."

Q: *Has it always been like that, do you think, or is it a recent phenomenon?*

A: "It is largely recent. It has to do with the problems that a large migration to cities creates. There are many young men that are homeless, away from the controls their families and their village impose. There used to be some houses of prostitution here, and this alleviated the problem a great deal, but these were closed down. This puts more pressure on men. They often have no sexual outlet of any sort."

Q: *What were you able to do for these small girls that had been raped?*

A: "All we were able do to was to resuture them, try to stop the bleeding and try to reassure the mothers that the girls would be all right. There is nothing else that we could do. The prime concern of the mothers every time is the virginity of the girl. They are afraid no one will marry her if we cannot repair the infibulation."

Q: *In other words, when you are able to fix matters so that the girl has an appearance of being a virgin, the crisis is over.*

A: "Yes, and especially if she is already circumcised. That is the central concern. You see, even if a girl is not a virgin, she can be resutured and no one knows the difference. Men, especially if they are laymen, cannot tell the difference."

Q: *So no one is really concerned over the physical or psychological trauma to which the child is subjected.*

A: "No, they are not worried about that at all. They do not even think about that. They think only of the virginity, not the child itself."

Q: *Can anything be done to help the child psychologically?*

A: There is nothing we are able to do for her. They want her sewn up, that is all. A psychiatrist would no doubt be useful in such cases, but here no one goes to a psychiatrist unless he is mad. Women, and especially small girls, never reach a psychiatrist at all."

Q: *Is there also much rape of grown women here?*

A: "If there are such cases, we never see them. We see only the children."

Q: *I hear a great deal about the new kind of circumcision that is reputedly being performed here now. I am told that educated people have a mild form of* sunna *done, or no circumcision at all. According to European women doctors and nurses, however, the girls are being pharaonically circumcised as before. What is your experience?*

A: "Actually my feeling is that educated people are telling you the truth when they say they are not circumcising their girls."

Q: *As a doctor then, do you actually see children who are uncircumcised or who have had a mild form of* sunna?

A: "Yes, I have seen a handful. The girls in my own family are not circumcised at all. But it is a tiny number of people that we are talking about, actually."

Q: *How many out of 10,000 would you say?*

A: "Pitifully few. Only those who have been educated abroad. Most of them are doctors' families, and there are not many doctors here to begin with. Even in my family our grandmother insisted, and my sister had a very difficult time preventing her from circumcising the girls. She actually had to hide them from her, in a boarding school some distance away. There were many terrible arguments about this. But as the older generation dies out, it is bound to become easier. If both mother and father of a girl are educated, she has a chance."

Q: *Do you think we are talking about 1% of the population here in the city?*

A: "Yes, it could in the near future reach 1%, although most likely it is not nearly that much at the present time."

Q: *We are talking about Khartoum. What about the rest of the country?*

A: "Far, far less. I would say change is virtually unheard of there."

Q: *Have you been aware of the campaign against female circumcision that is going on here in Khartoum? Do you hear about it frequently?*

A: "I have heard about it once or twice. Two years ago I took part in a pilot project at the town of Atbara some distance from here, and we had a very active experimental campaign for some time."

Q: *What was the effect?*

A: "Not much, considering the amount of effort that went into it. There was really no perceptible response to it at all. It was pretty well a total waste."

Q: *What about the law forbidding the pharaonic procedure?*

A: "The police do not attempt to enforce the law, and when something goes wrong, the families will not reveal the name of the midwife. It would be considered terribly shameful to do so, and it would be totally impossible for anyone who did accuse a midwife to remain living in the community. Such a person would virtually be driven out. Usually when something goes wrong the family prefers to let the girl bleed to death, rather than get involved with the authorities. Recently a 4-year-old girl was brought in bleeding massively from a pharaonic that had been a bad job. An artery had been damaged. The doctor on duty insisted that the family fill out a police form, naming the midwife so that she could be prosecuted. The family flatly refused. We were afraid we were going to lose the girl if we did not treat her. So we gave in. The midwife is doing a lucrative business as before. No one ever informs on her because she is of the same tribe as the people she does it for. If the girl dies, it is accepted as the will of Allah, and this absolves everyone of any moral responsibility.''

INDIAN MATERNITY NURSE

I spoke with a maternity nurse in the labor room of Omdurman Hospital. The decibel levels in this room and the adjoining delivery room approached total bedlam. The heart-rending shrieks and screams were so many and so loud that I had to pose some of the questions several times. It was nearly impossible to hear the replies that the nurse made to my questions.

Q: *What kinds of circumcision do you see on the women who deliver here at the hospital?*

A: ''Last year we had 6,000 deliveries. Maybe 50 of them were not circumcised. They were normal. All of them were from the South, from Wau or Juba.''

Q: *Were there any from Khartoum or any other parts of Northern Sudan?*

A: ''No. Not a one of them. They were all from indigenous southern tribes.''

Q: *What kinds of problems do you deal with most often?*

A: ''The circumcisions and infibulations create terribly abnormal and totally unhygienic conditions. People do these things because they feel it will keep the girls clean, but of course quite the contrary is true. All kinds of residue from urine and menstrual blood stays behind the tightly sewn-up part. It is impossible to wash it, and very fertile ground for infection exists constantly. We see the most terrible infections here.''

Q: *How long have you been working here?*

A: "For 5 years."

Q: *During that period have you seen any children over 10 or 11 years of age that were uncircumcised?*

A: "Two or three from the southern tribes only. No others. Actually we are beginning to see girls from the South with circumcisions now too. When they marry men from the North, the husbands make them do it, usually after the first child is born. I have heard these doctors here telling you that circumcision is no longer being done on some children now. That is not true. All girls here are circumcised same as before, same as women that come into the maternity ward. There is no change. They are circumcised without any exception. The younger generation does not want it, but it has already been done to them, and it is now being done to their little sisters.''

Q: *Why are the doctors lying to me?*

A: "They know it is wrong. They know that it ruins a girl's health. They are embarrassed because they feel you will think of them as barbarians. And there is also an element of wishful thinking. They would like their own families to be progressive and intelligent. They really do try to persuade them not to do it, and they feel very badly when they are not listened to, when they realize that in spite of all their education they are powerless. Many of them have been educated in different countries and they know what things should be like. They have seen normal women and normal births. Most of them leave the country at the first opportunity to work in Saudi Arabia. It isn't just the money that draws them away from here. They just can't stand the frustration after a while. Nobody can stand it for very long. The sad part of it is that when the doctors leave, more and more of their work is done by midwives, because there is no one else to do it.''

Q: *Are there any midwives in the hospital here who do circumcisions on the side?*

A: "They are all doing it, every single one of them. There are no exceptions whatsoever. That is their greatest source of income — that and what they call 'recircumcision,' the repairs they do after a woman gives birth. This job here pays very little, but circumcisions and recircumcision are very well paid."

Q: *Does the new law against pharaonic circumcision affect this practice of the midwives at all?*

A: "Nobody stops them. They all know they are perfectly safe in what they do. The ones who cut most drastically are the ones who are most in demand, and who make the most money, so of course they outdo themselves. The women themselves believe that if they are cut so that nothing remains but a little skin over the bones, the husband will find them more beautiful. They don't know any better and they can't be persuaded otherwise. It is such a foolish misguided practice. The whole thing is so awfully depressing. There seems to be no answer to it."

AN EDUCATED MALE

I found the attitudes of highly educated and Westernized Arab men particularly interesting. One day, while seated at a table in a Khartoum club, I was drawn into conversation by a man sitting at the next table with two French women, whom he introduced as his wife and sister-in-law. He spoke both English and French fluently, and his range of interests and experiences proved in the course of conversation to be considerable. He identified himself as the Syrian Press Secretary.

"I think I have heard about you," he told me. "You are a journalist, are you not? What paper do you work for?" As usual, when a question of this sort was posed to me, it did not take long before I established that I was a freelancer, and that I had a special area of interest. From there it became difficult to play it close to the chest, and we slid into a conversation about female circumcision. It always happened rather quickly, no matter how I tried to postpone it in order to be able to size up the other person before laying all my cards on the table.

"But of course it is dying out here," he said. I told him of my recent trips to Nuba and Jebel Mara in the west. "Not really," I said. "As a point of fact, it appears to be spreading more rapidly than it is dying out."

He expressed surprise. As we talked he kept returning to the same point: "Do you have any ideas of where and how this custom arose?" he asked repeatedly, and each time I assured him that I did not know, and that actually there was no *way* of knowing. Some mummies of women had been found in what is now the south of Egypt, and these mummies, 4,000 years old, *appeared* to have been circumcised and infibulated. Whether they were in a state of preservation that made this determination possible was something that I did not know. I had not seen them. There was also some doubt in my mind, even if this were so, whether these women had been thus dealt with during their lifetime, or if the procedure had been performed after death, since the process of embalming in ancient Egypt involved the removal of *all* the internal organs. In any event, I told him, the origins of the practice were only of peripheral interest to me. What concerned me was not how it began, but how it could be ended.

"But it is important," he said.

"And why?" I asked.

"Because I theorize that it began in those countries of Africa where the female parts are so hypertrophied that it is necessary to reduce them in size."

"Hypertrophied? What do you mean hypertrophied?"

"Well, there are women in Africa who are born with a clitoris that is far larger than is normal."

The hair on the back of my neck rose ever so slightly. "You know," I said, "the size of the penis among men the world round shows considerable variation. Were you to take the average size of the occidental, the Oriental, and Negro races, as well as those of the Arab and the Bushman, and even the fabled Dinka tribe of the Sudan, you would find that there would be some differences. Would you, therefore, having established a world average, advocate trimming down those penises that were too large to fit into your 'normal' category?''

"You are right," he said after some consideration. "I had not thought about it in that way. In an area where you find large penises you would expect to find corresponding female organs to fit them, wouldn't you."

"Precisely," I said. "So 'hypertrophy' is rather an arbitrary term, and it must be that the whole business is related to something other than correcting a form of pathology, as is implied by it. Large clitorides and labia may inspire some feelings of threat in the males or even the females of a culture, but they are not in and of themselves pathological.

"Among the Hottentots they were rather a sign of beauty and something to be greatly desired in a woman. The Hottentots enlarged and lengthened their labia by pulling on them from infancy on, giving rise to what has been described as 'The Hottentot Apron.' Unfortunately, during the slave trade they fell prey to Arab slave traders, and the so-enlarged female genitalia became associated with female slaves, while circumcision, the more severe the better, became interwoven ever more intricately with upper-class standing. No one knows how old the slave trade actually is. Saudi Arabia abolished it only about two decades ago, did it not?''

He shrugged. "But of course it is *still* going on."

"Most likely," I said, "and in the indigenous regions of Sudan women are ridiculed and shamed for not circumcising their children. They are told that it is the mark of a slave, that it is unclean and low class. So now they have begun circumcising their girls, and in their zeal to outlive these stigma, they are performing the most drastic operations possible. In their minds, lacking education to the contrary, it is the thing to do, for it removes from them the slave-stigma they so dread."

He shrugs. I realize fully that I have not even begun to alter his thinking. His attitudes are quite typical of even the most educated men here.

RESEARCH WORKER

I did not know anything about the operation at the time, except that it was very simple, and that it was done to all the girls for purposes of cleanliness, purity, and the preservation of a good reputation. It was said that a girl who did not undergo the operation was liable to be talked about by people, her behavior would become bad, and she would start running after men, with the result that no one would want to marry her when she was ready for marriage. My grandmother had told me that the operation only consisted of the removal of a very small piece of flesh from between my thighs, and that the continued existence of this small piece of flesh would have made me unclean and impure, and would have caused the man whom I would marry to be repelled by me. I began to be happy the day I recovered from the effects of the operation and felt as though I was rid of something which had to be removed, that I had become clean and pure.

23-YEAR-OLD GOVERNMENT CLERK

I am getting tired of hearing about all the dangerous and bad consequences of the pharaonic. It was done to us, and it was not our fault. No one asked us; they simply did it to us. How do you think we feel, hearing about all the bad things that will happen when we marry? We have enough fears. We do not need any more. It is very cruel.

AMERICAN MALE TRAVELING IN AFRICA

I have been with circumcised women many times in all the regions of Africa where this is practiced. It never occurred to me that they were mutilated women, and I don't think they thought of themselves as such. They were just women like any other women.

5. Voices of Reason

Despite the limited involvement of nearly all African national governments, female circumcision in Africa has increasingly gained international attention, particularly among women's groups. Beginning in 1958, when the United Nations Commission on the Status of Women called upon the World Health Organization (WHO) to undertake a study of the "persistence of customs which subject girls to ritual operations and of the measures planned to put an end to it" (Ogunmodede, 1979, p. 31), a number of international conferences and seminars have been held in recent years.

Since 1980, when UNICEF pledged assistance to community groups and organizations who were willing to work toward the prevention of the operations, several women's groups, some composed of Africans, Afro-Americans, and European women, have been organized. Among these are the Somali Democratic Women's Organization, Le Mouvement Femmes et Société (Senegal), Women's Group Against Sexual Mutilation (France), Union National des Femmes du Mali (Kouba and Muasher, 1985, p. 107), and the Babiker Bedri Foundation for Women's Studies and Research (Sudan). However, once more the attempts at effectiveness by these groups are largely thwarted due to lack of government backing and of financial support.

The subject of female circumcision has in the past and in recent debate been highly emotional, both among those who defend it as a practice, and among those who wish to see it end. Among the latter, there have been a number of dedicated Westerners whose unquestionably well-intended involvement has not always been welcome to African women, some of whom resent such involvement as an invasion of privacy, as interference in African affairs, and as yet another form of imperialism. This was made quite evident at the Mid-decade Conference for Women in Copenhagen in 1980, where the Association of African Women for Research and Development under the leadership of Marie-Angelique Savané of Senegal strongly denounced all forms of Western interference.

It has been my experience that this group does not speak for all African women, and that support without compulsion or direction is most welcome. Among the inflamed feelings that pervade the subject on both sides, one may yet hear clearly some voices of reason, and I quote several of them here:

> The types of female circumcision performed among traditional African societies and the medical complications arising from this ritual operation are sufficiently defined and documented in recent publications. During the last 12 years, a growing interest in this subject has generated research activities which have produced articles, reports and books providing evidence of the fact that female circumcision is a health hazard to millions of women and children in Africa. Most of this written material expresses a unanimous opinion of the need to eradicate this practice, labeling it as dangerous and unnecessary. Measures proposed for eradication vary, however; they depend on the understanding and the interpretation of traditional values attributed to female circumcision.
>
> Those who view female circumcision as a manifestation of the subordinate position that women have in the power relation of the two sexes, support the idea of total economic and social liberation of women as a primary and vital step in the campaign for the eradication of female circumcision.
>
> The health argument stresses education as a key note for creating awareness at both the individual and the communal level.
>
> There is also an emerging outlook which refers to the United Nations Universal Declaration of Human Rights and condemns female circumcision as child abuse and violation of fundamental rights. This party calls for legislation that prohibits the practice.
>
> While these opinions continue to be echoed at national and international forums, those directly affected by the issue pursue their traditional way of life, the values of which sometimes

impose obligations such as circumcision. Unaware of medical consequences, lacking a better alternative way of life, they preserve such ancestral values to ensure social cohesion and harmony (B. Ras-Work, 1984, p. 71).

Religion, if authentic in the principles it stands for, aims at truth, equality, justice, love and a healthy wholesome life for all people, whether men or women. There can be no true religion that aims at disease, mutilation of the bodies of female children, and amputation of an essential part of their reproductive organs.

If religion comes from God, how can it order man to cut off an organ created by Him as long as that organ is not diseased or deformed?

God does not create the organs of the body haphazardly. It is not possible that he should have created the clitoris in woman's body only in order that it be cut off in an early stage in life. This is a contradiction into which neither religion nor the creator could possibly be involved. If God has created the clitoris as a sexually sensitive organ, whose sole function seems to be the procurement of sexual pleasure to the woman, it follows that he also considers such pleasures for women as normal and legitimate and therefore as an integral part for mental and physical health. The physical and mental health of women cannot be complete if they do not experience sexual pleasure (Nawal Saadawi, 1982, p. 227).

Islam holds the human species in honor, and accordingly human beings should not suffer any harm, physical or mental. Islamic law and traditions preserve the wholeness of the individual, protecting him or her from everything that causes hurt, and female circumcision is nothing but a habit, a bad one, that should be fought. . . . Some people say that female circumcision preserves the woman's honor, but this opinion is rejected, for honor and virtue are the result of a good upbringing, not of clitoridectomy. . . . We must therefore fight against this custom, which is neither a religious duty nor even a recommended practice. All that has been claimed for it is that it is an honor to women, and even this does not seem to be valid in the light of modern medical knowledge. . . . It is time to increase public awareness by means of the mass media and conferences, and time for religious leaders to discharge their duties by enlightening people and combating this barbaric custom. For Islam preserves the wellbeing of both men an women. The Prophet said: "He who harms a believer harms me, and he who harms me harms God."

Modern medicine has demonstrated that this practice is harmful, and Islam is not an obscurantist religion. This custom should therefore be fought and abolished, since it does more harm than good (H. A. A. Sabib, 1984, p. 69).

There is still a large number of fathers and mothers afraid to leave the clitoris intact in the bodies of their daughters, and they often state that circumcision is a safeguard against the mistakes and deviations into which a girl may be led. This way of thinking is wrong and even dangerous, because what protects a boy or a girl from making mistakes is not the removal of a small piece of flesh from the body, but awareness and understanding of the problems we face, and a worthwhile aim in life, an aim which gives life meaning, and for the attainment of which we exert our minds and energies. The higher the level of consciousness which we attain, the greater our desire to improve life, and its quality, rather than to indulge in the mere satisfaction of our senses and the experience of pleasure, even though these are an essential part of our existence. The most liberated and free of girls is the one least preoccupied with sexual questions since these no longer represent any problem. On the contrary, a free mind finds room for numerous interests and the many rich experiences of a cultured life. Girls who suffer sexual suppression, however, are greatly preoccupied with men and sex. And it is a common observation that an intelligent and cultured woman is much less engrossed in matters related to sex and to men than is the case of ordinary women, who have not got much else with which to fill their lives. At the same time, such a woman takes much more initiative to insure that she will enjoy sex and experience pleasure, and acts with a greater degree of boldness than others. Once sexual satisfaction is obtained she is able to turn herself fully to other aspects of life.

In the life of liberated and intelligent women, sex does not occupy a disproportionate position but rather tends to maintain itself within normal limits. Ignorance, suppression, fear and all sorts of limitations exaggerate the role of sex in the life of girls and women and cause it to swell out of all proportion and to end up occupying the whole or almost the whole of their lives (Nawal Saadawi, 1982, p. 228).

A circumcised woman, never having had the chance to experience what it would be like to be uncircumcised, would be reluctant to believe that she had lost much. In her denial she would ensure herself of her intactness by allowing, openly or tacitly, her own or others' daughters to undergo the same procedure. She would justify her attitude through the belief that: "It preserves virtue by diminishing desire and I would like to protect my daughter from sin," or "For me it was a matter of tradition," implying she had no temptation to sin, even though her daughter would have. At the same time she might herself be enjoying sex and would use denial and projection to ward off her guilt: "It is my daughter, not me." To atone for her sin of enjoying sex she would punish her daughter. In the light of this, any statement that circumcision is harmful should be resisted by such women in an attempt to assure themselves of their intactness, and to alleviate the guilt they would have for having circumcised or condoned the circumcision of their daughters or others. What would be more appropriate is an approach that would focus on the uselessness of the practice coupled with sexual enlightenment geared to minimize the guilt surrounding sexual desire and enjoyment (M. Shaalan, 1982, p. 271).

It is indeed false to pretend to prevent sexual immorality through female circumcision and infibulation, since prevention of sexual immorality or protection of virginity is an ethical matter rather than a physiological matter. Sexual immorality can only be prevented through sexual and social education (E. Sayed, 1982, p. 156).

The wave of violent and uncontrollable reactions on the part of Western countries in denouncing these mutilations inflicted upon all these hardly mature young girls, is certainly a source of consolation and a show of solidarity by humanity. But when one examines closely this practice and its consequences, one quickly discovers that it is necessary to slow down a bit the ardor to eliminate it in order to be more effective and attain the objective envisaged, namely the complete abolition of the practice of sexual mutilation.

Africans do not always understand that the majority of Western countries which practiced, in their own countries, all these forms of genital mutilation considered today barbaric, have today begun a campaign of systematic denunciation, capable of provoking in those who are favorable to this practice the very complex problem of cultural animosity with unpredictable effects.

The situation is extremely disturbing and irritating even to people with the best intentions who, in fact, support these humanitarian actions. All these factors enable us better to understand the apparent discretion adopted by many Africans with regard to this burning issue. They have committed themselves strongly and resolutely, individually and collectively, to a persistent struggle for the final elimination on our continent of all these forms of corporal mutilation abhorred by the whole world, the victims of which are poor innocent young girls.

The African, like all the peoples of the world, likes to make even the most bitter criticism against his country and people, but finds it difficult to tolerate that others do it, especially at a time when Africa tries to find its own identity and unity.

We therefore contend that for understandable psychological reasons the task of sensitization of the public in this field should be left to black women (P. Correa, 1984, p. 56).

The solution to this problem can be reached only through African determination, understanding and education, with African resources and know-how and with African rationale and diplomacy which take into consideration the complexity of African reality, culture and heritage, while looking for sensible, practical and generally acceptable solutions to this major but preventable health hazard (E. A. Ismail, 1984, p. 121).

Clitoral circumcision . . . and infibulation of the vulva are deep-rooted customs affecting women from babyhood onward, causing suffering, shock, infections and even death, depriving them of sexual enjoyment, and keeping them in bondage and submission. Anthropologists may say that the initiative to stop this mutilation must come from the women victims themselves. But these poor, oppressed, frightened, superstitious, illiterate women enforce mutilation on young girls so that they will be accepted as members of the group or tribe and get a husband. And what can the baby girls do, but shriek and fight against the knife, while their arms and legs are pinned down by strong women who also wail in order to drown the shrieks of the victims? The only help and effective action can come from enlightened public opinion, through mass-media, through supporting groups and organizations such as the United Nations, UNICEF, and Save the Children Fund. The fight against manmade avoidable suffering is everybody's responsibility. Genital mutilation is a health-hazard and a total obstacle to social and economic development (T. Hakansson, 1982, p. 255).

Female circumcision exists on a large scale in Africa even though many of the traditional rituals and celebrations that accompany circumcision have been abandoned. . . . The reasons are manifold, the principal one being that the custom of female circumcision and the rationale underlying it are so entrenched in the societies where it is practiced that the operation is an integral part of the sociocultural system. The paramount importance of family honor, virginity, chastity, purity, marriageability and child-bearing in those societies that associate these attributes cannot be overstressed. Therefore, the benefits gained from these operations by the recipient and her family far outweigh any potential danger. . . . A sensible approach aimed at the eradication of female circumcision is embodied in a twenty year program . . . based on two areas; health education to increase knowledge of the dangers involved with the practice and to correct wrong religious beliefs, and health care to provide treatment and rehabilitation for the victims. The elimination of female circumcision in Africa will be a slow and complex process. While any program committed to its eradication must approach the problem with a great deal of sensitivity, traditional beliefs should not obscure medical reality. Those traditional beliefs which impact on women need to be modified by implementing broader policies aimed at improving the overall status of women in Africa (L. J. Kouba and J. Muasher, 1985, p. 109).

Certain Westerners have labeled female circumcision a barbaric mutilation of women and children, without first understanding the general oppression and underdevelopment of the continent. Indictments such as these have created confusion about the priorities and needs of African women. . . . It is important to bear in mind who these woman are. For the most part, these women cannot even satisfy their basic needs and have to struggle for their daily survival. They suffer from chronic malnutrition, excessive work, little obstetrical care and poor environmental conditions which are equally if not more mutilating than female circumcision. While the eradication of female circumcision should be called for, the practice should not be isolated from the whole range of debilitating conditions which constitute the reality of African women. . . . No campaign to eradicate female circumcision can be effective without the active participation of the women who are directly concerned with and affected by the issue. . . . While health education campaigns are important, it should be pointed out that "methods and techniques must take into consideration the deep cultural roots and the psychosocial ramifications of female circumcision" (Taba, 1979, p. 93) if they are to be effective at all. This can only be accomplished if there are adequate data to furnish the basis upon which such techniques can be formulated (B. W. Giorgis, 1981).

African women must stop being reserved and shake themselves out of their political lethargy. They must make themselves heard on all national and international problems, defining their priorities and their special role in the context of social and national demands. On the question of traditional practices like genital mutilation, African women must no longer equivocate or react only to Western interference. They must speak out in favor of the total eradication of all these practices, and they must lead information and education campaigns to this end within their own countries and on a continental level (Association of African Women for Research and Development [see B. W. Giorgis, 1981, p. 60]).

One of the recent seminars on traditional practices affecting the health of women and children in Africa was held in Dakar in 1984. It made the following recommendations aimed at the eradication of female circumcision in all its forms:

1. Governments should promote a clear national policy and set up adequate strategies to fight the practice of female circumcision with a view to its complete eradication.
2. Considering the fact that female circumcision is deeply rooted in African cultures and traditions, educational programs directed toward the people, traditional practitioners, circumcisers, community workers, village chiefs, religious leaders, and women's associations should be set up on a practical level, using both traditional and modern means of communication.
3. Special efforts should be made in the field of information and education in order to change the attitude of men.
4. Students in schools, colleges, and universities should be trained to motivate their families and local communities to give up the practice of female circumcision.
5. In view of the harmful effects of female circumcision on the health of women and children, and since such a practice is

medically unethical, all medical staff and health workers should be forbidden to carry it out.

6. The medicalization and modernization of the practice of female circumcision is condemned and regarded as inconsistent with medical ethics.

7. Social and medical assistance should be made available to circumcised women in order to alleviate their physical and psychological suffering.

8. In societies where the practice of female circumcision forms part of the initiation rites, which are in general positive and should be preserved, this practice should be excluded.

9. An alternative source of income should be found for those who gain their living from this practice in order to compensate for any loss of earning.

10. The problems of female circumcision should be brought to the attention of the Islamic League and raised at all conferences where the position concerning female circumcision can be clarified.

11. In order to carry out the programs aimed at abolishing female circumcision, the Seminar requests moral, technical, and financial support and assistance from the World Health Organization, the United Nations Children's Fund, the United Nations Fund for Population Activities, other international and bilateral organizations, and private initiatives.

12. The Seminar recommends that governments and national and international NGOs should collaborate to implement these recommendations.

Author's Note: To hasten the process of consciousness raising among the populace, I would like to add a final and very simple recommendation for the implementation of another kind of educational program, based on my experiences among the Sudanese and in other parts of the Arab world. As I traveled, I could not help but notice that what is known as "Television Soap Opera" is as popular there as it is in the Western world. Whenever I found myself in a place where a television set existed (and a goodly number are now brought in from Saudi Arabia), I would observe that at 7 P.M., when the soap opera originating from Cairo came on, people would congregate religiously to watch with great fascination, and would later discuss it with a tremendous amount of involvement.

The degree of interest in this type of program, I observed, far exceeded that which was elicited by the purely informative educational kind of program, since the emotional, social, and familial situations presented were easy to understand and could be identified with by everyone—those who were unschooled as well as those who had the benefits of formal education. The influence of this kind of program is potentially quite extensive.

It occurs to me, therefore, that television soap opera could be an excellent medium for raising consciousness by presenting all points of view surrounding this complex and highly emotional issue in dramatic form, addressing for example the convictions and fears of the older generation, the torment and aspirations of the young people, the bases for various erroneous beliefs and superstitions, and the medical problems women have to face. Such a program would reach large numbers of people, and would elicit a high level of involvement. It could be used to supplement the more standard educative documentary program, designed to give detailed scientific information. High level involvement in television soap opera already exists, and needs only to be utilized in creating an effective and relatively inexpensive consciousness-raising tool.

6. A History of Clitoral Excision and Infibulation Practices in the Western World

Excision and infibulation are by no means unique to Africa, and have at some time in history been practiced or are still being practiced in many other parts of the world. As Africans are fond of pointing out, and rightly so, the Western world has been no exception. I will briefly sketch out a history of those practices here, for the sake of completeness. The reader will note certain similarities.

Female clitoral excision was practiced fairly extensively in the English speaking world during the 19th century. The case of Dr. Isac Baker Brown is described by Wallerstein (1980, p. 173).

> Isac Baker Brown (1812-1873) was considered one of the ablest and most innovative gynecological surgeons in England. It is not clear precisely when Dr. Brown "invented" clitoridectomy and when he began to practice the surgery. . . . It is possible that several hundred or perhaps several thousand such surgeries were performed. . . . What is clear is that Dr. Brown was seeking a surgical solution to the vexing mental disorders of women. According to the doctor, the main culprit was masturbation. . . . The treatment was clitoridectomy.

In 1867 the British medical establishment repudiated Brown's claims to "cures," called his methods "quackery," and expelled him from the Obstetrical Society. Clitoridectomy was thereby largely abandoned in England. According to Fleming (1960, p. 1030), Baker was expelled from the Royal College of Surgeons not so much because of his uncritical advocacy and performance of the operations, but because of his colleagues' chagrin and envy of his fame.

In the United States, American physicians not only adopted clitoridectomy for quite a number of years after Baker's disgrace, but they enlarged upon the operation so that it included oophorectomy (removal of the ovaries) (Barker-Benfield, 1976, p. 89). There are no records of the number of clitoris-ovary operations performed in the 1870s. Wallerstein (1985, p. 74) estimates that the figure was in the thousands.

Although the combined clitoris-ovary removal surgery was largely discontinued by 1880, clitoridectomy continued on a large scale. Lesbian practices, suspected lesbian inclinations, and an aversion to men were all treated by clitoral excision (Money, 1985, p. 119) as were other female "mental disorders" such as hypersexuality, hysteria, and nervousness (Wallerstein, 1985, p. 27).

In addition to clitoridectomy another form of surgery was tried in the United States to prevent masturbation: the labia were infibulated. This practice continued to be used until 1905 (Spitz, 1952, p. 503).

In 1897 a Boston surgeon maintained that contrary to men, "the sexuality of the young woman does not reside in the sexual organs." He therefore contended that orgasm in women was an ailment and the removal of erectile organs like the clitoris was a necessity. A number of doctors resorted to excision for treating epilepsy, catalepsy, hysteria, melancholy, and even kleptomania. It was performed in mental hospitals until 1935.

As late as 1936, Holt's *Disease of Infancy and Childhood* recommended cauterization (circumbustion) or removal of the clitoris for girls as cures for masturbation (Bullough and Bullough, 1977).

Hosken, in 1980-82 issues of WIN News, maintains that the surgical procedures are now being taught to medical students in England. She further reports that the *New National Black Monitor*, a U.S. Sunday newspaper supplement, has proposed in an editorial that excision and infibulation be introduced in the United States to eliminate premarital sexual activity by teenage women.

A modern American woman reports on her own experience with excision (Bergstrom, 1981, p. 254):

My mother was fanatically obsessed with the idea that masturbation was the ultimate sin. When found guilty of this erotic pastime at the age of three, I was taken to a doctor who shared her legalistic background. He cut off the outer portion of my clitoris because it was "too large" and therefore causing arousal. (Later I was told that it was no different than that of my sisters.) The emotional effect on me as a child was to make me feel guilty for my very existence. Puberty was a struggle. . . . was I really once half male/half female? Young adulthood found me facing the question of my ability to function sexually as a normal female. Physically this has not prevented orgasm. Emotionally it has led me to internalize anger, to play the strong role, to be a peacemaker, to avoid deep trusting relationships . . . to face many situations as a child. I am learning now at the age of thirty-six to deal with reality as an adult.

From Germany I have received the report that there still are similar cases among German nationals as well (personal correspondence, Haas, 1985). One involves a German woman employed by an African embassy. This woman brought her 15-year-old daughter to a German gynecologist to be excised "because of excessive masturbation." She had been excised herself at the same age for similar reasons, she reported. The gynecologist flatly refused to perform the operation. Five years later, the daughter, by then married and pregnant, presented herself at his office once more. Upon examining her, he found that her clitoris and inner labia had been excised.

This same physician was approached in a similar manner by another German woman who said she wished to be excised "in order to improve relations" between her husband and herself. Again the gynecologist refused and tried earnestly to enlighten her. He felt that he had succeeded in dissuading the woman, but 2 years later, when he once more had occasion to examine her, he found that she too had had her clitoris and inner labia excised. Although it is assumed that such cases are relatively rare, they do exist, and it is apparently still not impossible to find a physician who is willing to perform such an operation.

7. Male Circumcision

Male circumcision is universal among all Muslim and Jewish peoples in the world today, and has been accepted as a religious rite since ancient times. It is still practiced extensively in the United States as an anti-mastubatory secular rite. The mission of my self-imposed research was simply to study female circumcision, and did not include male circumcision. However, a brief review of this custom may serve to remind us that the practice of female circumcision, which some of us may regard as barbaric and irrational, has had its parallels throughout history in procedures performed on men.

Male circumcision is of particular interest here in that it is still practiced routinely on the majority of male neonates in United States hospitals today. The phenomenon in its own way closely parallels some aspects of female circumcision in Africa. Its wax and wane as a practice could quite possibly supply us with at least some partial guidelines on how female circumcision might be abandoned as a practice. I will first present a brief historical overview of male circumcision in general, and then discuss its present form and status in the English speaking world today.

The procedures practiced on females have had their counterparts in male mutilations throughout history. Man in primitive societies was mystified by the fertility of the soil, the birth and death of animals and human beings, their sexual coming of age, and reproduction. In the course of time, he invented a variety of rituals whose intent it was to regulate, appease, or bribe the deities or spirits thought to control these phenomena. As a result, surgery is almost universally practiced in primitive tribal cultures, and is only rarely related to the treatment or prevention of disease. It seeks to secure for the individual and the tribe distinct benefits that are quite separate from physical health. This type of surgery may involve stylized alterations of the skin, head, ears, nose, teeth, extremities, and most particularly the external genitalia.

Circumcision is or has been ritualistically practiced by a wide variety of primitive as well as advanced peoples throughout the history of the world. It has existed in Asia, Africa, North and South America, Europe, Australia, and Polynesia. It was practiced by the ancient Egyptians, from whom the Phoenicians, the Arabs, and probably the Jews derived the practice. It is found among African tribes, Australian Aborigines, the Malays of Borneo, both North and South American Indians, the ancient Aztecs and Mayas, the Caribs, the Fijians, and the Samoans. In most cultures it is used as a manhood or pubertal rite, often as an immediate prerequisite to mating and marriage (Bolande, 1969).

Montague (1946) observes:

> For the original adoption of any practice there is always some reason, though subsequently different reasons may be substituted from time to time, and the original reasons be completely forgotten and lost. In some cases the operation may have fitted in with an already existing ritual or ceremony, in others it may have instantly solved a problem which had been troubling the group.

By sacrificing a part, the well-being of the whole is thought to be safeguarded. Circumcision rites thus assume a quality of purification. When a part of the reproductive organs is sacrificed, fertility and the entire process of reproduction is thought to be ensured.

It is quite likely that circumcision originated independently and for a variety of reasons in different parts of the world to satisfy specific local needs. In some tropical or water poor areas, it is not unlikely that circumcision was originally performed to remove foreign bodies such as sand, insects, maggots, or larvae that had accumulated under the foreskin (Weiss, 1966).

Remondino (1974) speculated that in some peoples circumcision may originally have been derived from the primitive custom of taking a part of the body of a defeated enemy as trophy or proof of manly prowess. This usually involved any part of the body that was easily detachable — quite frequently parts of the external genitalia.

Weiss (1966) claims that in parts of Australia, once established in a group, circumcision spread from tribe to tribe through simple imitation (much as female circumcision is known to spread in Africa.) A visitor to a neighboring group observes the custom, introduces it to his own group, it quickly becomes popular, and within a few years it is institutionalized.

Male circumcision in general ostensibly functions on two levels; one sacred, the other secular. Sacred circumcision is an obligatory rite; secular circumcision is elective. Wallerstein (1983) observes that most proponents of sacred circumcision deny any health benefits, claiming it solely as a religious ritual. Secular circumcision practitioners adamantly deny religious connotations, claiming only health benefits.

Among the Muslims, male circumcision began as a practice long before the birth of Mohammed. It has a hygienic and purificatory connotation. For the Jews, on the other hand, it has no connotation of cleanliness or promise of health benefits whatsoever. It is purely a religious act, establishing the covenant between their deity and his chosen people.

Maimonides, Hebrew scholar and physician in the Middle Ages, wrote that circumcision exercised a civilizing effect by weakening the penis, thus counteracting excessive lust.

Infibulation of the penis refers to the practice of drawing a ring or similar device through the prepuce or otherwise occluding it for the principal purpose of making erection painful and coition impossible. It is known to have been practiced by the Etruscans and later the Romans. It appears to have been restricted to performers and athletes who appeared before the public nude, and may be assumed to have been voluntarily submitted to in the interest of modesty (Schwartz, 1970, p. 965).

Infibulation later made its appearance once more in a far more sinister way in Germany, having for a period been practiced in the earlier part of the 1700s for the purpose of population control (Schwartz, 1970, p. 977) at around 1780. After this time the medical profession gradually began to accept it in ever increasing degrees as a remedy and prevention for masturbation in boys (Schwartz, 1970, p. 979). No physician of the 19th century would have denied that masturbation, unless stopped early, had lethal consequences, and infibulation was eagerly accepted by the English speaking world.

From 1800 to 1875 little was known about causes or cures of most disease. Emphasis was placed upon masturbation as the cause of almost every known disease. The question therefore became to find a way to prevent masturbation. With advances in medical science in the last quarter of the 19th century, a surgical "solution" to masturbation was widely sought. Thus "health" circumcision began as a practice.

Epidemiological studies of venereal disease in England in 1854 and in New York City in 1882 revealed that of all religious groups, Jews, who practice religious male circumcision, had the lowest venereal disease rate. This was easily attributed to circumcision. Other differences in life-style were not considered. Most important, it was claimed (erroneously) that Jewish boys masturbated less frequently than other children. Wallerstein (1983) maintains that for precisely those reasons non-religious circumcision was introduced. (It is actually only within the past few years that the prevailing medical view toward masturbation has become more relaxed. As Dr. Robert E. Gould writes in 1977: "Today it would be hard to find a sexual behavior expert who does not consider autoerotic activity within the realm of "normal" and "healthy.")

Male circumcision became fashionable in both England and America at about the same time (1870-1880), and infibulation reached its peak toward the end of the century, along with other manifestations of Victorianism. The "solitary vice," as masturbation was then called, was more severely condemned than ever before. To tolerate masturbation in a patient was inconceivable. It was not only a disease that had to be treated immediately and vigorously, but a crime to be punished by making the treatment painful, humiliating, and vindictive. Numerous treatments were added to infibulation by the highest medical authorities of that era. Among them were cauterization, neurectomy, excision of the spermatic cord, castration for males, cauterization of the labia, clitoridectomy, and oophorectomy for females.

In the United States, these brutal and punitive procedures were recommended in the extremely popular writing of Kellog (see Money, 1985, p. 99):

A remedy which is almost always successful in small boys is circumcision, especially when there is any degree of phimosis. The operation should be performed by a surgeon without administering an anesthetic, as the brief pain attending the operation will have a salutary effect upon the mind, especially if it be connected with the idea of punishment, as it may well be in some cases. . . . The soreness which continues for several weeks interrupts the practice, and if it had not previously become too firmly fixed, it may be forgotten and not resumed. . . . We have become acquainted with a method of treatment of this disorder which is applicable in refractory cases, and we have employed it with entire satisfaction. It consists in the application of one or more silver sutures in such a way as to prevent erection. The prepuce, or foreskin is drawn forward over the glans, and the needle to which the wire is attached is passed through, the ends are twisted together, and cut off close. It is now impossible for an erection to occur, and the slight irritation thus produced acts as a most powerful means of overcoming the disposition to resort to the practice.

The "health" benefits of circumcision were described in detail by Dr. Peter C. Remondino, who claimed that circumcision cured about 100 ailments, including asthma, alcoholism, epilepsy, rectal prolapse, kidney disease, gout, leprosy, plague, and tuberculosis (1891). (Remondino further suggested that males born with short or no foreskins are more intelligent than males with long foreskins (p. 10). His book, *History of Circumcision from the Earliest Time to the Present*, went through a number of printings, the latest being in 1974, and may still be found in current medical reference libraries. Its claims are still being disseminated, and quite possibly, believed.

Dr. Jacobus Sutor, another 19th century author who wrote about the sexuality of primitive peoples, claimed that the foreskin restricted the penis from growing to its normal length, and that circumcision provided for a larger penis size as well as enormous sexual prowess (see Edwards and Masters, 1963, p. 89).

From 1890 to 1923, an offshoot medical group, the Orificial Surgical Society, performed thousands of circumcisions on males and females, going beyond the masturbation cure, suggesting that headaches, arthritic hips, hydrocephaly, and kleptomania, among others, could be treated by circumcision (Wallerstein, 1983).

At the turn of the century, "health" circumcision of males was accepted only by English-speaking countries—the United States, England, Canada, Australia, and New Zealand. Today male circumcision performed in the newborn period, during childhood, or at puberty is practiced by fewer than 20% of the world's population. More than 80% of the people of the world reject it (Wallerstein, 1983).

Male circumcision ceased in England very abruptly soon after World War II, the reason being that the officials of the new national health insurance service decided not to pay for neonatal circumcision. Since 1950, the rate in England has dropped to less than 1%. In New Zealand the rate was reported to be less than 10% in 1983. In Canada and Australia it was about 40% and declining.

The United States is at this time the only Western country that practices nonreligious circumcision extensively. The rate was estimated to be approximately 85% by Wallerstein in 1983. In present day America many private medical insurance policies and public medical assistance continue to pay for it, and it remains a significant source of income for hospitals and doctors, along with other unnecessary surgery.

Routine male circumcision is usually performed in hospitals on the second or third day after birth, before the mother and infant are discharged from the hospital. The procedure is sometimes performed by a trained surgeon, although the task is generally assigned to residents or interns. In newborn infants anesthesia is hardly ever used, as it adds to the risk of the surgery. The infant must be restrained to avoid injury.

The foreskin is held by clamps and pulled away from the glans. One blade of a scissor or a scalpel is inserted between the foreskin and the glans, and the foreskin is cut along its full length to expose the glans. The incision is spread apart to expose the glans. Then, using a scalpel or scissors, the foreskin is completely cut off. Bleeding, unless it is profuse, can usually be controlled by pressure. Stitches are rarely required, except in older children or adults (Wallerstein, 1980, p. 205). In 1975 the American Academy of Pediatrics stated that there is "no medical indication for the routine circumcision of the newborn," a policy endorsed by other medical groups as well (Money, 1985, p. 102).

Social pressures are among the reasons why Americans to this day opt for circumcisions of their sons. "Everybody does it." "It looks better." Dr. George T. Klauber commented in 1973: "The practice lends itself well to the North American preoccupation with hygiene and banishment of all body odors (p. 445).

In the United States mothers have generally been blamed for wishing that their sons be circumcised so that the task of keeping the infant's penis clean will be less difficult, and so that it will require less handling — a task fraught with anxiety for many mothers. The circumcised penis tends to be less anxiety-producing to the mother. (Some have even interpreted this as meaning that the mother is hostile to her son's sexuality.)

Freud (1938) and later Reik (1962) pointed out that a close psychological connection between the compulsive actions of neurotic patients and ritualistic behavior exists. The rituals that various cultures develop may well be socially acceptable means of processing deep-seated primitive fears and impulses that would otherwise induce great conflict and anxiety.

Masters and Johnson (1966) observed no physiological differences in the sexual response of circumcised vs. uncircumcised men. However, psychiatrist Bettelheim (1962) suggests that neonatal circumcision may contribute to the development of castration anxiety later in life.

It is interesting to note that male circumcision was performed, initially, on more upper-class than lower-class infants (Wallerstein, 1985, p. 327). (Noncircumcision has generally been associated in the United States with low status minorities, and a dubious standard of hygiene.)

The initial drop in the circumcision rate following the introduction of the National Health Service in England followed a similar pattern: It was higher among the *upper* strata of society, who had also originally adopted the practice first. In other words, Wallerstein observes (p. 70), among the upper strata of society, there was a "first-in-first-out" phenomenon, with their example followed by middle and low-class strata. (These findings are of particular interest to the female circumcision issue.)

Wallerstein, who writes prolifically on the subject of male circumcision, speaks eloquently for the practices' opponents (1980,
p. 53).

> Circumcision opponents . . . maintain that study of the fore-
> skin's development and structure reveals that this tissue is in-
> deed useful. As a covering, it protects the glans from irrita-
> tion. The copiousness and sensitivity of the foreskin's nerve
> structure indicate that it is erotogenic tissue with a useful if not
> important role in coitus. Opponents of circumcision maintain
> that the supposed benefits that the glans is said to derive from
> the operation are myths and that, in fact, removal diminishes
> sexual sensation. . . . It is accepted medical knowledge that
> there is an element of danger in any surgery — including cir-
> cumcision. Life-threatening infection, hemorrhage, and injury
> are not rare; mutilations do occur, even an occasional death.
> The surgery may be physically and emotionally traumatic and
> removing erogenous tissue may actually inhibit, not enhance
> sexual functioning. (p. 3)

Scandinavian physicians take the definite position that circumcision is sexually harmful (Robertson, 1974, p. 48). The only study
on delayed circumcision complications (i.e., those that occur after
the neonate leaves the hospital) that has been conducted so far was
done in Canada. It was found that out of 100 cases, 24 developed
problems; among them bleeding that required sutures, infections,
meatal ulcers, meatal stenosis (narrowing of the urinary opening),
and one case that required recircumcision (Patel, 1966).

In addition, Money (1982, p. 251) cautions:

> Even when the operative procedure . . . in neonatal male cir-
> cumcision is performed with sterilized instruments and dress-
> ings in a modern hospital, morbidity is prevalent to a degree
> that would not be legally tolerated in test trials of any new
> clinical procedure. Increasingly, the term genital mutilation is
> being used to apply to the practices of circumcision, male or
> female, and of vulval excision and infibulation. Increasingly,
> children's advocates and the grown-up victims of these mutila-
> tions are attacking them as institutionalized infant and child

abuse, with an unknown magnitude and prevalence of adverse effects on adult eroticism.

The claims that circumcision prevents venereal disease have persisted beyond the middle of the 20th century. In a book published as late as 1973, urologist A. Ravich claims that both cancer and venereal disease can be prevented by circumcision. Within the past 10 years, there has been virtually no other statement that circumcision prevents syphilis or gonorrhea, and the New York City Bureau of Venereal Disease Control issued a statement in 1979 that circumcision was of absolutely no value in preventing genital herpes infection (Felman, 1979, p. 1964).

In spite of the general belief that circumcision prevents both penile cancer in men and cervical cancer in woman sex partners, no such relationship has ever been proven, and Grossman and Posner (1981), writing in *Obstetrics and Gynecology*, stated: "No one today seriously promotes circumcision as a prophylactic against cancer of any form. No significant correlation between cancer and circumcision has ever been proven."

There are also more subtle effects of neonate circumcision with possible long-term implications that have recently been reported: following circumcision, male babies showed an increase in the level of hormones related to stress, sleep patterns altered; and there was more crying and irritability (Morris, 1985).

Within the past decade dozens of articles have appeared in medical nursing and popular journals which questioned, criticized, or denounced nonreligious "health" circumcision. The editors of the *Journal of the American Medical Association* (1963), The American Academy of Pediatrics (1975), The American College of Obstetricians and Gynecologists (Wallerstein, 1980), Dr. Benjamin Spock (1976), and Dr. Sidney S. Gellis (1978) have all spoken out against routine nonreligious male circumcision.

There have been some dramatic results. At last report (Wallerstein, 1987) the rate of male circumcision has dropped from 85% in 1983 to 60% in 1987, and is clearly still declining. Data from no state, county, or city, nor from individual hospitals have shown an *increase* in the circumcision rate in more than a decade. Medical coverage for routine male circumcision has been dropped by a number of insurance carriers. In Canada and Australia, the rates have dropped to 25%. In Quebec it is about 6%; the Newfoundland rate is now zero.

In 1987 Wallerstein wrote: "Within the past five years the *non*religious circumcision rate in the U.S. has dropped from about 85% to 60%, a drop of 25 percentage points. Should this rate-drop continue unabated, by the end of the century the U.S. nonreligious circumcision rate will approach zero, the same rate as that of most (75%) of the world's population." He sums up by saying,

> There is no need for routine newborn circumcision. This is borne out by the experience of *every* European country, plus China, Japan, and dozens of others. . . . No country that abandoned the practice has even considered reinstating it. . . . The worldwide rejection of routine *non*religious circumcision provides overwhelming evidence that this is the correct course to follow. In the United States, every relevant medical society has taken a public position in opposition to routine circumcision. No medical society has taken a position in support of the practice."

8. Overview

Enlightened Westerners existing in a world far removed geographically and psychologically from the African countries' strange and disturbing manifestations under discussion may be tempted to disregard their practices as something that does not concern Westerners. I wish, therefore, to underscore certain similarities to practices in our own culture.

The reasons given for female circumcision in Africa and for routine male circumcision in the United States are essentially the same. Both falsely tout the positive health benefits of the procedures. Both promise cleanliness and the absence of "bad" genital odors, as well as greater attractiveness and acceptability of the sex organs. The affected individuals in both cultures have come to view these procedures as something that was done *for* them, and not something that was done *to* them. While the African rationalizes that women's pain threshold is far higher than that of men, we Westerners also rationalize that a newborn infant does not feel the pain of unanesthetized surgery.

Nor are we strangers to unnecessary genital and reproductive organ surgery for women. The clitoris has been seen to be cavalierly dismissed by some surgeons as being unnecessary to women, while the performance of hysterectomies, oophorectomies, and cesarian sections, whose necessity is often questionable, increases every year. Many of these procedures are performed routinely and have until very recently not been challenged. Only lately have women begun to protest.

The economic element of all these practices, both in Africa and in Western countries, is impossible to ignore. In both cases it is a matter of those who "oversell" to the gullible, conformist, easily cowed consumer in a culture that is hostile to sexuality.

Because female circumcision is so intricately related to complex social orders and traditional codes of behavior in African societies, changes concerning its performance are met with a great deal of resistance and may be expected to take place only slowly and gradually. Large-scale population movements from villages and small towns into African urban centers, although in many ways socially disruptive, also bring with them educational opportunities, well-paying occupations, and high social status for some. These privileged few are no longer economically dependent on their patrimony, and this, as well as the physical distance between them and their extended family, enables them to evolve new life-styles and to make decisions concerning their offspring independently, unfettered by their more conservative elders.

Factors affecting the decision of several families not to circumcise, as delineated in a preliminary study (Price, 1982), follow a predictable pattern: one or both parents are highly educated; there is a comfortable standard of living in an urban center; they are removed from the extended family; and a high level equality of rights, education, and social freedom for females within the household is found. The decision itself is agreed upon by both parents, with or without support from the extended family or larger society, when a belief in any valid reason for continuing the practice no longer exists. In this study all women interviewed expressed very positive feelings about not being circumcised, as did the husbands of the married ones. Ninety percent expressed the belief that a large-scale educational campaign should be conducted, aimed at women, men, and children.

Although people in Sudan and other African nations only recently emerged from colonial domination understandably resist Western interference in their internal affairs, there is now a growing awareness on the part of the educated that among the positive old customs that they wish to retain there are others that are not in the best interest of the country or its populace. While other damaging practices are rapidly being abandoned, female circumcision has hung on tenaciously to this date.

Within recent years, the morality of female circumcision has come increasingly into question. While most Sudanese may reject the ethics of the Christian-Judaic world, the influence of Saudi Arabia, the cradle of Islam, cannot be ignored. A dialogue between the two countries on the subject is expanding.

Another phenomenon which is very much on the increase in Sudan and all of Africa is the adoption of Western medicine and scientific method, and in view of this, the growing educated class is becoming ever more aware of the harmful effects of the practice on women, the family, the labor force, and the country at large.

With expanding educational opportunities for women, their voices have at this time become strong enough to be heard for the first time, and there are many that are questioning the necessity and advisability for continuation of the practice.

Over a period of years, the educated urban classes may be expected to be the first to perform successively less damaging procedures, and to ultimately abandon the practice altogether. Their example may be expected to eventually be imitated by the populace, over a considerably greater period of time.

The thrust of any program concerned with the abolition of the custom should therefore be aimed at those who can serve as potential educators. The universities should offer as part of their curriculum for health and social workers courses on all aspects affecting the health and welfare of women and children, including such topics as family planning, circumcision and its health consequences, sex education, and sound nutritional practices. Whenever possible midwives should be recruited into training programs, in order to preserve their prestigious standing in the community, and to offer them an economic alternative.

With the help of the World Health Organization, the United Nations Children's Fund, the United Nations Fund for Population Activities, and other international and bilateral organizations and private initiatives, the education of women needs to be further implemented, and the overall status of women in Africa raised. The brain drain of qualified medical personnel into Saudi Arabia could be counteracted by those NGOs interested in reversing the trend by adequately financing and training such people, especially women doctors, to treat and educate the population.

PART II

9. Images

PHOTO 9.1. This six-year-old girl was brought into a hospital emergency room in Port Sudan. She was hemorrhaging severely and required a series of blood transfusions over a period of two days. She had been subjected to an unskilled village pharaonic circumcision, and was suffering from severe sepsis. As this picture is being taken, she is in a highly disturbed emotional state and in a great deal of pain. She is babbling and crying with delirium, her eyes are rolling wildly in her head, and she tries to ward off anyone that comes near her with her frail little arms. Her abdomen, pubic area, and thighs are engorged and massively swollen. At the site of the fused labia, dark sutures are barely visible in the swollen flesh. She is one of very few girls that are brought into a hospital when things go wrong after a circumcision. Most of them are not so fortunate.

PHOTO 9.2. A village hut near Kadugli, in the Nuban foothills, where Muslim-Arabic Sudanese live side by side with the indigenous Nuba tribes. In this photo the youngest of a Muslim-Arabic merchant's three wives is seated next to her grandmother. Two of her daughters also appear in the picture. The bright-eyed, outgoing child on the right peering curiously into the camera is as yet uncircumcised. The girl on the left has been circumcised some months before. The markedly flattened, withdrawn expression of her eyes is characteristic of girls at that period in their lives. As the girl becomes adapted to what has happened to her, there tends to be yet another change, which can be seen reflected in the faces of womanhood here. High spirits have permanently left those faces. What can now be found there is passivity, resignation, and a deep inner balance.

PHOTO 9.3. Wedding party at Suakin, in the ruins of this former slave port near Port Sudan in Red Sea Province. This photo shows three generations of women. The older ones are wrapped in traditional *topes*. Their faces are heavily marked by tribal scars. The younger women and children are unscarred and wear Western-style clothes. Every female in this picture may be assumed to have been pharaonically circumcised. The practices in Red Sea Province are particularly severe, and exceptions are as good as unheard of.

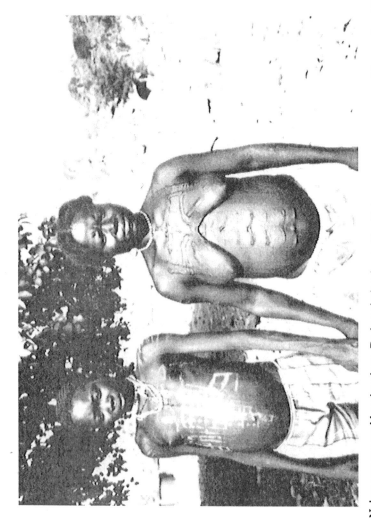

PHOTO 9.4. Nuban woman and her daughter. Body painting is used by Nuban women as a means of decoration. When they reach maturity, they generally opt for extensive body scarring. In a way of life where beautification takes the form of such a painful alteration of the body, circumcision quite logically follows if it facilitates an advantageous marriage.

PHOTO 9.5. This Nuban woman is the wife of an Arab-Islamic trader. Although Nubans have traditionally never practiced circumcision, the woman and any children born to her are subjected to the rite in such a marriage, as will be any of their offspring.

201

PHOTO 9.6. Wedding portrait.

202

PHOTO 9.7. Wedding portrait.

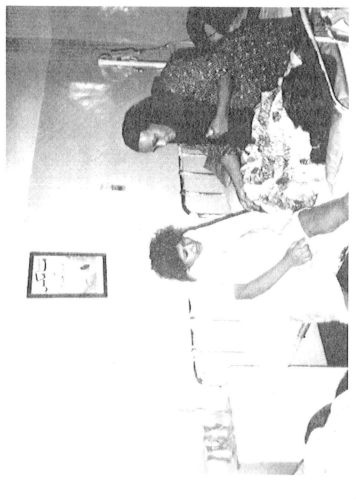

PHOTO 9.8. The labor room at Omdurman Maternity Hospital. The facility is so crowded that there are two women in each bed. As the women go through their tortuous labors, they fill the room with wailing and piercing screams. The older woman in the photo comforts her daughter, who is lying on the bed.

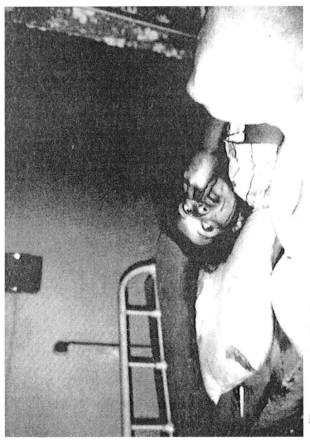

PHOTO 9.9. The young village woman in this photo has given birth some hours earlier. Here she is lying on a bed in the delivery room, waiting for the midwife to come and repair the two three-inch anterior cuts that have been made into her infibulation scar to allow her rather large baby to be expelled from her body. Her dread of the imminent pain is clearly written on her face. She is wrapped in her daily *tope*, in which she has also given birth. She is too poor to give the midwife an extra sum of money, and so when the midwife comes to sew her up, she does so without first allowing the analgesic she has been ordered by the doctor to inject to take effect.

205

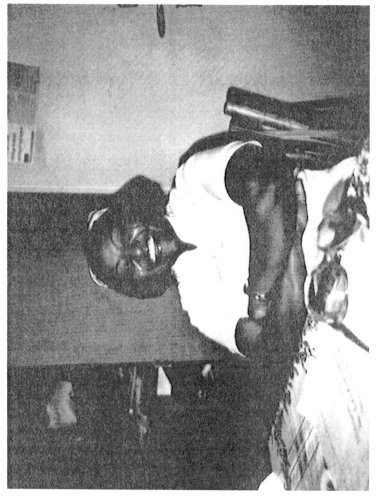

PHOTO 9.10. Head nurse and midwife at Khartoum University Teaching Hospital.

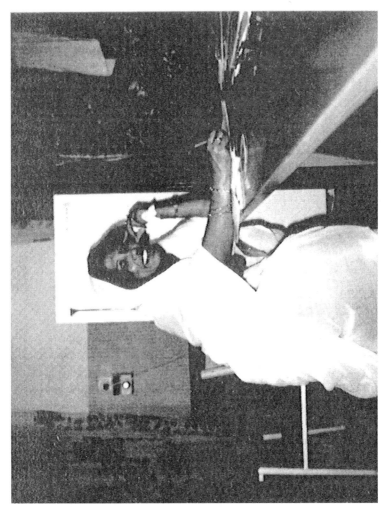

PHOTO 9.11. Sudanese doctor. She is one of a mere handful of women in the medical profession in Sudan.

10. A Sudanese Odyssey

Female circumcision is an issue that must be examined within its cultural context. As I traveled extensively in Sudan to learn about this pervasive practice, I got to know an enchanting people rich in beauty, compassion, love, enthusiasm, and delighted generosity, and a place bedeviled by unsolvable paradox. My experiences are valuable not merely as adventure and anecdote, but as a backdrop to the seemingly insurmountable circumstances of the people who live there. It is my hope that the vignettes related here will provide the reader with a clearer picture of Sudan, and with an impression of how I worked to obtain my information.

GARDEN

The stretch of desert from the southern Egyptian border at Wadi Halfa to the Sudanese capital is like no other geographical phenomenon on the face of the earth that I know of. It can be described only as a total absence. For a distance of some 200 or 300 miles along a 360 degree horizon, there is nothing to be seen but perfectly flat sand. There is a complete absence of all vegetation. There are no animals, no birds, no boulders or stones. There are not even flies, except for those that the train harbors from its point of origin. There is nothing but wind driven eddies of dry brown dust that swirl about aimlessly, unendingly under a merciless, scorching sun.

After some days within this void, on the ancient train that wends its way laboriously along this stretch, the mind begins to hunger increasingly, and finally has to turn inward in search of sustenance. It searches more and more acutely among the riches of the inner landscape. Feelings surface and become magnified. The more the senses are deprived, the more intensely one feels. The fantasy life expands, and as the days and nights blur into one another and one becomes ever more weary and sleep deprived, standing or crouching in the crammed compartments, one may even begin to hallucinate.

Along this route, in the course of this seemingly endless journey, the train periodically comes to a halt at a series of small stops, where there are perhaps two or three forlorn huts, and some large jars filled with water. It is at one of these stops, when everyone has piled out of the stifling compartments, that I notice a ring of passengers that is growing in front of the huts, and I am aware of a current of excitement that emanates from it. Everyone is looking at something within the center of the circle.

I make my way to the periphery, and like others in this shifting human mass gradually work my way into the center, to discover the reason for the excitement. Because I am a white woman, everyone makes way for me, and I see, in the center of the circle, a small collection of stones in the form of a ring—in and by itself a noteworthy series of objects in this vast, dust-driven void. But this is not what everyone is gaping at. Within the circle of stones, there is one tiny grasslike plant with five stunted leaves. That is all. What I am looking at is someone's garden.

I stare at the tiny plant, transfixed. It is the first green I have seen in 7 days, since I began my journey along the barren dunes that flank Lake Nasser in Egypt. I cannot take my eyes away from it. What a miracle! A living green thing growing here in this endless emptiness! I suddenly realize how something in my being has hungered for the sight of something green. I stare and stare, as if to fill the emptiness in my eyes, my nerves, my brain.

At the same time, another part of my mind is snickering derisively. "You are absurd! Surely you are joking! You have seen a rain forest! You have seen the splendor of botanical gardens in all of Europe! You have, for heaven's sake, seen the Redwood Giants of California!"

Why does this little plant move me so? I drag my eyes away reluctantly to look at the faces of the others in the circle. I see the same look of wonder and happiness in all of their transfixed eyes.

It is hard to explain the magic of the desert to someone who has not experienced it. The more arid it is, the stronger is the magic. All living things are treasures here, because they are so improbable, so rare, and so miraculous. I have never felt such an intensity of love and joy and oneness with the universe as I have in this desert. It is my first experience in Sudan, and it is here that I begin to love the Sudanese people who manage somehow to survive in their harsh and barren environment.

THE KNIFE EDGE OF MAHFEE

To understand the Sudanese and the context within which they live, one must first understand the full meaning of two all important words, and those are *fee* and *mahfee*. *Fee* means there is, and *mahfee* means there isn't.

You might ask a man *"Moyah fee?"* (is there water?) or *"Akil fee?"* (is there food?), and if he has any food or water, he will equally share them with you, with visibly great joy, while he praises Allah with all his being for having allowed him to give them to you.

Sometimes you are face to face with *mahfee*, and then it is truly and irrevocably *mahfee*. There is no food, there is no water, there is no transportation, there is no medicine. There is only the pitiless sun, the endless sand, the unshakable faith in Allah the Merciful. Most Sudanese live out their lives on the knife edge of *mahfee*.

They are first and above all other things Sudanese and Moslems, and the ultimate meaning of their existence is to serve Allah and his Prophet. They are fierce warriors who die gladly for Islam, certain that to die in the service of Allah ensures their place in Paradise. At the Battle of Omdurman, history teaches, they plunged into battle against British cannons armed only with swords and fighting sticks and broke the English line of defense. They perished by the scores of thousands, leaping into battle over heaps of their own dead, to be mowed down in turn.

To the Sudanese to serve Allah is happiness, and the multitudes of Islamic schools are crammed with eager little children, chanting joyously in unison: "Allah the all-merciful! Allah's will be done! Praise be to Allah!" Five times a day, everything grinds to a halt while they pray—wherever they find themselves. They leave their occupations, their wares, their open money boxes and do obeisance to Allah, singly or in groups, in the Mosques, in the market place, by the wayside, kneeling, touching their faces again and again to the ground, oblivious to all around them. At the knife edge of *mahfee* the goodness and infinite mercy of Allah are everywhere.

Alan Moorehead (1960) gives this vivid description in his historical account *The White Nile*:

> Even today the traveler on the Nile must be struck by the power of Islam in the North and Central Sudan. It would seem that there is little enough to thank God for in these appalling deserts, and yet the poorest and most wretched of the inhabitants will be seen throughout the day to prostrate themselves upon the sand with a simple concentrated fervour that is hardly known in the green delta of Egypt. No village lacks its minaret even if it be nothing more than a ramshackle scaffolding of poles, and the muezzin, calling the people to prayer, at once brings to a halt all sound and movement on the ground below. Here every precept of the Prophet, every injunction that governs the great fasts and feasts, appears to be observed to the letter.
>
> Perhaps it is the very austerity of life in these arid wastes that predisposes the people to worship. Mecca lies only a short journey away across the Red Sea, and the Prophet Mohammed himself lived and received his inspirations in just such an environment as this. An immense silence possesses the surrounding desert. The heat is so great it stifles the appetite and induces a feeling of trance-like detachment in which monotony dissolves into a natural timelessness, visions take on the appearance of reality, and asceticism can become a religious object in itself.

ON THE ROAD

Near the very beginning of my first sojourn into Africa, in a Khartoum hostel, I met Ros, an American woman who had been trailing through Africa for 5 years. She had lived in villages among the people, a sort of self-appointed, self-motivated, one-woman Peace Corps. I was very much impressed by how knowledgeable she was, and by how easily she flowed from one African experience into the next. I asked her if I might travel with her for a little while, so that she might teach me what one had to know as a woman trailing through Africa alone.

I learned some very useful things from her. She advised me strongly against finding an African man who could serve as my translator and porter. There were to be many such offers along the way, from desperate young refugees from Ethiopia or the south, strong, honest young men, willing to work for a pittance. In traveling with a man in Sudan, she said, you automatically had to accept his rank and social standing as your own, and you thus forfeited the great advantage your solitary condition gave you.

She told me that as you traveled through the countryside and you came to a place that had no hostel or resthouse, or, as often happened, where they would not accept a woman lodger, as they had only dormitory rooms for men, there were a number of places that would always give you a place to sleep, and it was not too difficult to find them.

You can stay at police headquarters where the police force also slept at night on the floors if you followed this simple procedure: You present yourself at the station, as night falls, and announce that you are a woman traveling alone, and that you wish to spend the night at the station. You can then expect them to tell you emphatically that this is completely impossible, that they have no facilities for you. You then say that you appreciate that it is indeed a difficult problem, but you have no place to sleep. Then you smile helplessly and hopefully and stand there, as they talk excitedly among themselves.

Pretty soon they ask you to sit down while they talk some more, their voices gradually returning to normal. You have to sit and continue to smile sweetly and trustingly. Then, eventually someone brings you a cup of tea, and as you sip it, you can observe the men warming more and more to the idea of how *interesting* it would be to have you there. In the end, someone always finds a solution. You can certainly sleep on the lawn, or in the courtyard, or whatever, and you will be very safe there. They lock up your gear in the arsenal, while you are doing whatever you had come to do, and in the morning they provide you with letters of introduction to people who will accept you into their homes. The important thing is to keep smiling, to praise Allah at every opportunity, and to be very, very patient.

If there is no police station to take you in, you can always count on a school, which lodges both teachers and students, and in a real pinch, you might even resort to a medical installation, although this is not a very desirable solution. If you are in really desperate straits, as you sometimes can be in the city, you know you will always be safe in a cemetery. No African will enter a cemetery during the night, Ros said. Fortunately I have never had to test the veracity of that statement.

I always liked the police stations best, although they were in their own particular way a bit taxing. To bathe, for example, one had to creep to the faucet in the yard in the dead of night when one was certain all the men were asleep, and to perfunctorily perform one's necessary ablutions in haste, with clothes on and under the cover of darkness. You had to learn to change your clothes inside your sleeping bag. There was always a row of chairs like a grandstand around you when you popped your head out of it in the morning, each chair occupied by a police officer, holding his cup of coffee, waiting for you to awaken, waiting for the show to begin.

Because you are big entertainment. Just walking down the road you are big entertainment. Best of all, the private show that you gave, squirming around in your sleeping bag, and emerging finally, fully clad, was like a command performance. The part they liked most was the combing of the hair. That was always the feature act, to be marveled at and exclaimed about, and they never seemed to tire of it.

Ros also taught me that if a man offers to take you to his mother, you can trust him. When he says that, he is honor bound to respect you and protect you as if you were an honored member of his own family. The fact that I was traveling alone without the protection of a man was so inconceivable and tragic to the Sudanese that this offer was made wherever I went. It went beyond their code of honor, which stringently demands kindness to strangers and an incomprehensibly generous hospitality. To them, a woman traveling alone was a helpless creature, without protection, totally at the mercy of the unspeakable, someone that had to be sheltered and kept from harm.

Generally it was very sweet and comforting to be thus taken into the bosom of a family, but it could also be a dreadful nuisance. If I was the guest in a man's house, I was forever being admonished to "take your rest," when I was not being plied with endless meals and round after round of sweet tea, syrupy coffee, and sugary lemonade.

It was often difficult to make them understand that I had rested enough, eaten and drunk enough, and that I now wanted to go out and do what I had come to do. They then stretched their concern for my welfare still further by offering to find someone who would go with me. If I waited for that to happen, I sometimes had to wait a very long time. So I had to explain quite firmly that I was quite accustomed to doing things on my own, and then go and do them. They generally bowed to this, but with visible misgivings.

I loved above all to sleep under the open sky. The African night, in the clear, dry, unpolluted atmosphere of Sudan, is studded with an unimaginable myriad of stars. The Milky Way, seen by comparison only dimly elsewhere, stretches like an immense highway from horizon to horizon. There is a constant panorama of shooting stars, pulsars that truly pulse, and fast moving satellites, from dark to dawn. The nights are fragrant and cool. I can think of no greater happiness than to wake up to this magnificence in the middle of the night, lying in the reassuring cocoon of my sleeping bag. Sometimes I must elude my protectors to be able to do so.

On one occasion I stayed with some teachers at a girls' secondary school in a small town. When night fell, I announced my intention to sleep in the garden of the school courtyard. My announcement was greeted with exclamations of horror from the young teachers. They fluttered about me nervously, like hens whose duckling charges are hastening toward the water.

"Oh, you must not do that!" they implored. "It is terribly dangerous."

"But how can it possibly be dangerous, here in the garden?" I asked.

"Robbers will rob you!" they exclaimed.

"How can there be robbers when there is a high wall around us, the gates are locked tightly, and there is a watchman outside the gate? Do not be afraid. No one will rob me."

"Oh, you must not do it!" they pleaded. "The wild dogs will eat you!"

"The dogs are all outside the gates, and cannot come in. Do not worry. The dogs will not eat me."

"But there are evil spirits that come in the night, and they will harm you!"

"There are no evil spirits, and even if there were, closed doors would not stop them. No, all the spirits are good, and Allah will watch over me."

"But the watchman will see you!"

"Well then, the watchman is a kindly old man, and if he sees me, he will watch over me. You will see. Nothing bad will happen." They stood there, wringing their hands, helpless and frightened.

"But we are afraid," they finally said.

"Why are you so afraid?" I ask.

"Because they teach us to be afraid. From the beginning, when we are little, little girls, they teach us to be afraid."

"Afraid of what?"

"Afraid of everything. Everything. We sleep wrapped up in our blankets, with the covers over our heads, with all the windows bolted and shuttered, and the doors locked. We huddle together, and still we are afraid. We are always afraid."

And they did indeed all sleep wrapped round and round tightly like mummies, in their hot airless chamber. I came into their room in the morning, after one of them had unlocked, unhooked, un-latched, and unbolted the door. The little room was airless and sweltering with the heat of many bodies, and I could hardly bear to enter it. One by one they crawled out of their cocoons, and each embraced me, as though I was freshly risen from the dead. They were so happy and relieved that indeed I had come to no harm.

"Allah is merciful. Praised be Allah!" they exclaimed over and over again. "But were you not afraid?" they marveled. "Were you really not afraid?"

Later we spoke together of their greatest fear, the one that is always with them, the one that has been with them from early child-hood on, the one that never leaves them. It is the most terrible, potent fear of all. It governs their waking hours and pervades their dreams. It is their fear of being raped.

SCISSORS AND KNIVES

Whenever I travel in Sudan, I carry a bag stuffed full of little gifts to give to people. I collect these things over a period of time, and there is something for everybody. Perfume is welcome everywhere. Coins are particularly popular with children, especially the Danish 25 øre piece, which has a hole in the center and can be worn about the neck. In the villages, any kind of costume jewelry, beads, even safety pins, paper clips, can openers, and keys cause great delight. Everything metallic is a potential source of adornment. I carry small utilitarian items also. Matches, empty medicine bottles in which to store them, aspirin, small coin purses, plastic bags and needles and thread are treasures to people who own literally nothing except their bowl and the few scraps of clothing on their bodies. For the doctors, I carry magnifying lenses, which are unobtainable in Sudan.

At the very bottom of my bag, there are three small pen knives and two pairs of good scissors. At the end of each journey I find them, all still there, and I realize that once more I have not found a single soul among those who want them to whom I would also entrust them. Unjust perhaps, but this is how I feel. The idea that they might wind up being used to circumcise a little girl terrifies me.

So they remain at the bottom of my bag for the next journey. Or the next, or the next. I will keep on trying. Who knows, perhaps some day I will be able to give them away.

THE ARM OF MY UNCLE

I was asked frequently by deeply troubled mothers what I thought they should do in regard to their daughters' forthcoming circumcision, and while everything inside of me wanted to scream aloud that they should leave the children as nature had made them, I knew that this would not bring the desired results; that too many factors militated against it. I therefore had to learn to deal with this question strategically. As happened so often in Sudan, I would make my point by calling upon my own life experience, and I would relate the following story to them:

When I was a child, I had a dearly loved uncle whose life philosophy largely shaped my own. When he was a young doctor, he was in a devastating accident in which his left arm was crushed. There seemed to be no alternative other than to amputate his arm. He begged his surgeon not to amputate at the shoulder, but to leave him a stump. He felt that if he kept even one third of his upper arm, this would make it possible for him to continue practicing medicine. The surgeon told him that unless he took off his entire arm at the shoulder, he might not live. My uncle answered that he did not want to live if he could not continue to practice his chosen profession, and when they wheeled him into the operating room, he insisted that they give him no more than a local anesthetic – not very effective for such a major operation, and a truly heroic feat on his part – to make certain that they left him the stump he so ardently desired. He recovered and continued to practice medicine, skillfully using his good right hand and the stump of his left arm, until nearly the end of his days.

When I finished this story, I would say to the woman:

Cut away as little as you possibly are able to do. Leave her a stump. Leave her an opening, so that she will suffer less. Perhaps, if you leave her something to work with, she can do a little less for her own daughter, and that one in turn may do yet less for *her* daughter, and perhaps in time, there will be no cutting at all. If you show courage now, this will give *her* courage when her time comes to make this decision. Do not take the arm off at the shoulder. If you must, take it at the elbow, or at the wrist, or best of all, take only a fingernail. Your daughters will bless you for it when they are grown.

ENGLISH IN SUDAN

Anticolonial sentiment in Africa notwithstanding, I found much evidence of pride among the Sudanese in the fact that their country had been an English colony. They are inordinately proud of their well-functioning English-style schools, their dilapidated English hospitals, and their deplorably cumbersome bureaucratic and banking systems, also of British origin.

An English of sorts is taught in the high schools and colleges, which is quite difficult to understand until one gets used to it. It was sometimes extremely puzzling for me to extract the correct meaning from a word or phrase used with such enjoyment at their being able to speak the language.

My favorite example stems from a conversation with Bythena, a head nurse, who informed me that Sudanese women always had sexual intercourse in the machinery position, since any other position branded them as wanton.

"The machinery position?" I queried, feeling that I was about to learn something new. "Can you describe it to me?"

"Yes, of course," she exclaimed. "In the machinery position the man is on top, and the woman is on the bottom."

A light dawned brightly. But of course! The *missionary* position!

CAUTIONARY TALES

Wherever I traveled in Africa, I allowed myself 3 pounds of carried weight in small articles for gifts, such as matches, water disinfectant pills, magnifying glasses for the doctors, strong thread and rust-free needles, iodine tablets for people in the interior hill country where goiter is rampant, antibiotic eye drops, and beads. I steadfastly refused to carry razor blades, even though I was often asked for them, and I kept my nail scissors extremely well hidden.

The reason for these maneuvers was a cautionary tale I heard from a nameless missionary, who had involved himself in trying to abolish circumcision in the village where he taught school. He despairingly told me that he had failed miserably in all his efforts, and that he was ultimately reduced to the heartbreaking circumstance of supplying the midwives of the village with clean razor blades to substitute for their dirt-encrusted, rusty knives, if only to save a few of the little girls' lives.

There was yet another cautionary tale which made me most reluctant to force my own cultural preferences upon people who clearly had theirs. It involved another missionary who had taken it upon herself to forcefully dissuade the women of a village from having their daughters circumcised. The midwives of the village did not take too kindly to this endeavor, since she was tampering not only with their livelihoods, but with their high status in the community as well. They in turn actively labored to persuade the villagers that the missionary lady was dangerous, and that she must be stopped. The events that followed can only be reconstructed by the evidence on her body, when it was found one morning by a fellow missionary. Her clitoris and labia had been excised, and she had died of a massive hemorrhage.

AN ISLAMIC TALE

It is a pitch dark night, and the ancient train packed with human freight labors its way through the bleak and arid desert. Inside sealed, airless compartments the women crouch in the searing heat in silence. The men lie unsleeping in front of the locked doors, cradling their gleaming naked swords, keeping watch. They are Hadendewah tribesmen, the Fuzzy Wuzzys of Kipling fame, fierce and wild desert dwellers of incredible beauty.

There are two sides to every coin. In this land where women are the unquestioning servants of men, I remember an Islamic tale I recently heard in the capital: When man and woman first came to live upon the earth, man went forth into the marketplace to earn his bread. Woman stayed behind in her house, where she cried bitterly. "What will become of me? How will I live?" she wept. "I am a poor, weak, defenseless creature. I cannot go into the marketplace." Allah reassured her. "Do not be afraid, woman," he said. "That is why I have made man to serve you."

ENCOUNTERS

I carried with me on my back a veritable arsenal of medications and ointments to combat infections, parasites, fungus, malaria, hepatitis, and all other manners of evil that beset one constantly in Africa, along with a slew of bandages, disinfectant, vitamins, and water purifier. Had it not been such a problem to carry it all, I would have taken a great deal more to dispense where it was needed. Sickness was a constant danger, and the greatest fear I had to face in traveling alone was the ever present possibility that fever or dysentery would overtake me in some remote village, and that I would be too sick to get myself back out, and into a town where at least the rudiments of medical care were available. I did get sick quite often, at least at first, before my immunity had a chance to build up, but I always managed to get myself back out.

The rivers are dangerous to swim in, not only because of crocodiles, but because of electric fish which claim the lives of many foolhardy travelers who venture innocently into their waters, even when there are no crocodiles. Worst of all are the schistosomas, parasites that invade the body of the swimmer, lay their eggs, and wreak havoc.

The people themselves were only rarely dangerous. For the most part, they were sweet, open, kind, and generous as no others I have encountered in my rather considerable travels. Yet a woman traveling alone in an Islamic country among sex-starved men would certainly be living in a fool's paradise if she did not expect a great number of sexual or romantic overtures, even when she is in her well-preserved 50s. Few of these overtures were offensive, and even fewer dangerous. They often took the form of earnest proposals of marriage. The village men were particularly taken with me, and would inquire whom they would have to negotiate with in order to buy me. Sexual overtures tended to occur more in the cities and came more from Westernized men and from officials or merchants. There was rarely any real unpleasantness. Once or twice, however, things got a bit sticky, and I had to rely on my New York City "street smarts" to get me out of trouble.

The mountain villages of Port Sudan are quite remote and are accessible by lorry only during part of the year, along a deeply rutted dirt road. During that time, about once a week, one is never sure when, a lorry turns off from Sudan's only paved road, which stretches from Khartoum to Port Sudan, and travels into the mountains. One must sit by the side of the road and wait until it comes by, and pray that it will not be too many days. At the end of a day-long, bone-wrenching journey atop the lorry freight winding up into the mountain, one arrives at a small village that consists of a tiny, ramshackle market, the usual ruin of a British rest house, a boarding school for boys, and a few huts made of sticks and twigs.

I was traveling at this time with Dale, a young American pre-med student I had met in Suakin, who like me had drifted down to Sudan from Egypt. He carried with him a tent and offered to share it with me, and I eagerly seized this opportunity to penetrate an area to which I would otherwise not have had access as a woman alone.

The little village was safe enough, but the mountains surrounding it were inhabited by Hadendewah, the fierce, wild, beautiful warriors described by Kipling as the Fuzzy Wuzzy tribe, so named because of their wild and bushy hair. Among Hadendewah, a lone female stranger needed the protection of a male.

We wandered around the little *suk* (market) in search of food, little of which was in evidence. A few onions, some milk powder donated by the Dutch government, little else. At one end of the *suk* there was a tea shack, where some men were playing a gambling game. We stopped to watch them. Several wizened old men squatted in the dust near the shack. All of them stared at us, smiling broadly. Suddenly one got up and ambled over. He pulled a small bottle out of the folds of his robe. It looked like a medicine bottle. He opened it, shook out a bright purple pill, and popped it into his mouth, leering at me. "*Kwaiss?*" (good?) he questioned. I was intrigued. "Good for what?" I asked. He flexed his right arm, patted his biceps to indicate strength, and made unmistakable piston-like thrusting motions with his fist. Again he looked at me expectantly as he popped still another pill. "*Kwaiss?*" he repeated.

I held out my hand for the bottle in order to look at the label. Why the old rogue! The pharmaceutical label on the bottle of bright purple pills showed that it was of French origin, and that its contents were testosterone, the male sex hormone. How, in the name of heaven, had it found its way here, into these wild, remote mountains? I laughed aloud. "*Kwaiss!*" I assured him.

Out of the depths of his robe he now pulled an ancient pocket watch, his ultimate treasure, given to him long ago, no doubt, by some British colonial. He urged it on Dale, and gestured back and forth between himself and me, clearly offering an exchange. Dale, who loved and enjoyed the Sudanese as much as I did, smilingly shook his head and wrapped his arm around my shoulders. "No, I can't," he said half apologetically. "She's my mom."

The next day we took our gear and followed a tiny, intermittent trickle of water into the desert. On our way, we saw several small groups of women who were washing clothes in the distance. They ran off in panic as soon as they saw us and disappeared into the dunes, leaving their wash by the waterholes they had dug into the sand. We walked for 3 hours until we found an oasis about 5 miles away, where there was a miniscule waterfall perhaps 1 foot wide and 2 feet high. Its water seemed potable. Here we pitched our tent. I began to wonder if the little stream led to a more remote village, and after 3 days in camp, curiosity got the better of caution, and I decided to follow it while Dale remained in our camp to watch the tent.

I walked for perhaps half an hour in total solitude when suddenly, from out of nowhere, five tall, fierce-looking Hadendewah men suddenly appeared. Each was carrying a long, naked sword and a dangerous-looking fighting stick. The biggest one stepped in front of me and I was instantly surrounded by the others.

"Huwen rajah" (Where is your man?) he demanded imperiously. I remembered what Ros had told me to answer whenever this question—which was almost *always* the first question anyone asked of me in Sudan—was asked. I drew myself upright to my fullest height and answered defiantly in a loud voice, stabbing my forefinger toward the ground for emphasis. *"Heenah!"* (here).

He looked around him, and laughed contemptuously. "He is *not* here!" He took a step forward as if to seize me. I stood my ground as if planted in it, raising clawed hands, prepared to rake my nails across his face. *"Heenah!"* I snarled, the very picture of fiery defiance. He backed off, uncertain. They muttered for a minute among themselves, glancing unsurely in my direction. Then they decided against it. The big one spat on the ground.

They disappeared into the dunes as swiftly as they had come. With shaking legs I retreated in haste toward the safety of camp, when yet another figure materialized out of the dunes. This one was a young boy, about 12 or 13 years old, also carrying a naked sword and fighting stick. He spoke a greeting, and began to walk alongside me. He looked benign enough, even in my adrenaline-saturated state, and I was rather relieved at the presence of another being, as he appeared to pose no threat.

As we walked I noticed that he was studying me with sidelong glances, and assumed that he was curious about my clothes, which must have seemed strange and unfamiliar to him. Suddenly, he shifted his fighting stick into the crook of his elbow, and his free hand shot out and grabbed at the part of my anatomy he coveted.

Oh, no! Not again! I pushed his hand away angrily, cursing vehemently on the top of my voice. His young voice implored me insistently, while the hand once more made clear what it was he wanted. He was smaller and lighter than I but very strong. I was not sure that I could fight him off, if he resorted to his weapons. I screamed for Dale — Dale who was fully a mile away and could not reach me, or even hear me — screamed his name in the direction of camp, as if he were about to descend upon this hapless boy and wreak a terrible bloody vengeance.

The hand dropped away. "*Chalas*," (finished) the boy said softly and sadly, looked at me with eyes full of longing and pain, and turned to walk away. He too was swallowed by the dunes, while I ran back to camp as if possessed by demons. That was my first and last lone excursion into Hadendewah territory.

Two weeks later, I was once more in Suakin, a seaside village on the Red Sea near Port Sudan, the country's only modern seaport. I had spent the day among the ruins of this ancient slave port, built by Turkish slave traders along the sea, and just before night fell, walked the 2 miles to the village where I stayed at the hut of my friend Sidahamed's third wife, Moonah. When night falls this close to the equator, the transition from daylight to pitch dark takes place in a matter of minutes.

Somewhere along the path I took the wrong turn, and in trying to correct it, went even further afield. Darkness descended like an enormous bird of prey, and as I stumbled along, I suddenly became aware of a hulking dark figure that was following me. I stopped, and it stopped too, maintaining the distance between us. I walked on, and it followed. This happened three times. Finally I stopped, picked up two sizable stones for weapons, and waited.

After hesitating for some moments, he slowly walked up to me. "What are you looking for?" he asked me in English. "You should not be here alone. This is a very bad place. This path leads to the prison."

I clutched my stones. "I am looking for the house of Dr. Sidahamed," I said.

"It is far from here, you must go back to the crossing. We can find it from there." He stood in my way.

"Step back so I can pass," I demanded. He did so without a word. Good heavens, but he was enormous! When I did not move, he stepped back still further.

"It is better if I walk with you," he said softly. "Very well," I said, and keeping a tight grip on my stones, raised them so he could see that I was holding them.

"You do not have to be afraid. I will not harm you." His voice was so gentle and musical that I believed him, although I could not make out his very black face in the darkness. We began to walk, and he told me that he was from Juba in the South of Sudan, where he had learned to speak English at the missionary school. There was no work to be had there and no food, and his family was starving. He had come to Port Sudan to find work, but had met with no success. There were so many others like him, and besides, there was much ill feeling between the Muslim tribes of the North and the Christian animists of the South, and a long, bitter civil war between them had only recently ended and threatened to resume.

We walked until we came to the crossing, where there was a tea shack and a solitary lantern.

Ah yes, I saw now how I should have gone. In the light of the lantern I was able to see his young, eloquently honest face, and dropped my stones to the ground. "When have you eaten last?" I asked him. "Three days ago," he said, softly.

"Thank you for helping me," I said, and tried to give him some money.

"You do not have to pay me," he objected, putting his hands behind him. "I only did what was right and my duty."

"Then allow me to do what is right also," I said, and when he did not move, added gently, "You must eat. You will need all your strength."

This time he took the money. "Do you know where I can find work?" he asked hopefully.

"Come to the house of Dr. Sidahamed in the morning," I said.

"Perhaps he can help you." We shook hands and parted company. I never saw him again.

AIR TRANSPORT

Over the years of my sojourns in Sudan, I became more and more knowledgeable about the ins and outs of obtaining the necessary shelter, entry, permission, and above all, transport. There is an official Sudanese airline, also known affectionately as "Enshallah" (God willing) Airlines. It is at best a very "maybe" sort of thing. Maybe there will be a plane, and maybe there will not. If there *is* a plane, maybe there will be petrol for a flight, and maybe not. Although the people in charge bravely continue to schedule regular flights, which are always supposed to leave at 6:30 in the morning, and for which one must appear at the airport by 3 A.M. if one wishes to obtain a seat, morning after morning no such plane appears.

At this point it becomes a matter of how many times one can drag one's gear the 2 miles out of town to the airport and back again, how sleep deprived one becomes, and how much frustration one can endure. Chances are that on the 4th or 5th day (enshallah!) there will be a plane, and there will be petrol, and then if one commences one's vigil at the airport at midnight, one may obtain a seat. Sometimes, of course, it takes much, much longer.

"Enshallah" Airlines flies to Port Sudan, El Obeid, El Fasher, and once in a great while when there is petrol enough (enshallah!) to Juba. From these points, if one wishes to go further, one must find a lorry, or if one is lucky enough to make contact with a government official who is returning to some remote outpost, it may be possible to catch a ride on his government vehicle. I usually begin my scouting for further transport when I am in the airport, waiting for a plane to materialize, and by the time the aircraft lands at our destination, I am already armed with letters of introduction that will pass me along to people who will be of further help to me.

The Department of Agriculture, which employs a number of Westerners, has its own small passenger plane, and I had the good fortune of making the acquaintance of Curly, their pilot. Curly, an American, is a former racing driver who smashed himself up badly in a race. Thereafter he became a jet pilot for a number of years, and has recently been disqualified by Sudan Airlines for health reasons, due to a spiraling weight problem. He is a huge, flamboyant man who admits to 350 pounds, but who tips the scales at well over 400 by my calculations.

Curly is a gentle, unhappy man who suffers greatly from depression. He takes me along on a number of flights, glad for my company, and relegates the empty co-pilot seat in his cockpit to me. I soon find out what my role on these flights is to be. As soon as Curly gets the plane into the air and on course, he sets the automatic pilot and promptly falls stuporously asleep. Periodically, I have to punch and pummel him into a sufficiently awake state so that he can check the instruments before he once more relapses into his stupor. It is a little nerve-wracking, but I soon get used to it because I see that he always manages to get himself together when we approach the landing field, and he always sets the airplane down flawlessly.

No one in the cabin behind us is any the wiser. For all I know, they think I know how to fly the plane. I don't.

THE MILITARY INSTALLATION

The lorry has brought me to Atbara, a small desert town, through which flows a shallow and sluggish river, spanning at this point no more than 30 feet, and teeming with activity. Immediately beside the ford in the river, camel drivers are watering their herds, and flocks of goats stand knee deep in the water, drinking. A little to the side upstream, women are busily washing clothes, and at yet another point, where the water runs slightly deeper, they are filling their water skins and loading them on to stoically patient donkeys.

I have been warned by the lorry drivers that there is a military installation here that guards the dam some distance up river. I must therefore go to the police station immediately to inform them of my presence, and to find out what is permitted to me here and what is not.

The police station is not hard to find, a short distance away into the desert. It is the usual concrete box-like structure, dating to an earlier, British dominated time. As I approach it, I see that there are also a number of out-buildings, and as I pass one of them, I recognize the heavy iron bars of a jail. Intrigued, I approach it. Within the confines of the single, cagelike cell, there sit perhaps 10 or 12 old men, in heavy chains and leg irons, silent and patient in their somehow terribly incongruous, spotlessly white Islamic garb. Outside, within the shadow of the jail, squat a number of mournful old women. I greet the women, and then I tentatively walk over to the bars of the cell, where the old men reach out to shake my hand. What gentle, saintly faces they have! What terrible wrong could they possibly have done to warrant these manacles?

"Why are you here?" I ask them. They regard me with sad resignation. "It is the will of Allah," they answer, laying their hands over their hearts. "Allah be praised!"

I enter the police station, and after a short wait I am shown into an inner chamber which is reminiscent of a stage set for a Kafka drama. A stern-faced, powerful-bodied official sits high on a grotesquely elevated magistrate's bench, designed to dwarf anyone standing before it.

He sizes me up for some moments, and then, with measured tread, slowly descends to greet me ceremoniously. He shows me to yet another room, bids me be seated in one of two comfortable chairs, lowers his considerable bulk into the other one, and loudly claps his hands twice. The haste with which a quivering subordinate answers his summons serves to reinforce my ever growing conviction that this is not a man to trifle with, and that I had best mind my manners. He orders tea to be brought, and it promptly appears.

We sit and chat. He asks me where I come from, and what my purpose is in coming to Atbara. I tell him that I am on my way to Suakin, and that I am here to await the coming of the train that will take me to Port Sudan. It is to arrive the next day, is it not? "*Enshallah*," he answers. Not waiting to be prompted, I hand over my papers. They are all in order. "Do you carry a camera?" he asks. "No, I do not," I answer quite truthfully, having left it with friends in Khartoum. I open my small pack and push it toward him, so that he may search it. He holds up a hand. "That will not be necessary. But I must warn you that to take photos of the dam is very dangerous. The penalties are most severe. You must not go within 1 mile of the dam. It is heavily guarded, and the soldiers have my orders to shoot anyone on sight. *Anyone*. Do you get my meaning?"

It is a little appalling. I assure him that I have no desire to see the dam, that it is of no interest to me. "I have seen a great many dams in my own country. When you have seen one, you have seen them all," I say lightly, in an attempt to jest.

He does not return my smile. I realize that this conversation is not unusual. Anything, no matter how remotely related to the military, is always in absolute dead earnest. It is not allowed, for instance, to take photos in the tiny airports, although I fail to understand the connection.

There is a heavy silence while we sip our tea. "I would like to ask you a question," I finally venture. He nods. "As I entered the station," I continue, "I could not help but notice the jail, and the old men incarcerated in it. Tell me, what crimes have these men committed?"

"They are murderers," he replies sternly. "Murderers?" I marvel, remembering their sweet pious faces, "Is it possible?"

"Yes, they are all murderers," he repeats, and then adds severely: "Or they are *suspected* murderers."

He stands up. I sense that the interview is over. Once more he claps his hands loudly. A subordinate appears as if spewed out of the ground.

"Is there anything else?" the magistrate asks. "No," I answer, and thank him profusely for his hospitality. He gives swift orders.

"This man will escort you on your tour of the town."

I exit under guard, as it were, breathing a sigh of relief.

SUDANESE HOSPITALITY

I had been told that the bus from Kadugli to El Obeid in Western Sudan would take 5 hours, and arrive at 2 P.M. at its destination. Although such buses to anywhere are nearly always reputed to take 5 hours, and although sad experience had taught me otherwise, I took it anyway. Like most Sudanese buses in the outlying areas — rattletrap 1930s vintage wrecks, excessed from various places in Europe — it broke down continuously, and so it arrived finally in the pitch dark of a moonless night at what I presumed to be El Obeid marketplace, at 3 in the morning.

I began to roam the deserted streets with a 50 pound backpack on my shoulders, vainly looking for a place where I could sleep. Those few inns that opened to my pounding on their door had dormitories for men only. No one would accept the responsibility of lodging a woman traveling alone. Growing more and more weary and desperate, I grimly staggered on. Suddenly a young man stepped out of the darkness and in English asked what I was seeking. "A place to sleep," I told him. He held out his hand to me and said, "I will take you to my mother."

Those magic words! I had had such experiences in the towns and villages of Sudan before, and understood their code of honor and hospitality toward strangers. To be told that one would be taken to a man's mother meant safety. Without the slightest hesitation I took his proferred hand in the darkness, and followed him to a living compound. His mother immediately arose from her sleep, joyously greeted me like an old and dear friend, carried water for me to bathe, and prepared a magnificent feast for me — all at 4 o'clock in the morning.

PERMITS

The permits one must obtain from the African bureaucracies are endless, and no matter how much one tries, there are nearly always some that are overlooked. So it happens that when I am in transit to the villages near El Obeid, where I stay at the house of a merchant who has generously extended his hospitality to me, I am stopped by a man in uniform as I walk in the *suk*. He wants to see my papers. I haul them all out for his inspection, and all seems at first to be in order until he discovers that among the dozen or so places listed as those that I wish to visit, no mention is made of El Obeid. An oversight on the part of the official who has made out the permit, I assure him. All the same, he insists, I must accompany him to police headquarters. I am in El Obeid illegally.

We walk for perhaps a quarter of a mile until we arrive at the police station. We enter, and find that there is not a single soul in attendance. "They have all gone out for breakfast," he grumbles. For 2 or 3 minutes he paces up and down, obviously annoyed. Then he makes his decision. "You must sit here and wait until someone comes. Now I will go out and have *my* breakfast. I will take care of this matter later." He leaves.

After another 2 or 3 minutes, it occurs to me that I have not breakfasted yet either. I slip out of the door, make sure he is nowhere in sight, and amble back to the *suk*. If I should see the uniformed man again, or rather, if he sees me before I see him, I will explain that I went to get my breakfast, and then could not find my way back to the station. Then, as always, I will smile sweetly and trustingly, and wait for the problem to be solved.

As it turns out, I never see him again. Two days later I find a lorry to take me from El Obeid to the villages, and that is the end of it.

THE OUTBACK

In the outback, most of the populace have still never seen a single *chiwadja* (white woman), or at best only one or two. When I step down from the lorry and walk through the village, they are often confused about my gender because my appearance is so different from their own women. They cannot sort out my cotton trousers, my sunglasses, my short haircut, my general appearance, my voice, my fearless demeanor. They will argue about it among themselves as I pass, or they will accost me and ask me outright: "Are you a man or a woman?" Generally I laugh and tap my breasts, those more than generous portions of proof that I am indeed a woman. Then they all laugh in recognition, and chatter happily about this phenomenon, this strange anomaly that has entered their lives. It is as if the circus has come to town, as if the parade with a full brass band were passing through.

It is very heady stuff to be the constant focus of all eyes, the subject of a myriad of smiles, the object of such happy excitement. There are always children that come running, with joyfully glowing eyes, to shake my hand, to carry my load, to bring me water.

When the time comes to find a place to sleep, I need only sit down in the marketplace and wait. It is not long before someone brings me tea, and after that everything evolves quite naturally. In the villages I feel very safe.

A CLASH OF CULTURES

In dealing with the authorities, one has to expect a certain amount of patronization, and more than a bit of benevolent despotism. Women in Sudan are generally regarded as helpless, somewhat defective, and potentially wayward children, who, because they are also loved, have to be protected against their own folly. It is as if they are an inferior species that must be treated with a kind of "noblesse oblige," directed and guided by those in charge. On occasion this attitude extends also to me, and there are times when I lock horns.

In Nyertete, a small town near the Chad border, there is a government rest house built by the British in colonial times for their own use. Like other such rest houses in Sudan, it is a squat, no-nonsense cement structure, bare and stark, devoid of all furnishings. Its window glass has long since disappeared, and its ramshackle doors and windows only occasionally sport the tattered remains of long-defunct screens. Its unswept floors are littered with rubbish that has been discarded by previous wanderers passing through. All in all, it offers little motivation for use, other than as a depository for one's gear.

The second time I arrived in Nyertete, on my way back from the Jebel Mara mountains, the rest house was inhabited to overflowing by a group of Khartoum University art students of both sexes, and their chaperone professors. They were on a field trip, and had arrived early that morning, by lorry.

As usual, I was immediately welcomed, feasted, and entertained. In the small room occupied by the girl students, all the trash had been pushed into one corner, and the room was crammed with sleeping mats and all manner of makeshift luggage. Still, somehow, with a lot of shifting about and pushing together, a narrow space that barely accommodated my pack and sleeping bag was cleared, and I was graciously urged to move in.

I contemplated the prospect of sleeping in this tiny, oppressively shuttered room with growing claustrophobia and a sense of real desperation, and so at dusk while everyone was at prayers, I searched for a safely secluded spot where I might spend the night. Some distance away, I found an ancient, friendly looking tree whose overhanging limbs formed a sort of shelter. Silently I whisked my sleeping bag out of the room, and disappeared into the darkness. I remember waking several times during the night and feeling an overwhelming sense of well-being and happiness at having escaped that dungeon of a room.

As the sun rose, I returned to the rest house and was immediately confronted by one of the professors, a rather imposing figure of tremendous girth and height in his flowing robe. He came at me like a frigate in full sail.

"I have been told that you did not sleep in the women's room last night, as you were supposed to!" he announced in stentorian tones.

"That is true. I did not sleep in the room," I answered calmly.

"Then you will tell me immediately where you did sleep!" This in the stern and censuring voice of one disciplining an errant child.

"Outside. Under a tree."

His voice climbed. "How could you *dare* to do a thing like that?" he demanded imperiously. "You did not have my permission! You did not *ask* me for permission! I never would have allowed it!"

I felt the last remnants of a smile leave my face, but forced my voice to remain quiet and steady. "I appreciate your concern, professor, but you must remember that I am not one of your students. I am fully as old as you are. You are not responsible for me, and I have no *need* for your permission."

He began to sputter. "I am very angry with you! What you do is terrible and dangerous!"

I shrugged. "I thank you for your concern, professor," I said, my humility by now worn rather thin, "but I come from a different culture. I am not accustomed to asking permission from a virtual stranger." Smoothing my ruffled feathers, I walked quickly to the dreaded room, gathered my belongings together, and said my goodbyes. As I passed him on the way out, he was still sputtering.

SUDANESE HUMOR

Since I had to carry everything I needed over 6-month periods in Sudan where nothing was replaceable, the weight of my backpack was a constant problem to me, and I could not collect even the most desirable souvenirs along the way. I began, therefore, another type of collection that would not add materially to my burden. I collected a small number of wedding photos, and whenever it seemed opportune, I asked people to tell me jokes. Both collections proved to be extremely telling, and I present parts of them here.

Jokes are known to reflect the anxieties and concerns of a given individual or culture. In Sudan the vagina is regarded as an unclean, malodorous organ, and uncircumcised women are considered to be dirty and low class. The practice of cunnilingus, if one is to believe what men admit to in Sudan, is virtually unknown, and if it does exist at all, is publically despised and not admitted to even privately.

A male doctor in Khartoum contributed this story: "A girl from Latukka (where female circumcision is not practiced) will never wash her vagina. When you ask her why, she says: 'Because it loses its flavor.'"

Another joke along those same lines was told to me by a male university graduate: "A man tells his friends that he is having a card game that night with a prostitute. If he wins, they have agreed, he does not have to pay her. If he loses, he will have to perform cunnilingus on her. The next day the friend meets him on the street and asks how the card game went the previous night. 'Tui! Tui!' the man spits. 'Don't ever play against that woman! Tui! Tui! You have no idea what a good player she is!'"

Another such joke was told to me by a Sudanese merchant who had spent 5 years in the United States. I had heard this joke in New York some years ago, and as retold by the Sudanese man, it had undergone an amazing transformation. Here is the original story: "Picasso had an inflammation of the eye, and went to see an eye doctor who treated his condition successfully. Picasso wished to pay the doctor, who out of respect for the artist's genius would not accept payment. Picasso thereupon drew a picture of an eye and presented it to the doctor as a gift. As he left, the doctor was heard to mutter: 'Thank heaven I am not a proctologist!'" When retold by the Sudanese merchant, the last line was different: "Thank heaven I am not a gynecologist!"

Feelings about sexual restraints that Sudanese men are subjected to find expression in the following joke told by a mathematics professor: "A man is riding home on the bus, his salary in his pocket in the form of a roll of coins. As the bus becomes more and more crowded, he is pushed against a woman, who misinterprets the feel of the roll of coins against her thigh, slaps the man's face, and loudly accuses him of misbehaving. He pulls the roll of coins out of his pocket, explaining that this was what she felt. The woman apologizes to him. The following week, the man is riding the bus home once more, and finds himself again standing next to the same woman. This time he decides to misbehave (sic). The woman turns to him smiling, and says: 'Congratulations on your promotion!'"

Educated Sudanese are well aware that their culture abounds in Catch 22s that even their faith in the unending mercy of Allah does not appear to be able to resolve. A Port Sudan headmaster told me this story: "All the leaders of the Muslim nations of the world have convened so that Allah may speak to them. Each one offers up a prayer and asks a question. The Ayatollah is first. 'Oh Allah!' he begins, 'My country has many problems. My people are divided, and there are those who do not believe as I do. When, oh Allah, will these problems be solved?' The voice of Allah is heard from above: 'Not in *your* lifetime, Ayatollah!' Mubarak speaks next: 'Oh Allah! my people are hungry and diseased. My country is poor and I cannot help them. When, oh Allah, will these problems be solved?' Again the voice of Allah is heard: 'Not in *your* lifetime, Mubarak!' And so on down the line. Each leader presents the problems that afflict his country, and each in turn is told by Allah that they will not be solved in his lifetime. The last to speak is Sudan's Numeiri. 'Oh, Allah,' he begins. 'My country has the worst problems of all. My people are ignorant and stubbornly unchanging in their ways. We are poor and getting even poorer. When, oh Allah, will our problems be solved?' There is a dreadful silence for a moment. Then the clouds part with a terrible lightening bolt, and Allah's voice is heard to thunder: 'Not in *my* lifetime, Numeiri!'"

A sociologist discussed social changes and Islam in Sudan with me, and offered the following wry saying:

Three Sudanese Muslims are three Muslims. Two Sudanese Muslims are two Muslims. One Sudanese Muslim is *no* Muslim.

The following story told to me by a Sudanese nurse is totally lacking in wit by our own standards, but is tremendously revealing: "A bridegroom is penetrating his bride on their wedding night, and in the process the woman dies of fright. 'I cannot understand it,' he complains, 'I was covering her mouth with my mouth, and I was plugging up her vagina with my penis. Out of what hole in her body did the soul fly?'"

It is difficult to get past the initial statement here: "A bridegroom is penetrating his bride on their wedding night, and in the process the woman dies of fright." But of course, this could not be an unheard of occurrence; it must happen here all the time. And although there is the sly implication that the man has somehow been remiss in not plugging up other sexual orifices, quite possibly her anus (see Bolling, 1976), there is also the suggestion of a masochistic revenge. No matter how totally the bridegroom dominates his wife's body, he is powerless to stop her death and the escape of her soul.

I cannot help but wonder. The incidence of AIDS among African women is equal to that of African men. Can this be related to female circumcision and a prevalence of heterosexual anal intercourse there?

A LETTER HOME: NAIROBI, KENYA

Dear Herta,

Your letter has certainly started me thinking. You pose some interesting questions. Let me try to pull it all together. The relationships between tourism, prostitution, female circumcision, venereal disease, and AIDS in Africa are as yet elusive, but also most provocative. They should certainly be studied.

While prostitution is not openly tolerated in an Islamic society like Sudan, there is a great demand for such services, especially among the upper classes in the capital, and every evening at sunset one may see numerous automobiles slowly cruising along the Nile Avenue, near the Kartoum Hilton, and the commercial district near the Aarak Hotel downtown. They will stop near any woman who is walking alone or who is standing along the road, and the driver will offer to take the woman to wherever she is going. It is all very low key, and a refusal on the part of the woman merely tells the man that he has made a mistake and he quietly moves on. I have often accepted such rides in daytime or early evening and have been able to obtain some very interesting interviews. There has never been any unpleasantness.

The women along the road are generally beautiful, delicately featured Erytreans or Ethiopians and graceful Nigerians—refugees from war or famine or personal tragedy, who support themselves and their families in the only way possible to them.

A few also appear in the hotels or public clubs. Some wear the traditional *topes*; the more daring among them wear blue jeans, a garb that practically identifies their profession in this tradition-ridden land. It is all very soft and low key, and no woman ever actively solicits. It is only the anonymity that a large city affords that makes the existence of the phenomenon possible in Sudan at all, and prostitutes are periodically rounded up by the authorities, along with the ubiquitous lepers and beggars around the mosques and in the marketplaces, to be imprisoned (or quite possibly dumped, heaven only knows where, out in the desert).

Kenya, by contrast, is wide open for all manner of prostitution. Whatever the tourist from the West desires is catered to there. For example on Lamu, the small island off the coast where I lived for several months, I spent many hours of conversation with an intense, slight, middle-aged Italian professional man, married to a high ranking woman in the U.S. military who is stationed in a German city, where they reside together. He is a closet homosexual pedophile, who spends his summer vacations in various places of the Third World, where small children can be obtained for a pittance. There are a great number of others like him.

Lamu is one of Kenya's various "Sin Cities" and teems not only with prostitutes of the more conventional type, but a multitude of panderers who offer the eager tourist whatever other exotica he may desire. The whole island is actually little more than a mass of barely concealed brothels of various types, and the commerce is aggressive and highly competitive.

A rather pathetic story I can relate here concerns an Anglican abbot from the United States, a lovely, truly kind, and spiritual man, with whom I became friends while I lived on Lamu, who related it to me with a sense of bitter disappointment that his presence there should have been so grossly misinterpreted.

After having taken his vows of chastity, poverty, and obedience and having been immured in a monastery for 20 years, he was persuaded by a wealthy relative to accept an all expenses paid vacation to any place in the world on the occasion of his 50th birthday. He naively chose Africa, in hopes of finding spiritual nourishment there, and was directed to Lamu by a travel agent he consulted.

Full of good will and anticipation he arrived on the island, where his immediately tangible generosity to the luggage carriers that descend upon tourists as soon as they step off the plane made him an instant target. He was immediately beset by all sorts of offers. "A beautiful girl, a virgin?" He thanked them in his gentle way. "A *little* girl? Only 8 years old!" Again he thanked them and tried to explain that his religion forbade such things. "Oh! We understand! We have just what you want. A little *boy*, very beautiful and small!" This was his introduction to Lamu, and the continuous siege never stopped in the weeks that he spent on the island until he finally fled.

Mombassa is a crowded, bustling seaport that thrives on its influx of many tourists and sailors. It is well above average in terms of the general African city, in that its garbage levels are within endurance in the more affluent, which is to say tourist-frequented, quarters of the commercial district. Yet here too are the ubiquitous beggars, lepers, and other unfortunates suffering from advanced stages of the most horrendous tropical diseases seen in Africa. A little outside the city one finds the posh houses of Europeans or white Kenyans, and luxury hotels along pleasant but unspectacular beaches. In the evenings, there is not much by way of entertainment. The hotels feature discos with outdated American records played at deafening decibel levels by native disc jockeys, an occasional Bingo game, and not much else.

What then attracts the tourist to Mombassa? A well known budget-type German travel agency catering to the small businessman offers (or certainly was still offering in early 1984) its extremely popular "Sun and Sex Safari" package to its male clientele. This package includes air-fare and hotel accommodations, as well as an optional prophylactic injection of antibiotic on the return flight, to take care of whatever venereal disease the client may have contracted on his vacation. The agency's customers have cynically nicknamed the flight to Mombassa "The Sexpress Express," and the return flight "The Tripper Clipper." ["Tripper" means gonorrhea in the German vernacular.]

The hotels along the Mombassa and nearby Melindi beaches teem with relatively well-dressed Kenyan prostitutes, who sit and sip affordable government price-controlled Pepsi Colas, waiting passively to be picked up. In the center of town at the New Castle Hotel, the action is a great deal more interesting, and the soliciting quite open. One may sit there in the sidewalk cafe on an afternoon or an evening and watch the black market money changers, drug dealers, and prostitutes ply their trade. The girls are for the most part very young innocents fresh from the upcountry villages, dressed in their touchingly naive conceptions of American chic.

When the fleet is in, one may observe the more experienced and pretty among them negotiate with groups of four or five sailors and then shortly thereafter haul off the lot of them. Tourists tend to be unattractive, middle aged, and willing, but less inclined toward grouping. Sailors come in droves from ships of all nations, stay in port for a short while, and indiscriminately buy out all of the souvenir shops and whatever else is for sale. After a few days they are replaced by a new batch from a different ship, from a different land — all eager for the novelty this African seaport affords. Mombassa thrives on them all. Nairobi, with some variations on the theme, is not much different.

Venereal disease is reputedly rampant in Kenya. An unofficial source in Nairobi at this point claims that 10% of Kenyan men and women test AIDS positive, though the government's official statement is that there is no such thing as AIDS in Kenya.

In talking to European medical personnel treating the Masai out in bush country, I am told that close to 100% of the Masai, a slender, graceful, much photographed Kenyan tribe, have syphilis and that the men come in droves to the medical installations to be catheterized so that they can urinate. They look for Kikuyu women to marry, blaming their women for giving them the disease, which they then pass on to their Kikuyu wives and any resulting offspring. One hundred percent may be a rather shocking and barely believable figure, but it is easy enough to spot the plainly visible suppurating sores on the bare arms and legs of the Masai children and cowherds one passes while driving through the game preserves in Masai Mara, and one would be wise not to touch them. Syphilis among the Masai must be a relatively recent phenomenon, brought to this formerly proud and now dying tribe from who knows what outside source. If it were not relatively recent, the Masai, a former warrior tribe turned herdsmen, would have been killed off or died out long ago. Both the Masai and the Kikuyu practice clitoral excision. Kikuyu alone accounts for 50% of the population, Masai for another 10%. Including other smaller tribes in the figure, one may therefore safely assume that two-thirds of all Kenyan girls are circumcised. A nurse at a Lutheran mission station informed me that contrary to what I believed to be true, the Turkana do not circumcise either males or females. Because of this, they have a lot of problems with the Samburu, a tribe that circumcises both. The Samburu think the Turkana are "dirt" because they are not circumcised. This is an attitude seen fairly often in Africa. Additionally, African tribes who circumcise generally consider those who do not to be "little children," i.e., not brave enough to undergo the initiation and hence not brave enough to be a mature man or woman. A Luo field worker described cases she knows of, where uncircumcised Luo men living among the Masai were tormented and ridiculed so much that they eventually got circumcised, and now feel very proud of it! No doubt things are much the same where it comes to circumcised and uncircumcised women.

Prostitutes have been cited as one of the high risk groups for contracting AIDS. Female circumcision, which tends to lead to coital tears and bleeding in women and possible abrasions in men, would quite logically increase the risk factor still further, especially among prostitutes, but also in the population at large when there are multiple sex partners. This is true even though the bulk of the current AIDS epidemic seems as yet to be centered in Zaire and Rwanda, in areas where female circumcision appears to be relatively rare, as far as is known.

It has been my experience that African officals are an exceedingly poor source of information on the medical state of affairs in their countries. Whether they are deliberately smoke-screening or they simply do not themselves know what is going on is often not clear. If one wants to know what the facts actually are, one must talk to non-African medical personnel working out in the bush, up-country in the medical installations, who are in a position to observe what is going on and who have no motivation to falsify what they know. It is for this reason that I have related what has been told to me by such sources. I believe them to be valid. In most African countries the subject of female circumcision is totally taboo, and cannot be discussed by Africans with people from other countries or tribes.

AIDS is also unknown in most African countries *if one is to believe* African Ministries of Health, who shrink from naming any figures whatsoever, fearing for the economy of their countries. Whether AIDS did or did not originate in the Central African countries of the Congo is still a matter of conjecture. Africa is a huge continent, however, and in my own opinion there is little doubt that AIDS is being spread into other parts by outside sources, from Zaire and Rwanda, and yes, Europe and America by other high risk individuals from those places. Prostitute carriers in places like Kenya spread it still further to Western tourists and African clients alike. Furthermore, the role of heterosexual anal intercourse among the populace is still to be investigated—not an easy topic to research. The commonly used hypodermic needle that makes intravenous drug users a high risk category for AIDS in the First World has its counterpart in the nonsterile common cutting implements and needles employed in male and female circumcision, defibulations, recircumcisions, and scarring procedures in Africa by nonmedical personnel. Asma el Dareer told me in Sudan that midwives told her that Sudanese women who have multiple sex partners (another high risk group) frequently come in groups of five and six every few months to be recircumcised. Scarring practices, although on the wane in urban areas, still abound in Africa, and there is a great deal of migration from rural areas and villages into the cities, where the incidence of AIDS is the highest.

Yet another mutilating procedure has sprung up in Uganda in

recent years, which is becoming ever more widespread. It involves digging out unerupted incisors of infants, and is the invention of local medicine men as a "treatment" for fever and whatever other ailment may befall the hapless child. The unerupted teeth are explained as having been deposited in the child's mouth by malevolent spirits, in place of the true teeth. These false and evil teeth, the medicine man explains, must be excised to save the child. If the infant bleeds to death or dies of infection as a result of the procedure, the medicine man explains this to a frightened and profoundly superstitious parent easily enough. He tells them that the spirits are angry because the medicine man was not consulted soon enough or given enough recompense for his valuable services. The populace has responded to this by rushing their infants even earlier to be excised. Needless to say these operation are performed with totally unsterile implements, the same as other mutilating procedures.

Whether AIDS has actually originated in Africa is not important to my way of thinking. But there is little doubt that it is carried in and carried out at a frightening rate, that it spreads like wildfire in Africa where everything seems to favor its propagation, and that somewhere in the chain of circumstance female circumcision plays its role.

IN THE DESERT

The train has stopped in the desert. It has broken down along the route for the fourth time in one afternoon. This time it looks as if we are stuck for a long time. Everyone eventually piles out of the hot dusty compartments and climb off the roof of the train in the cool evening, to sit or lie on the desert sand, to pray, to play cards, to talk, to await the coming of the repair car. It will come, *enshallah*, by morning, they tell me, along the single track that stretches from Port Sudan to Khartoum. By morning the track will be free and not before, so we will all sleep in the rapidly cooling desert under the stars.

I have my warm sleeping bag, and I eagerly await the desert night, whose silence is beyond silence, whose darkness is made glorious by a vast blanket of stars, stretching over the entire sky to a completely flat 360 degree horizon. The unrelieved, empty landscape which stretches for hundreds of miles has the effect of a sensory deprivation tank. It turns you inward, into the depths of your emotions, and you relate to others on the train with an openness and honesty that you might not be capable of otherwise. I feel as if I had known people on the train all of my life, as if they were my closest friends.

I am joined in the darkness by three soldiers who are on their way to Kassela, a garrison along the Ethiopian border. Night falls rapidly in the desert, and we draw close together in the quiet darkness, barely able to make out one another's faces. They ask me many questions about my life which I answer, and then they tell me about their own.

The tall one is from a village near Wad Medni, a town along the Nile. He is 33 years old, he tells me. Am I married, he wants to know, and what has it been like for me? He himself has never been married, he says. He is still saving all of his earnings to be able to afford the bride-price and the very costly wedding. It takes many, many years. Perhaps by the time he is 40 he will have enough money. He has never been with a woman, and he is very curious about what it would be like. There are no prostitutes in the area where he lives. There was one at one time, but she was driven out. Perhaps he will find one in Kassela. He hopes so. His own life history is very similar to that of most of the men in his village. Only the richest merchants can marry while they are still young.

The dark one comes from Juba, in the south of Sudan. It is an indigenous, Christian, and animist area, and circumcision is not practiced there. He is very unhappy about his term of service in Northern Sudan. Things are much more natural between men and women where he comes from. He does not understand the ways and customs of the people here, he says. It is so difficult. He misses having a girlfriend. "I always had girlfriends, ever since I was a boy," he tells me. "They liked to make me happy, and I liked to make them happy. It was not complicated at all." The tall one looks at him with envy and amazement.

The slim, soft-spoken one says that he too is experienced with women. When he was 16 years old his uncles took him to a nearby town, where they knew of a prostitute. "She was Syrian, not Sudanese," he hastens to inform me. "They told me what I must do, and I did it with her."

"Was this the only time?" I ask.

He expresses surprise. "Yes, of course. That was the only time." He tells me he is getting married soon. "I am glad that I am experienced in these matters of women," he says with obvious satisfaction.

I turn to the tall one. In the deepening darkness I sense rather than see him. "Tell me," I say, "when men do not have access to women, what do they do?"

"Other things."

"Other things? With men?"

"Yes, other men."

"Animals?"

"Yes, animals. Sheep mostly."

"Little girls?"

"Yes, little girls sometimes too."

"What happens when it is little girls?"

"Well, in my village a little girl was raped. She told her father that it had been a neighbor who had done it. Her father went to the neighbor and told him he would do nothing for revenge if the neighbor moved away from the village and left the father his hut for restitution. He was to tell no one about the incident. This was done, and that was the end of it."

"And what about the little girl?" I ask.

"They took her to the midwife, who repaired her circumcision. Eventually she got married to someone else in the village, so no harm was done to anyone."

I hear a stifled moan in the darkness, and realize with a start that it has issued from my own throat. We sit in silence.

THE HOSPITAL

The University Teaching Hospital of Khartoum reminds me in many ways of the inner city high school in New York where I used to be a teacher, and where I held the strong conviction that if anyone was able to teach or learn anything there at all, among the chaos and overwhelming sense of futility of that place, it was truly a miracle. My view of the hospital is equally jaundiced. It is a miracle that anyone *survives* it, or any other medical installation in Sudan, for that matter. I shudder at the mere thought of ever having to be a patient there.

The Khartoum University Teaching Hospital is housed in a series of seemingly sturdy concrete structures, built by the English sometime before 1956, in colonial days. From the outside, it appears to be a reasonable state of preservation, but when one enters, one sees immediately that everything inside the building has fallen into total wreck and ruin.

My hospital dealings are exclusively with the obstetrical ward, housed in a remote wing of the main building. The entrance to the ward has to be approached with great caution, as I soon discover, to avoid the buckets of slops heaved from the second floor balcony. Patients are clustered in the overcrowded ward, on sagging cots covered by stained, evil-looking mattresses, innocent of all bed linen. The delivery room sports a battered, peeling delivery table, covered with a blotchy, liver-colored oil cloth. Several resident cats are at their posts in the proximity, crouching expectantly, awaiting heaven only knows what scraps.

The nurses are rarely in evidence on the wards, and the patients take care of themselves, or some female relative tends to them. One may generally find the nurses in the nurses' room, eating breakfast, having tea, or just resting.

At another hospital in Omdurman, where I was able to obtain a number of interviews, its highly capable chief of gynecology left the country to attend some scientific meetings in London. He returned one afternoon after 2 weeks to find his staff asleep in the ward beds. The rooms had not been cleaned or swept since his departure. No one was taking care of the patients.

There are power failures almost daily, and nearly as often there is no water. The sanitary facilities for patients make one weep, and defy all description. Only pictures can convey the horror of these stinking disease pits.

I am wracked with pity for the gynecologists. Their faces are shrouded in deep depression, and they are pervaded with a sense of futility so profound that it is almost palpable.

THE MIDWIVES

They called me *El Shadida* — the Strong One. There was a standing joke between us. Whenever I came to the hospital in the morning, one or the other of the midwives would sidle up and ask me in a discrete whisper whether I had been circumcised yet. Playing the game, I would assume an apologetic stance and reply, no, I had not. She would then conduct me ceremoniously to the delivery table and offer in a most affecting way to help me out of my shameful predicament. It would be very quick, she would assure me, and not at all expensive. It would instantly remedy my scandalous state. I would always thank her with profuse and elaborate politeness for her kind concern, and then conclude with an emphatic: "but all the same, I prefer to keep what I have!" This would set of shrieks of laughter all around, and after we had all enjoyed our laugh together, we would amble out to the tea shack to have our morning tea. All of us were excellent friends.

THE DELIVERY ROOM

One morning, on my way into the delivery room at Khartoum Hospital, I practically collided with one of the young interns, who was pushing his way out through the door. His eyes were blinded by tears, and his voice was choked with rage and grief. "How can we help them when they come here in that condition? There is nothing we can do for them! We are helpless," he rasped harshly and slammed his clenched fist into the wall.

I followed him back into the delivery room. On the table lay a festively clothed, beautiful, delicate-featured young woman. She was surrounded by bloodied clothes and pans of blood — the whole room seemed red with blood. She had obviously hemorrhaged. Her skin was a bluish shade, and she was shaking uncontrollably with shock. I took her hand and held it, trying with all my being to send her some strength. She was too far gone to even register my presence. She died within a few minutes.

APPENDIX I

Interviews with Women

HISTORY #1:

This 50-year-old village housewife has deeply pitted tribal scars on her face and blue lip tattooing. She has had no schooling. She received no analgesic at her pharaonic circumcision, which was performed when she was 6. She claims that there was no pain whatsoever, and that some native herb was given to her. The only pain she recalls was at attempting to pass urine after the operation, from distension due to the smallness of her opening. She says she has had "no problems at all" because of her circumcision, and is very happy about it. She feels that circumcision is a good practice.

She married at 14, before menarche commenced. Penetration required 4 to 5 months. There was a great deal of pain, she recalls, but practically no bleeding.

She has had two sons and three daughters, and was cut and refibulated to pinhole size with each birth. Repenetration required 2 to 3 months with each child, and was very painful. Her daughters have been pharaonically circumcised, same as she was, as have her granddaughters. Two of her grandchildren died of what appears to have been tetanus sometime after circumcision, but she is not aware that these two events could be related in any way. At first she is very emphatic in asserting that she has never enjoyed sex. Occasionally she has had orgasm, or something like it, but it was not very strong. She avoided intercourse whenever she could, she says. On closer questioning she admits that sometimes she *did* like sex, but feels strongly that this is very shameful, and she would never make such an admission to her husband. Her husband wanted very much for her to have pleasure, but she felt compelled to hide her response from him.

She says that most of her body is very sensitive, especially her breasts. She feels no sensation in her scar area, but it is very strong inside her vagina. She really is not interested in sex at all, she reiterates, but her obvious zest and laughter as she talks negate her words. She admits that two or three times out of ten she has had orgasm, and that she would sometimes drop pots and pans in the middle of the night to awaken her husband when she desired him.

There was no verbal communication between them in connection to this. She never allowed the slightest response to show, she says, and so he finished when he finished. Sometimes this elicited orgasm in her, more often not. "He is dead now," she says sadly, and then laughs again. "He was a good man, and we were happy together."

She feels circumcision is a good thing, because men like it. Women do it for men, she says. She feels it is a bad thing for women, because there is so much bleeding after delivery, with all the cutting and stitching they have to go through. With no great feeling she says that it is all done for men, and because the religion demands it.

HISTORY #2

This attractive, articulate 21-year-old housewife has had 12 years of schooling. She was pharaonically circumcised at 11, leaving a 1/2 inch opening. Because of the relative width of her aperture, she has had "no problems" until marriage.

Penetration was accomplished in 1 month, and the pain was not severe, she says, and shrugs. In spite of this she does not enjoy sex at all. She feels that this is so because of the circumcision. "Everything is closed," she says. She tells me that she has no negative feelings toward her husband. She simply has very little erogeneity. She loves her husband, although her marriage to him was arranged. She has no sexual feelings for him, or for any other man for that matter, although she very much enjoys the company of men. She would feel happier if she never had to have intercourse again. She accepts it as her duty, but avoids it whenever she can.

She feels that circumcision is a crime. Her relatively late circumcision has allowed her to realize what she has lost. She has read books on sexuality and feels that she has been greatly robbed. Her feelings of rage are quite clear as she talks about this. She expresses hatred toward her parents for allowing this to be done to her. "No matter whom I married, it would have been the same," she says, sadly shaking her head. Her despair and sense of loss show plainly on her face.

She has two daughters, whom she says she intends to leave uncircumcised. "Times are changing," she says, "and they are still very young." If she puts off their circumcision and holds the grandmothers at bay, she may succeed in her intentions, she feels. "I hope the old women die soon," she says defiantly. "That will make things a lot easier."

HISTORY #3

This 35-year-old practical nurse has had 11 years of schooling. She was circumcised pharaonically at the age of 8 with no analgesic. She married at 14, before she began to menstruate. Her husband was very impatient, and penetrated her in 2 days. He felt deeply guilty and hated himself, she says, because he had not meant to do it that way; he just lost control. She fainted from pain and lost a great deal of blood. The wound then became infected, and he had to stay away from her until it was finally healed, 3 months later.

Her initial terror gave way to enjoyment, when intercourse was resumed. She loves her husband very much, she says, and it is clear in her happy laughter and glowing eyes as she talks about him. "We are like one person," she says. They are able to have intercourse only four nights per week, she sighs, because he is a musician and works nights. If they had the opportunity, they would make love "all of the time." Neither of them initiates; they are just drawn together like magnets.

She becomes orgasmic almost as soon as he enters her, she says. Her orgasms are extremely strong and long lasting. She has strong sensation in her breasts, pelvis and lips. Her scar area is extremely sensitive, as is the mouth of her vulva. The strongest feeling is in her cervix. She describes her orgasms vividly: "I feel as if I am unconscious and shaking. It is almost unbearably sweet in my whole body, and if my baby fell out of the bed, I could not pick it up."

She tells me again that she is very happy with her husband. The more mature she becomes, the better sex gets. If she had the chance, they would have sexual relations "10 times per day."

She has six girls and one boy. Four of these daughters have been circumcised in the modified way. Half the clitoris and half of the inner labia have been excised, and they have all been infibulated to pinhole size. She does not want to do the remaining two at all, because her circumcised daughters have had complications. She herself has to be cut extensively for each birth and has been resutured with each to pinhole size. She wants to save her children from having to go through this.

HISTORY #4

This 60-year-old supervisor of practical nursing comes from a small town in Western Sudan, and has had 10 years of schooling. She was one of the first girls to be circumcised in her village, which until then had not practiced circumcision at all. Her mother told her that this was "the new way," and that it would keep her clean and free from disease. Her drastic pharaonic circumcision was performed when she was 6, with no analgesic. She developed a huge cyst at the operation site, with a great deal of pain, pus, and bleeding, and she could not sit or walk until it was excised.

She was married at 11, before she began to menstruate. Her husband made an agreement with her mother not to touch her until her menses began, and he lived up to his agreement. When he attempted to penetrate her, he was totally unable to do so, due to the massively hardened scar tissue. He maintained his efforts for over a year. She had been sewn so tightly that even after marriage it took her an hour each time she attempted to urinate, to force out her urine drop by drop. Menstruation, which commenced at 12, became an agony.

Finally at 13 she was cut open by the midwife's knife. It was only then that she was able to pass the built-up menstrual blood clots that had accumulated behind the infibulation. Until then, she says, she was constantly crying with pain. Some weeks after she was cut open the pain ceased, and her husband, a much older, generally kind and gentle man, began to want intercourse with her daily. She was in a constant state of terror and frequently ran away. She never enjoyed sex because she could never get over her fear, she says. Although he was very loving and she did have orgasm perhaps 20% of the time, she could not enjoy it due to her extreme fear. She constantly sought to avoid intercourse. She did have some pleasurable sensation in her lips, her breasts and around the scar area, but it was overshadowed by her overwhelming fear.

Eventually when she was 16 they decided that it would be best to divorce. She never remarried, because she says: "I could not love him; I could not love any man; I hated marriage! The little pleasure was not worth all that pain."

She says that in her village there were many girls with similar experiences, and all of them got divorced. There was just too much pain.

During her marriage she had two second trimester miscarriages. There were no live births.

She has adopted eight children—five girls and three boys. These were all illegitimate, unwanted children that she obtained at the hospital. She had only part of the clitoris taken with the first two girls "because I did not want them to suffer as I did, and I want them to enjoy sex." She hopes not to circumcise the other three at all, and since they are all illegitimate, there will be no one to oppose her. "If they want to have themselves circumcised when they marry, they can do so, but I will warn them about what a terrible thing the pharaonic is, so that they will not want to do it," she says firmly.

HISTORY #5

This is a 35-year-old woman who was born in Saudi Arabia of Sudanese parents. She has had, much to her regret, only 3 years of schooling. Her sternly religious father strongly opposed any education for women. She wanted desperately to continue school, she says, but he would not permit it, although both her brothers were allowed to finish high school. She now makes dresses at home, and dreams of earning enough money to send her daughters to European universities.

She was circumcised pharaonically at the age of 11. Her mother returned to Sudan with her for that purpose. The operation was performed by a trained midwife under local analgesic, and appears to have resulted in no immediate complications. She was able to urinate after 1 hour and was back to what she calls "normal" within 2 weeks. Passing urine thereafter presented only a slight problem, in that it took 2 to 3 minutes to empty her bladder. Menstruation presented some problems until her marriage, but again apparently not severe ones. She guesses that this was because her infibulation left a half centimeter opening.

When she married at 18, penetration took 3 weeks. With a great deal of convulsive laughter she relates that she cried and screamed so much during that period that all the neighbors knew about it. Nonetheless she tells me that the marriage was a love match. Her husband is a distant cousin, and they have loved each other from early childhood on. She has seven children, four boys and three girls. After each one she was refibulated to pinhole size at the urging of her grandmother. Each of her repenetrations took over 3 months, and was severely painful. She has had so much pain that she wants no more children, she says. However she believes that "recircumcision" is a good practice, "because it gives your husband more pleasure."

She enjoys sex very much, and claims to have orgasms nearly 100% of the time after she heals. She laughs convulsively again. "I have seven children as a result," she says.

When asked what parts of her body are sensitive, she laughs anew and explains that most of her body is quite sensitive. The scar area is highly erogenous, but her greatest pleasure is experienced inside her vagina. She claims that sometimes it takes her only 1 minute of penetration to achieve orgasm. Sometimes she has two or three orgasms, she says. Most of the time her orgasms are quite strong, but sometimes less so. She laughs again. "Sometimes there are distractions; I have so many children!" When she does not feel up to having sex, she refuses her husband's advances. However, she also lets him know when she is interested, and how he can please her. She knows that "most women feel that this is shameful," but she does not agree. She feels that it is only normal. She is unable to describe what she feels during orgasm, but her animated demeanor in talking about it make it convincing that she is well familiar with the subject.

Her first daughter has already been pharaonically circumcised. The others will be done in the same way. She says that she thinks pharaonic circumcision is a good practice, and feels she has lost nothing by her own circumcision. (In this interview we were left with the impression that this woman was playing the role of "the good wife" by exaggerating her pleasure with her husband. There was something agonized about her convulsive laughter, which created an aura of desperation, rather than mirth.)

HISTORY #6

This 32-year-old practical nurse has had 9 years of education in the capital. She was pharaonically circumcised at 12 with local analgesic. She says that she urinated almost immediately after the operation, and that she only had 2 hours of postoperative pain. She resumed normal activities after 10 days.

She began to menstruate at 16 and had much clotting and pain until she was married for the first time at 17. On the fourth day of her marriage, her husband succeeded in creating a tear which bled profusely. Two days later he enlarged this tear, which by that time bled so much that she had to be taken to a dispensary for help. They treated her there, but told the husband to continue in his attempts so that she would not heal shut again. After 2 weeks, he succeeded in penetrating her completely, and after 15 more days, she says, things were normal.

She did not love this husband. He was a distant relative, and the marriage had been arranged. He drank a great deal, and was often abusive. She did not enjoy sexual relations with him because he was rough sexually and entered her without any preparation. He was involved in politics, and spent much of the 10 years she was married to him as a political prisoner. Finally he left Sudan for Saudi Arabia, and was not permitted to return. They were divorced consequently. She did not miss him at all, she says. She felt that she had been treated very badly by him.

Her marriage to her present husband took place a few months after her divorce. She says that she is extremely happy in this marriage. They love one another passionately, and she has an extremely enjoyable sex life. She absolutely glows with happiness as she speaks about it. She has strong orgasm simultaneously with his every time they have intercourse, she tells me.

Her breasts, mouth, inner thighs, and scar area are very sensitive. Greatest sensitivity is inside her vagina. She never directly initiates intercourse, but signals receptivity almost every night with smoke and oil.

She has three boys and one girl by this second husband. She plans to take only half the clitoris from this girl because of the many gynecological problems she sees in her work. Also, she wants to spare her the pain of penetration and resuturing. She points to her deep facial scars. "My parents did this to me because they thought it was beautiful," she says. "I don't think it is beautiful at all, and I have not done it to my girl." She feels that both scarring and circumcision are bad practices, and would like to see an end to them. Still, she does not dare to leave her daughter entirely uncut. She must have some sort of circumcision, she says, or people will look down on her.

HISTORY #7

This 24-year-old practical nurse comes from a village in Western Sudan. She has had 5 years of schooling. She was pharaonically circumcised at the age of 4, and remembers very little of the experience except that she cried a great deal.

She began to menstruate at the age of 12, and her periods were consistently very painful for 10 days each month until her arranged marriage at 16.

In the village where she lived, custom demanded that the man penetrate his bride in 1 night. The experience was so brutal that she was terrified of him for half a year afterwards. Then, as he was quite gentle with her following this initial trauma, she adapted to a degree. She was never able to enjoy sex with this husband, however, and implored her family to arrange a divorce for her. This was done after the birth of a son, when she was 17. She was resutured to make her ready for a second marriage, but this time a 2 centimeter opening was left.

She remarried a man that she had loved since childhood. There was only 1 day of pain in repenetrating her. He is patient and gentle, she says, and she feels secure and loved with him.

She has strong orgasm with him 30% of the time. She enjoys being kissed, and has a highly pleasurable feeling of "shock" in her lips. She also enjoys having her scar stroked. The strongest sensation is experienced at the contact of his penis with her cervix, and her orgasm, when it occurs, is precipitated by his ejaculation. She has strong vaginal pulsations, and feels as if she were under sedation. Orgasm occurs after 20 minutes of intercourse. The other 70% of the time she is unable to climax, even if intercourse is prolonged or repeated. Her body is simply too tired on those occasions, she states. Still she feels happy and relaxed afterwards just from the contact with his body. "There is a slight feeling of disappointment" but she realizes that "it has to be that way," that her body "simply cannot respond more often than it does."

Even though communication is very good between her and her husband and he cares deeply about keeping her happy sexually and in all other ways, she is too shy to initiate intercourse directly. She was brought up to believe this would be extremely shameful, and she therefore resorts to smoke and perfume when she is receptive. He immediately understands, and responds every time she signals this way.

She recently has had to separate from him, because of an intractable mother-in-law problem. She now lives with her own family again, and misses him acutely. They meet at her sister's house, and no privacy is possible there. The mother-in-law wants him to divorce her, and so far he has refused.

She has one daughter whom she intends to circumcise in the modified way, leaving a 2 centimeter opening. She has been deeply impressed by the difference in the penetrations by her two husbands and does not want her daughter to suffer as she did with the first one.

This decision is one of the main bones of contention between her and her mother-in-law, she tells me. Her daughter lives with her now, so the mother-in-law cannot get at her so easily. But she is really afraid, especially since she works and is away from the house all day, so that she cannot watch her daughter all the time. She sighs and then says resolutely: "Allah will protect her. Praise be to Allah."

HISTORY #8

This is a 38-year-old maintenance worker in a school for girls. She appears far older than her years. She comes from a small village, and has had no schooling. At the age of 7 she was circumcised pharaonically by an untrained midwife. She received no analgesic, and had massive bleeding. Unable to urinate for 2 days and nights, she suffered great pain. On the third day she was transported to the nearest medical installation (a considerable distance away) to be catheterized. There she was partially reopened to 1 centimeter. The wound was badly infected, and she had to remain at the installation for 40 days treatment.

She married at 11, before the onset of menstruation. The husband was unable to penetrate her, and maintained his attempts to do so with a great deal of brutality. After 2 years, he succeeded. During this entire period she was in continuous pain and in a constant state of terror. She continued to lose a lot of blood and again suffered infections which were never able to heal because of the husband's onslaughts. At 13 she began to menstruate. The menses have been consistently painful, even to the present date. She has had seven children, and required multiple incisions to give birth to each. She had herself refibulated with two of them. With the other five, spontaneous refibulation appears to have occurred. Sex has been very painful to her, and she has never had an orgasm.

To her great relief, her husband died 2 years ago. She states that she will never marry again, and fears all men.

She has one daughter, who has been circumcised by a trained midwife under local analgesic. The labia majora were left intact, and a 1 centimeter aperture was created. She will permit exactly this, but no lesser procedure to be done to her granddaughters, because she cannot defy custom. Even so, she says that she takes solace from the thought that her daughter and granddaughters will have less suffering than she has had.

HISTORY #9

This 30-year-old housewife has had 8 years of schooling. Her husband is a university graduate.

She was pharaonically circumcised at the age of 9. She had to be hospitalized for 7 days and required 5 blood transfusions. She was unable to urinate, and when her wound reopened at the hospital, a large blood clot was found to be causing the blockage. She was allowed a 2-centimeter opening, and consequently had no further urinary difficulties, once she healed. There were also no menstrual problems as a result of having a relatively large opening.

She was married at 14. Penetration took 15 days, with very strong pain and much bleeding. Intercourse continued to be painful for another 3 months, and then became normal. When asked if she enjoys sex, she laughs and retorts: "Is there any woman that doesn't?" She is able to have very strong orgasm close to 100% of the time. She has little sensation in what remains of her sex organs, except for the scar area. Her strongest feeling is in her breasts and also in her hips. At orgasm she feels as if she were under sedation, and she experiences strong vaginal contractions. This is followed by complete relaxation. She appears to be very proud of her husband, and laughs happily as she talks about him.

There are five children, two girls and three boys. After each birth she had herself refibulated to a 1 inch opening. Her husband wanted her very small, but she did not agree to the pinhole infibulation. "Enough is enough," she says. "I don't want any more pain." He is quite happy with her anyway. Repenetration involves a week or so of discomfort, but no strong pain.

She uses smoke and fragrant oil, but it is "to smell good, rather than to signal," she says. She does not feel that it would be shameful to let her husband know by more direct means when she is interested. "It is not necessary," she says. "He never gives me a chance to sit down." They have intercourse whenever possible, often three times a day. She comes to orgasm after 15 to 30 minutes of intercourse.

The first of her two daughters has been pharaonically circumcised. This child nearly died of blood loss. She has decided not to circumcise the second one, since in her family there have been too many such complications, among her sisters and their daughters as well. Her husband supports her decision. They plan to send the girl to a distant boarding school, so as to remove her from members of the family who do not agree with their decision.

HISTORY #10

This 42-year-old trained midwife has had 9 years of schooling. She was pharaonically circumcised at the age of 6. She experienced a great deal of pain when she began to menstruate, and was married after her first two periods. She was then only 11.

Her husband tried for 3 months to penetrate her, but was unable to do so. She had so much pain that she ran away. She was by then pregnant without his having penetrated her.

He left for a job in Saudi Arabia for 2 years, and when he returned, the first child had been born, and her infibulation had been cut open and sewn back to pinhole size. This time, it took 15 days to penetrate her. After discontinuing intercourse for 2 weeks she healed, and after this she experienced no more pain. As soon as the pain was gone she began to enjoy sex. She likes to have her breasts and belly stimulated. The area of her scar is pleasurably sensitive to an extreme degree. However, the strongest sensation is inside her vagina. She has orgasm 90% of the time and becomes "completely unconscious." She laughs happily as she describes this. She lubricates very much, feels a pleasurable shock, and then relaxes completely. She never overtly initiates sex, but signals frequently with sandalwood smoke and oil.

She has two daughters, and will do only a partial clitoridectomy on them, she says. She has seen so many birth complications in her capacity as a midwife, and has had so much pain in giving birth herself, that she feels this is best. Both her mother and mother-in-law are already dead and this will make matters easier. Her husband, having worked in Saudi Arabia, where he has on occasion been ridiculed for "this barbaric practice of the Sudanese," is already convinced, and supports her decision.

HISTORY #11

This 35-year-old practical nurse comes from a village in Western Sudan and has had 9 years of schooling. She was circumcised pharaonically at the age of 7, along with her two younger sisters, both of whom died as a consequence of the circumcision. She knows of no details, only that they died. She suffered from infection and fever for 2 weeks after being circumcised and had considerable problems with urination and menstruation until her marriage at 16. Penetration required 2 months, and was extremely painful. Her husband was impatient and inconsiderate. "He did not seem to care how much he hurt me," she says in a matter of fact way. "But, eventually everything became normal and pleasant."

She sometimes enjoys sex, but not too often. Too many things get in the way. Sometimes she is too tired and very often they quarrel. "There are money and family problems so much of the time."

They are really not suited to one another, she says. They seem to disagree on everything. Still, she says, they love one another, and the sexual relationship is a good one. She likes him to caress her breasts, her neck, her buttocks, and her hips. She has strongly erogenous sensation in the scar, as well as in the walls of her vagina and her cervix. She has orgasm about half of the time. Intercourse lasts for 1 hour, and it is so important to him that she reaches orgasm that she pretends when she is unable to do so. He initiates and maintains a dialogue on what her wishes are, and she has no anxieties about letting him know what pleases her. When she is receptive she can indicate this by the use of sandalwood smoke and fragrant oil. In spite of their strong communication during intercourse she cannot overtly initiate it. "It would be shameful to do so. He would not like it."

She has two daughters and three sons, and was cut and resutured to pinhole size with each birth. She says she has had far too much suffering.

She intends to take only part of the inner labia with her daughters and to infibulate to a 1 inch opening. She feels she has lost a great deal of sensitivity, and does not want this for her daughters. Also she wants to spare them the suffering she has had in childbirth.

HISTORY #12

This 35-year-old highly intelligent head nurse has had 16 years of schooling. She received a modified pharaonic at the age of 5. Her outer labia and a quarter of the clitoris remain, and she was left a half inch aperture. The actual surgery is remembered as being extremely painful, but after she urinated on the second day she had no further problems, she says. At 27 she was married to a physician.

In spite of her only partially closed vaginal opening, penetration was performed with a great deal of pain over a period of 10 days, she tells me. She sits pensive for a moment and then says: "But I *liked* that pain." "Do you generally enjoy pain?" I ask. "No, not at all. I hate pain as much as anyone. But I enjoyed *that* pain."

For 15 days after penetration she continued to feel pain. After that "everything was normal." She has had orgasm ever since. "It is like electric shock inside my cervix, pleasurable shock. I feel as if I am fainting. Everything in my body becomes completely relaxed after orgasm. Sometimes I actually become completely unconscious, and sometimes there is some loss of urine," she says. "The whole thing is entirely pleasurable." It takes about 15 minutes of foreplay and a half hour of intercourse to elicit orgasm in her. "He has excellent control. He is a wonderful lover," she laughs happily. She has orgasm every time, she says, and when possible they have intercourse twice per day. She is aware that the stump of her clitoris is ultrasensitive and that it is erectile. The scar site is also particularly sensitive. In spite of having lost three quarters of her clitoris and all of her inner labia, she still feels "complete."

She tells me that her daughter has not been actually circumcised. When peer pressure became too strong, she performed a small cut on the 5-year-old child's clitoris and told her that she had been circumcised. The daughter has never questioned this.

She admits that she does circumcisions and that her great skill causes her to be very much in demand. When I ask her what type of circumcision she does she looks at me piously and says: "It is something called a 'sandwich.' All I do is to 'freshen' the inner surfaces of the large labia, and then suture them together. This creates a very easily broken, thin scar. Nothing is actually excised."

I ask her how many people request this. "Many," she says.

"And of course the rest ask for the pharaonic, and you give it to them to the best of your ability?" I retort.

"I give them whatever they ask for," she says, looking me straight in the eye.

(After I get to know this woman better over a period of months, I realize that she likes to fabricate a great deal, and I doubt her entire story. This impression is reinforced when I meet her husband, an elephantine, pompous bank manager, tremendously inflated by his own importance, an obviously insensitive man.)

HISTORY #13

This is a 39-year-old housewife. She was born in a village, and has had no schooling. She was circumcised at the age of 7 by an untrained midwife, without any analgesic. The pain was so great that she bit the block of wood that was placed in her mouth in two. She was not able to urinate until the second day. She was given a modified pharaonic. The labia majora remained intact, as well as part of the labia minora. She was infibulated to 2 centimeters, but appears to have spontaneously infibulated further. The type of procedure she suffered was done to everyone in her village, because this was the technique employed by the midwife practicing there. Later another midwife came to the village, well versed in the pharaonic, and a lot of people returned to the older custom of circumcising their daughters pharaonically, even though the new midwife got far more money for this. Everyone felt the pharaonic was more "proper."

When she was 9, a grapefruit-sized, painful, infected dermoid cyst developed at the operation site. She could not walk or sit until the cyst was surgically removed. She began to menstruate at 14, and experienced a great deal of pain at each menstruation, until marriage. She was married at 16. Penetration took 1 month. Her husband was patient, gentle, and loving, she states, and tried not to hurt her. She has a happy marriage, and enjoys sex very much. The remainder of her labia are very sensitive, as is the area of her scar. The greatest sensitivity, however, is inside her vagina. She has strong orgasm 90% of the time, she says.

She has six daughters and three sons. With the first child, she was hung from the roof of the hut by her wrists, "in the old way," while the midwife squatted in front of her and cut her open. She was resutured after each child to 1 centimeter. Repenetration required from 7 days to 2 months and involved a great deal of pain.

Four of her daughters have been circumcised the same as she, and the same will be done to the others. She feels that her own circumcision has created much havoc in her life, but sadly states that she must do the same to her children, because it is the custom.

HISTORY #14

This is a 25-year-old housewife who was raised in a West Sudanese town and has had 12 years of education. She was pharaonically circumcised at the age of 5 by a trained midwife, under local analgesic. Her wound became badly infected, and she suffered severe bleeding and fever. The wound remained open due to infection, and a year later when it finally healed, she was resutured. She had tremendous pain during the entire period. The refibulation was so tight that it took 30 minutes to empty her bladder. She suffered greatly from depression.

She began to menstruate at 17. The menses were exceedingly painful, with much clotting and very little flow, due to the extreme infibulation. This continued until her marriage at 21. Penetration required 2 months with a great deal of pain and heavy bleeding, even though her husband was gentle and considerate. She does not have much sensation in what remains of her sex organs, except possibly the area of her scar. She is able to have very mild orgasms about half of the time, after two prolonged periods of intercourse. Her operation was a very drastic one, and she feels that this has greatly weakened her sensation and sexual response. "With the pharaonic, you cannot really feel your man," she says. She is happily married, and loves her husband very much. He is "exceedingly good" to her. In his capacity as a medical technician in a gynecological hospital, he has seen so many complications of circumcision that he did not want to circumcise their two daughters at all. She agreed, but while both of them were away from the house, the grandmothers had both girls pharaonically circumcised. She feels very badly about this, she says. She has had four children, and has had herself resutured each time. Repenetration took 2 to 4 weeks each time. She says she is terrified of the idea of having to go through so much pain again, and has persuaded her husband to obtain contraceptive pills for her.

HISTORY #15

This 39-year-old trained midwife has had 7 years of education. She admits that she does circumcisions, but denies she performs the illegal procedures. I look at her long and hard, but without comment. She shrugs her shoulders and says, "I do what people ask me to do. They are all satisfied with my work. That is all I can tell you."

She herself was circumcised at the age of 3. She remembers nothing about it herself, although she has been told she bled heavily. Her clitoris and inner labia have been excised. Her outer labia are intact, and she was infibulated to a pinhole. She had the usual menstrual difficulties, from the onset of menstruation at the age of 12 to her first delivery. Then it became normal.

She married at 13. Her husband was totally unable to penetrate her, and after 3 years of marriage she was cut open to enable delivery of her first child. She now has four boys and two girls. Resuturing after each birth was to a 1 centimeter opening, and repenetration was accomplished each time in 1 day. She has had two husbands, and loved the first one very much. The sexual adjustment between them was excellent, she remembers. They had intercourse daily, and she enjoyed daily strong orgasm with him. The marriage lasted for 20 years. Then he left the country for a job in Saudi Arabia, and simply disappeared. After 2 years and a fruitless search for him, her family divorced her from him through the courts. She continued to wait for him, but he never returned.

Her first husband cared very much about her feelings and her sexual response. She had strong sensation inside her vagina and in the area of her scar. It was less there, she says, because of the pharaonic, but it was pleasant. He never gave her a chance to initiate sex (although she feels she might possibly have done so), because he wanted her constantly. She laughs happily as she recalls this. She hardly ever refused him, only when she was really sick. She played the role of being shy and having intercourse only for his pleasure, but she loved it, and he saw through her game completely, and loved her for it.

With her second husband sex doesn't matter one way or the other, she says. She does it only because she has to, and rarely comes to orgasm.

Her two older girls have been circumcised with a lesser procedure than her own. She has had the clitoris and a small part of the inner labia excised, and they have been left a 1 inch opening. She says it is no use to do to them what was done to her. It causes too much suffering. She does not want her girls to suffer as she did. The youngest girl has Down's syndrome. She will not have her circumcised at all. "There is no need. She will not be able to marry," she shrugs.

HISTORY #16

This 23-year-old third year college student comes from educated parents. They excised her glans clitoris when she was only 3 years old, to prevent the older members of the family from having her pharaonically circumcised. There has been much ill-feeling and bitterness in the family as a result, she says. The driving force behind saving her from the pharaonic had been her chronically ill mother, who had herself been pharaonically circumcised and had had life long complications as a result. The mother died at a relatively young age.

The student has recently married. Penetration required 1 night, and there were no problems of any sort. She tells me that she feels exceedingly lucky when talking to her friends, and is immeasurably grateful to her parents for saving her from the pharaonic.

She is very happy in her new marriage, and feels that she is fortunate in having had a good sex life from day one. She has sex one or two times every day, and has orgasm every time on the first intercourse, but generally not on the second one.

She feels she is "not conscious" during orgasm. "At that moment I love him very, very much," she says. He says he can feel her vaginal contractions, which are moderate, but appear to be getting stronger as she relaxes into her new role of married woman.

She does not feel that she has been in any way mutilated. "I feel absolutely complete," she says. She wants very much to get pregnant, but does not want a girl. It would create so many problems that she would not have to face if she had a boy. Then she laughs and says: "Well, if it is a girl, I'll just have to assert myself. My mother did it for *me!*" She would not circumcise her daughter at all, and her husband feels the same as she that it is best to leave a girl "as Allah made her." It will be easier for her, she feels, since all the dire predictions by older family members that she would become a prostitute and would not be able to find a man to marry her have been proven to have no foundation. She has a strong case, she feels, and even the most vehement proponents of pharaonic circumcision in her family have begun to soften somewhat because of this.

HISTORY #17

This youthful and spritely woman looks far younger than her 68 years. She comes from a small village and has had no schooling. She was circumcised pharaonically at the age of 8 with no analgesic. Salt and very hot water were used to sterilize the wound. She had pain for 15 days, and then resumed her normal routine.

Her menses began at 13, when she was already married. She had severe menstrual problems because her husband was unable to penetrate her. She conceived after 3 years of marriage, and was cut open to allow her to give birth. She was then refibulated to a pinhole. It was a new practice then, she says, and was done to give her husband more pleasure. "Now all the women do it, because it is the best way, and keeps men from taking a second wife." Penetration after the child required 1 month and was exceedingly painful. She had great difficulty in urinating, and was unable to sit down for yet another month.

She has had 11 children and was refibulated to a pinhole with every second one, to normal size with the others. Her three daughters and all her granddaughters and great-granddaughters have been pharaonically circumcised, same as she.

She feels the pharaonic is "a good thing for the woman with her husband." She is still active sexually, and enjoys it. It is better that he does it with her than another woman, she says. She still has intercourse one or two times per week, and has orgasm 20 to 30% of the time. When she was younger, it was 50 or 60% of the time. She says that her husband is a wonderful lover, and that they would have intercourse more often, but they live with her children and grandchildren, and it is difficult to find privacy. She cannot calculate how long intercourse lasts, but it is a very long time, she says.

She only rarely refuses him, when she is tired. Her denial that she ever initiates intercourse is unshakably emphatic. "It is far too shameful." She never even uses smoke or perfume, she says. She is much too shy.

Most of her body is very sensitive. Her scar area is still the most sensitive area, and she has no sensation internally at all. She is too shy to tell her husband what her desires are, but he knows anyway. He can feel it, she says. It is very important to him to please her, and she is not too shy to let him know when she is pleased. She makes no attempt to hide it.

HISTORY #18

This shy, soft-voiced woman is in her 9th month of pregnancy. She has had no schooling, and is not sure of her age, but guesses it to be around 30. When as a result of peer pressure she asked her mother to have her circumcised around the age of 7, she was told that she had already been circumcised at the age of 2. She had absolutely no recollection of this event. She has had a full pharaonic, and it required about 5 minutes to empty her bladder when still a virgin. Her menses were extremely painful. She was married at about 14. Penetration was accomplished in 3 weeks. There was so much pain, bleeding, and infection that she had to stay in bed for 6 weeks thereafter. She has had seven children and three spontaneous abortions. With each delivery she was refibulated to a pinhole because her husband "wanted me to be tight." Repenetration took 7 to 15 days each time, with "little bleeding, but much pain." Her three daughters have had modified circumcisions. This involved excision of the clitoris and infibulation to pinhole size, "so that they will be tight." This particular technique was something she saw done in Egypt and she was told by her uncle that it was better than the full pharaonic.

She enjoys sex once in a while, and has orgasm perhaps 10-20% of the time. She does not know if she has lost anything by being circumcised. She has no erotic sensation around the region of the scar, but it is sometimes pleasurable on the inside of her vagina. She never initiates sex, mostly because she has very little desire for it, and in any event "it is shameful for a woman to do so." Sometimes when she wants her husband, she signals him indirectly with sandalwood smoke. Sometimes she does this without any desire on her own part, but merely to please him and to hold him.

If the baby she is pregnant with now is a girl, she will circumcise her in the Egyptian way, like the others. She feels she has suffered a great deal herself by being pharaonically circumcised, and feels very sorry that this was done to her. She feels that her whole life has been destroyed by it. Her daughters are lucky by comparison, she says, but she fears for them. She is afraid that their future husbands will not stay with them if they are not circumcised pharaonically as she has been.

HISTORY #19

This sad-faced, 26-year-old secretary was born in a small town and has had 10 years of schooling. She received a modified circumcision at the age of 8, and was the first one in her family not to be pharaonically circumcised. Her clitoris and parts of the outer labia have been excised, and she has been infibulated to a half centimeter opening. Her inner labia remain. She was circumcised by a trained midwife with local analgesic. She was unable to urinate for 48 hours, and had considerable bleeding after the operation. Within 1 week the pain wore off. Urination, however, remained difficult and often painful, and when she began to menstruate at 14, her periods were protracted and painful.

At 24 she was married. Penetration required 1 week, and she experienced pain for 1 week after. She has one son, a forceps delivery. A great deal of cutting and resuturing were involved in the birth, with considerable blood loss on her part. She was refibulated to a pinhole opening. The child has suffered brain damage (most likely due to the difficult delivery).

The 1 week of repenetration was even more painful than the initial penetration. It was begun after the customary 40 day period following birth. She feels that this was too soon, and that the time was insufficient for her healing.

She very much enjoys sex. Her whole body is extremely sensitive, especially her breasts. She began to have pleasure 1 month after marriage, and now that she has had her baby she enjoys sex even more. She has external and internal vaginal sensitivity. The scar area is highly sensitive, as are the remaining inner labia. The inner walls of her vagina are also sensitive to a lesser degree. She experiences strong orgasm perhaps 40% of the time, following a 10-minute period of intercourse. His orgasm precipitates hers.

She lives within her husband's extended family. There are marital problems due to the interference of her mother-in-law. It is not a good arrangement, she says, and lately her husband has changed a great deal toward her. They quarrel a lot now, and she is subject to spells of depression. When she is depressed, she is unable to have orgasm.

She feels that she has lost a great deal by being circumcised. When asked what, she says "a part of my body and a degree of pleasure." She is convinced that she would have had far more sensation had she not been circumcised.

Her husband is considerate of her in his lovemaking, and concerned about pleasing her. She tries to hide her pleasure because tradition requires this of her, but when he asks her about her orgasms, she can admit them to him. She sometimes refuses his advances when she is depressed. She is too timid and tradition-bound to make advances herself, but uses sandalwood smoke to signal when she is receptive. If she gives birth to girls, she intends to do a lesser procedure than what has been done to her. She will have the clitoris excised, no more. She will do this so "they will not have desire before marriage." She plans to do no more than this due to the many problems she has had herself. She can do no less because she must satisfy tradition, and because she cannot defy her family.

HISTORY #20

This 40-year-old secretary has completed 2 years of a technical college education. She remembers that she was very pleased at the prospect of her circumcision. She felt that it was something good that had to be done. She was told that this was what Muslims did, that it would purify her. "You will be narrow and enjoy sex more," she was told, "There will be no discharge and you will not smell bad."

She was pharaonically circumcised at the age of 8. She suffered a great deal with the first urination, and continued to have pain in passing her urine until she was married. Menstruations until that time were also painful and difficult.

It took 1 month for her husband to penetrate her. She says she hated sex at that time because of the pain. She had pain for 4 months more. The first two of her seven children were born in England, and she was not resutured after their births. She then returned to Sudan, and beginning with the birth of her third child, she was resutured to pinhole size after each subsequent birth. Her grandmother had insisted on it. "Your husband will like it," she had urged her, "You will be tighter." This was done even though her husband had in no way been dissatisfied after the first two births. Nor was he consulted in the matter.

She began to enjoy sex after 5 months of initial pain following her marriage. She has orgasms, and says about them, "I feel as if I am shivering in my belly. The entertainment before it helps. Sometimes the whole thing takes hours. When I do have an orgasm it can take 2 or 3 hours before it happens. The sex act itself can take 1 or 2 hours. With a lot of control on his part, I can have an orgasm. It depends on emotional factors as well." In describing her orgasm she says, "It feels like an electric shock going around my body, and very sweet. It seems to last for minutes. It is very strong. When it finishes I feel as if I'm going to faint. Then I feel very sleepy. When I have a repair I like it better, and he likes it better because it is tighter. But it is not *very* tight, so it only hurts for 4 or 5 days.'' She has orgasm 50% of the time, and when she doesn't, she pretends. Fear of pregnancy sometimes interferes with her pleasure. She has tried contraceptive pills with ill effects. They use nothing now except withdrawal. She is able to have orgasm before he withdraws.

She has three daughters, who have had a partial clitoridectomy performed on them because they insisted on being circumcised. She felt it was medically better not to do a full pharaonic. She was convinced that she was losing something as a result of the pharaonic having been performed on her.

HISTORY #21

This 24-year-old social worker is a college graduate. She was circumcised at the age of 9. Her pharaonic was modified by leaving an opening that would admit an index finger. She was very much afraid and did not want to be circumcised, but her parents told her it was necessary and would make life with her husband more enjoyable. Her grandmother warned her that if it was not done she would smell bad, and her husband would not be pleased with her and order her to be circumcised later. This wore down her resistance and with many doubts and trepidations, she finally agreed.

She had no immediate complications, as she recalls. Menstruation, however, proved to be exceedingly difficult and painful. During her college years the entire genital area became highly sensitive to urine. She was treated, and after 2 years the sensitivity receded.

She married at 23 and has no children so far. Penetration took 1 month and the pain continued for 4 months after. Since then everything has been normal, she says.

She likes sex very much now and has it daily. Sometimes she even initiates it. She has orgasm 90% of the time, and describes it vividly: "All my body feels like it is tingling. Then I have a shock to my chest and my legs and it gets tight inside my vagina and I have a feeling of great pleasure. I am totally unable to move. I can't move for 15 minutes. Then I feel wonderfully relaxed. I have this happen almost every day except when I am very tired or worried."

She is presently trying to get pregnant. If she has a daughter, she plans to take only the clitoris, this to save the girl from having to be circumcised when she gets married, possibly in a much more severe way.

When she first got married, she hated marriage and sex. Now she loves both. It takes her 20 minutes to reach orgasm, 10 minutes of preparation, and 10 minutes of intercourse. Her husband has good control and waits until she comes to orgasm, even when it occasionally takes her much longer.

HISTORY #22

This 25-year-old village woman has 6 years of education and was circumcised pharaonically at the age of 8. She remembers an extremely painful first urination, and that the pain continued for 3 days.

Her first menses at 15 was extremely difficult. She was married within 3 weeks of this event and menstruation subsequent to this has been normal. She describes her husband as considerate of her in the process of the initial penetration, and says it took about 1 month.

She has heard about the anticircumcision conference that has taken place in Khartoum, and it has made her think. She still plans to pharaonize her two daughters because she cannot break with the culture and oppose her family. Her husband wants her to do a lesser procedure, but her mother and grandmother insist on a pharaonic. There are many emotional family scenes.

She enjoys sex very much. Her body is sensitive all over. The area of her scar is very sensitive, but she experiences her most pleasurable sensation inside the vagina. She used to have mild orgasm about 50% of the time, but not any more. She is taking contraceptive pills and registers surprise when I inform her that this is quite possibly related. She has had a number of spontaneous abortions lately, which have weakened her. She says she loves her husband and certainly radiates those feelings. Still, she rejects his sexual advances frequently, because she is usually so tired. When she is in the mood, she uses sandalwood smoke and fragrant oils to signal her interest. She would never admit it when she wants him, because she feels it would be very shameful. She was refibulated after the birth of both her children to pinhole size because her husband wanted it and felt it would give him more pleasure. She had a lot of pain on reopening, but she felt it was important to have it done because she wanted to please him. Repenetration took 7 days each time. When she enjoys her husband's love making, she does not hide this from him. "It is not shameful," she says. "It makes him happy."

HISTORY #23

This unschooled village woman is not sure of how old she is, but believes she is about 35 or 36 years old. She recalls little of her pharaonic circumcision at the age of 6. She remembers only that after 15 days she was back to normal. The rest has been blocked out of her memory.

She was married at the age of 12, before the onset of menstruation. In attempting penetration, her husband tore an artery and caused so much bleeding that he had to rush her to a hospital to be repaired and transfused. The doctor opened the remainder of the infibulation surgically and advised a 1 month abstinence period while she healed. After about 4 or 5 months more, she began to experience sexual intercourse as pleasurable instead of frightening.

She describes herself as being very sensitive to touch. There is virtually no sensation in the area of her scar, but very strong sensation inside her vagina. She has orgasm about 80% of the time and describes her orgasm: "I shake all over and I hold my husband very tightly inside and feel like I am going up in the air." She says she has a very strong love relationship with her husband, which is quite apparent in her face and the joy with which she speaks of him.

Sometimes when she is very tired or if one of the children is ill she refuses him, but that is fairly rare. She herself never initiates intercourse because she is too shy, but she uses sandalwood smoke, perfume, and anything else she can get her hands on to entice him. Sometimes she will even rattle pots or drop dishes in the middle of the night when she wants him, she says.

She has eight children, three of whom are girls. Two of these have been circumcised and sutured to a pinhole. She has heard about the conference on circumcision and has seen television programs that describe the resulting complications. She plans not to circumcise her third daughter pharaonically. Her husband was opposed to the circumcision of the first two daughters because of the suffering she went through with each birth, but his mother insisted and had her way. His mother has recently died, so this obstacle is now removed. Her sister-in-law has traveled to London with her husband, and was deeply influenced by what she learned there. This woman has also had serious problems in giving birth, and has had three stillborn children. She has left her three daughters uncut, and the subject is using her as an example. Her own mother is a more progressive person than the mother-in-law was, and will be satisfied with the removal of a part of the clitoris, so this is what she plans to do with her third daughter.

HISTORY #24

This 42-year-old unschooled village housewife gives the impression of being slightly demented. Nonetheless she emanates a zest for living. Her physical appearance is painfully plain, but her easily elicited laughter when it rises from her very depths is exceedingly attractive.

She was pharaonically circumcised and infibulated to a pinhole by an untrained midwife at the age of 7. No analgesic was used. She remembers tremendous pain and that she suffered from vomiting throughout the procedure. There was very little bleeding, and she did not become infected. She was able to urinate on the second day, and had pain for 1 week more.

Urination thereafter took at least 10 minutes to accomplish. She began to menstruate at 12, and her periods were consistently painful. She had great difficulty in passing her menstrual blood, due to the extreme tightness of her aperture.

She was not able to marry until quite late, and it was not until she was penetrated at 40 that her menses became less difficult. Penetration took 45 days, with a great deal of pain, but again little bleeding. Her husband tried to be gentle and considerate.

She was divorced from her husband after 1 1/2 years due to his preference for another woman, which she was unable to tolerate. During the earlier phase of their marriage she enjoyed strong orgasm each time they had intercourse. As things deteriorated, it became weaker and more infrequent. She attributes this change to her unhappiness with the situation.

Her body is extremely sensitive, she says, especially her breasts. Her circumcision scar was at first painfully sensitive, later became pleasurably so. Before the marriage deteriorated, they had intercourse two to three times weekly. It took her 15 minutes to achieve orgasm. She very rarely refused his advances. She would have enjoyed more frequent intercourse, but could not make any advances, because, as she most emphatically states, this would have been exceedingly shameful. She was never even able to give any evidence of her enjoyment. He would definitely not have tolerated such behavior, she is certain. She did everything within her power to create interest, however. She used sandalwood smoke, perfume, and oils. She constantly searched for aphrodisiacs and magic charms to entice him. When the marriage failed, it was very difficult for her to deal with.

Her husband left her without giving her divorce papers and she will not be able to remarry. It is for this reason only that she will not have herself refibulated. She has had no children.

HISTORY #25

This 24-year-old practical nurse has had 8 years of schooling and comes from a small town in West Sudan. She was pharaonically circumcised at the age of 8, with no anesthesia. She vividly remembers the entire scene, and with many dramatic gestures describes the asthma attack that she had as it was taking place. Her pain following the surgery, she maintains, lasted for 12 hours only and she appears to have healed very rapidly.

She began to menstruate at 11, with much delay and pain. This lasted until the birth of her first child, a boy. She has a great deal of pain menstruating even now.

She was married at the age of 16. The marriage was arranged by her family, and she says simply, "He was the wrong man for me. I loved another man. I had never even seen this one before."

Penetration took 45 days. Even though he was considerate of her, it was a terrible experience for her. She had absolutely no libido for her husband and regarded marital relations with him as an unpleasant duty. She has rarely had orgasm, even though he was able to maintain an erection for over 1 hour and by her admission did everything he could to try to please her. She emphasizes once more that she really did not like it. Eventually she divorced him. She has not yet remarried, even though she has been refibulated to a pinhole once more. She feels that if she had the right man, her sexual response would be entirely different.

She has had no girls. If she ever has a girl, she hopes that times will be such that she can leave her uncut.

She does not agree with the common Sudanese attitude that the female sex organ is ugly and impure. She feels that a normal organ is a beautiful thing. She wishes her circumcision had never been done to her. She sees many terrible things on the gynecological ward where she works. She feels it is a terrible practice.

HISTORY #26

This 30-year-old housewife comes from a village near Khartoum, and has had no schooling. She was pharaonically circumcised at the age of 6. The operation was done with her squatting over a hole in the ground which was used to catch the blood and cut parts. Some sort of native drug was given by mouth, and there was little bleeding, she says, and practically no pain.

Closer questioning elicits the information that in her tribe an admission of pain concerning circumcision is shameful. A paste of egg white and sugar was used to cover the wound. She withheld her urine until the second day, and this would appear to contradict her assertion that she had no pain.

She also asserts that menstruation, which began at 11, was not painful, but when asked whether it was easier after her marriage at 12, admits that it was. Penetration required 1 month, and is described by her as having been exceedingly painful, in spite of her husband's earnest effort to make it as easy for her as possible. She has nine children, and is presently pregnant. She has to be cut for each delivery and is refibulated to a pinhole each time. Repenetration is accomplished each time in 1 night. Her husband, she says, is very considerate of her, and again maintains that it does not hurt. Her daughters have been circumcised in the same way she has.

She loves her husband deeply, and has very strong orgasm nearly 100% of the time. Her body is very sensitive all over. She has no sensation at all in the scar area, but it is very strong along the walls of her vagina and the cervix. She describes orgasm as: "Going up and up and up, an electric shock in my body, and I hold him very tightly inside."

She says she never refuses him, even when one of her children is sick. She never tells him directly that she is receptive, but uses smoke and oil frequently. She never hides pleasure from him, and does not have to tell him what she likes. He feels it, she says. Intercourse lasts for half an hour but he spends up to 2 hours preparing her. She feels "the pharaonic is a good thing, because that is what men like."

HISTORY #27

This 32-year-old lecturer at a women's college has had 2 years of postgraduate study in London. She is highly articulate and a willing talker.

She was circumcised at the age of 6 in the modified fashion. A part of the clitoris remains under her infibulation, although it is hard to determine how much. She was allowed a 2 centimeter opening. She had some difficulty healing and had 15 days of postoperative pain, for which she was given aspirin. Although she had slight pain at menstruation the first 2 years, it seems to be unrelated to the circumcision, she feels, since she was not sutured very tightly.

She married at age 28. There was some pain, especially at urination for 4 days, and they discontinued intercourse for this reason. He then left for a job in Saudi Arabia and she did not see him for a year. They resumed intercourse upon his return and after 1 more week of moderate pain, everything became normal. She has had one boy. If she has a girl, she plans to do no circumcision at all because of the pain and because of the way a circumcised vagina looks. She feels it is not pleasant to look at in that condition. She has also read and heard a great deal of all the adverse effects of circumcision. She had no difficulty giving birth and did not have to be cut. She cannot explain why this was not necessary, but is very happy about it.

She has an equal amount of sensation in the area of her scar and inside her vagina. The scar itself is not sensitive. She has strong orgasm close to 100% of the time. She has no reservations about telling her husband when she wants sex. "Of course I do!" she says. "Every time I ask him, he is smiling. I ask him why, and what he thinks of me for asking him, and he says: 'I like it!' " She feels that hers is an excellent marriage. There are no barriers between them. She feels that her exposure to Western education has modified her outlook toward sex. She was able to talk freely to her married friends in Europe, and they told her a lot of things and made her realize the importance of sex for both men and women in marriage. She began to realize how normal and healthy her feelings were, and that she did not need to hide them as is customary for women in Sudan.

APPENDIX II

Interviews with Men

HISTORY #1

Dr. Mohammed at 28 is an outgoing, energetic young doctor, who appears eager to contribute his story. I have known him for 2 months, and we have had many conversations. He has had 7 years of training in Romania, which have impressed him deeply in terms of the cultural differences he observed there. There is a large burn scar on his left arm, and I question him about it. It was caused by boiling oil when he was quite young. I ask him for more detail. Is the area sensitive? Yes, he says, the burned elbow is far more sensitive to touch than the unscarred one. It is even a little bit erotic.

His first heterosexual experience was with a married, pharaonically circumcised woman at the age of 18. It was difficult because he did not know how to proceed. He had caught glimpses of sex organs of an unmutilated woman from southern Sudan who worked at his parents' home, so he knew what they were supposed to look like. He had not seen a circumcised woman's organs before, and his first experience came as a real shock. In this and later experiences with circumcised women he found penetration very difficult, since they all had had frequent incisions and repairs, and the introitus was exceedingly small and inelastic.

When I asked him if there was any difference in his own response to the two types of women, he emphatically replies, "Of course." For one thing, the sight of a pharaonically circumcised vagina is repulsive to him. "It is too abnormal!" he says. The pleasurable stimulation he gets from touching the genitalia of his partner is absolutely absent. "It is only a hole," he explains. I ask him if the response of the women is different. Again his answer is emphatic. Custom in Sudan dictates that the woman act completely uninterested, he tells me, even if she strongly desires sex. Each partner has to play an assigned role. She acts the part of the rape victim, and he acts the part of the rapist. "Everything proceeds quite normally after that," he says.

Once intercourse is initiated, do circumcised women behave differently from uncircumcised women? "Very differently indeed," he says. "Uncircumcised women communicate their preferences more clearly. They tell you what they like, either by their actions, or verbally." The concentration of a circumcised woman has to appear to be entirely on satisfying the man, he says, and this, to him, detracts from the enjoyment. If he tries to determine her preferences, her pleasure, she will not tell him, and he finds this to be the source of considerable frustration.

There is also a characteristic difference in movement, he informs me. There are of course individual differences, and some uncircumcised women as well as circumcised women do not move at all. But the circumcised woman, when she does move, will rotate her pelvis in a continuous circle, whereas the uncircumcised woman moves up and down. The rotation produces more vaginal sensation, he assumes, and the up and down movements more clitoral sensation. He further speculates that the fact that the woman does move indicates the stimulation she receives is pleasurable to her. The general tendency on the part of a circumcised woman, however, is to suppress all movements, to give the appearance that she has had little or no experience, because to appear in the least bit sexually experienced is considered to be very shameful. So the circumcised woman tends to hide both interest and pleasure.

He has had experience with married and unmarried circumcised women. "How do the unmarried ones hide the fact that they have had premarital experience?" I ask.

"They have themselves refibulated before marriage," he answers, "and the husband does not know the difference." But he ventures to guess that premarital sex happens very rarely in Sudan. Extramarital affairs are far more common.

I ask him about orgasm among circumcised women. "There are psychological, social, and religious factors that come into play in this," he tells me. "A woman who has frequent orgasm is regarded as wanton, and so she tries to hide her orgasms." He, however, is one of those men who clearly perceives them from her vaginal contractions, overall behavior, and bodily tensions, in spite of her attempts to hide them. He feels quite certain that a woman could not hide her orgasm from him.

"Is there a difference in the intensity of orgasm in the two types of women?" I ask. "Yes, definitely," he says. "It is almost consistently stronger in the uncircumcised women. There is definitely a serious crippling effect as a result of circumcision, in proportion to its severity."

He tells me he has had a sizable number of experiences with Romanian, Yugoslav, Polish, Hungarian, German, Greek, and uncircumcised central African women, and he volunteers that even among the various nationalities differences in response can be observed. He has had many conversations with his peers on this subject, and they all agree. "It seems to be largely a question of cultural factors and temperament," he says.

In his capacity as a doctor the most common complications he sees at the hospital are cystitis, bladder infections, and kidney infections. Great numbers of women suffer from lumbar pain due to infections of the renal system. They are not able to relate this to their circumcisions or to the many incisions and penetrations they suffer, and so do not mention it if they are asked if they have had complications at any time due to circumcision. Infections are caused by urinary deposits that collect under the infibulated area, but women are ignorant of this fact, he says.

HISTORY #2

This 35-year-old medical technician is an intensely serious, slight man, who leans against a desk as he talks, his body poised as if in imminent flight. I wonder if he will answer all my questions, or if he will in fact flee from the room at any moment.

He tells me that he is about to be married, that the papers are in the process of being drawn up, and that this is very much on his mind. Yes, he has had sexual experiences with both circumcised and uncircumcised women, but nonetheless he is very worried about his coming marriage. He says that the uncircumcised women in his experience were consistently more pleasing than circumcised ones. He comments that he is well aware that the uncut woman obviously has more pleasure herself.

How does he know this?

He can feel it, he says, and she shows evidence of wanting to repeat the sex act frequently. The circumcised woman gives no such indication. Also, he perceives more and stronger vaginal contractions on the part of normal women. He can perceive such contractions clearly.

Is he marrying a circumcised woman?

Yes, she is pharaonically circumcised.

Does he have any anxieties about what he will have to do to penetrate her?

He takes two involuntary steps forward as if to flee, and then returns to the desk. He expects to have some difficulties, he explains in a stifled voice, but he hopes to help her to understand that it must be this way, and to enlist her cooperation.

What if he is unable to penetrate her, or if her pain becomes unbearable so that she cannot cooperate?

If penetration proves to be impossible, he says, they will go to a midwife to have her opened surgically.

How does he feel about female circumcision?

He feels that it is a terrible thing to do to a child because of the health problems it creates for her, and because it deprives her of her most sensitive parts.

What does he intend to do if he has daughters?

He hopes to leave them entirely untouched. His brother is a doctor and has already set a precedent for this in the family.

Has he had a sizable number of experiences with both circumcised and uncircumcised women?

Most of them were circumcised. There were only three that were not.

Was the difference between the two types as he described them consistently the case?

Occasionally a pharaonically circumcised woman was able to express pleasure more than an intact one. There was some overlap between the two types but all in all his observations in regard to each holds true. "Normal women generally respond more," he says, "a not too surprising finding."

Can he think of any positive reasons for circumcising girls?

"There is not a single mitigating reason for it anywhere," he says, "I can find nothing good about it, no matter how I look at it. The practice is simply a bad custom that is perpetuated for no other reason than that it is a custom."

If his intended wife were not circumcised, would he marry her?

Yes he would, and gladly. But where the woman he loves is concerned, what is done is done, and so he must deal with it as best he can.

HISTORY #3

This is a vigorous, youthful looking man of 40. He is a medical technician and has had 8 years of schooling. He was married at the age of 25 to a pharaonically circumcised woman. They have four female children. Three of them have had 1 centimeter of the clitoris removed.

What will he do with the fourth one?

Nothing, because he no longer sees any reason for circumcision. All of his medical experiences in the hospital cry out against it.

Have any of his three circumcised daughters had any complications?

No, but his wife has.

Will his family give him any problems in regard to his decision about the fourth girl?

He quarreled bitterly about the first three with his mother, and she broke off all contact with him for 3 months. Then she gave in and ceased opposing him.

Does he anticipate problems in marrying off any of these girls?

No, because times are changing here very rapidly, he feels, and they will change more. Educated men above all are changing their minds about the sexual desirability of pharaonic circumcision in their wives, and there may well come a time very soon when this will affect the marriageability of a girl and her bride-price as well. Parents with small girls are giving the matter some thought.

Is his wife pharaonically circumcised?

Yes, and she has had many problems. Delivery has been exceedingly difficult for her, and two of the children were forceps deliveries. She has had much cutting and it takes her 2 months to heal each time.

Were there any problems in penetration?

He flinches, then tells me that his mother-in-law begged him before the wedding to take his wife to a doctor, and to have her surgically opened. His pride prevented him from doing this. He penetrated her forcibly in 3 hours and created a medial tear. She bled severely and he had to rush her to a doctor for emergency repair.

How did he feel about this event?

His face plainly shows it. "I felt like a criminal," he says. "I could hardly bear to live with myself." He had to wait for 2 months for her to heal before he could approach her again.

Is his wife able to have sexual enjoyment?

After the initial trauma wore off, he says, he noticed that she began to have enjoyment. It now takes her two sessions of half hour intercourse to come to orgasm.

Has he ever had sexual contact with uncircumcised women?

Yes, with Ethiopian girlfriends who were prostitutes.

Does he feel there is a difference in response between circumcised and uncircumcised women?

Yes, uncircumcised women are able to have orgasm more quickly and more often. Also, in his particular experience, as well as he could determine, orgasm intensity is greater for them, and this appeared to be consistently so.

Is his wife able to express passion toward him, or does she, in the manner of so many Sudanese women, hide it from him?

She does not hide her feeling. He is very frank with her, and consequently she is able to be frank with him as well.

Does she have herself resutured to pinhole size after each child?

Yes, she does, and it creates many problems for both of them. It is exceedingly painful for her to be repenetrated, and it is painful for him as well. But she insists on doing it for "aesthetic reasons" and he does not stop her. He feels that she does it because she is ashamed to be loose, as she is bound to be due to the damage inflicted on her.

"But why not a more reasonable opening?" I ask.

He shrugs. "It is women's business." He does not interfere. He knows she orders the midwife to do it for his pleasure, but he feels if she were sewn less tightly it would be easier for him and easier for her.

Why does he not tell her this?

"Women do not allow you to interfere in this," he insists. "It is their business, they tell you."

"What is the explanation?" I ask. "Do women get satisfaction from pain?"

"No," he says, "they do not enjoy pain. They do it because they feel it will make them sexually more attractive to their husbands, and they will tolerate a great deal of pain for this. It is a misguided act of love." He tells me that he is losing his desire for his wife and cannot explain this because she is a good, loving wife to him. Perhaps it is because she has no passion for him any more, and seems to have sex with him only out of a sense of duty.

How does he explain this?

He can only guess at the answer, he says. Probably she has simply suffered too much.

HISTORY #4

This man is a soft-spoken, 28-year-old physician, who gives the appearance of being a concerned, sensitive human being. He received his medical training in Egypt, and is now practicing medicine in Khartoum. He has been married for 2 months to a pharaonically circumcised woman. She has been infibulated to a 1 centimeter opening. When they married, he tried to penetrate her very slowly and carefully because she was extremely afraid. There was much pain and much blood. He used an anesthetic spray to lessen the pain for her, and succeeded in opening a partial wound. Every few days he would enlarge it. After 2 months she is now open, but is still very narrow and still suffers periodic pain.

He says that for the first 2 weeks he could experience no pleasure. He passes his hand before his eyes and shakes his head, frowning. "It was something other than sex." Causing her pain was making him feel very depressed, although he hastens to add that he did not have any potency problems during that period, as some me do.

Her reaction at the beginning had been extremely fearful, he recalls, but she got over this gradually as pain diminished. Then she began to react sexually and to cooperate. She now comes to orgasm after a prolonged period of intercourse, and he is able to discern this event when it happens. Also, his wife is able to discuss her feelings and reactions with him.

He has had sexual experiences with uncircumcised women before marriage. Two were long-term relationships, others were brief encounters with prostitutes. He has known his wife for 6 years, and has a strong, emotional relationship of long standing with her, although he had never even kissed her before marriage. He feels that a noncircumcised female is a lot less difficult to satisfy. "In the sexual process, it is easier for a noncircumcised woman to cooperate. The movement, the response are quite different," he says. He feels that circumcised women lose a lot. He has the impression that most of his wife's pleasure is emotional. Her physical reaction is weak by comparison. However, the possibility still exists that she will develop along those lines, since their marriage has been so recent. "there is cause for hope," he says.

HISTORY #5

This 30-year-old resident medical officer had his university and medical training in Alexandria, Egypt, over a period of 8 years. A thoughtful, gentle, soft-spoken man, he is as yet unmarried, but hopes to find a wife in the near future. When I first question him, he tells me that he has had sexual experiences with circumcised and uncircumcised women.

His first experience was in a brothel at the age of 16, at the goading of an older friend. The woman was pharaonically circumcised. He relates that the experience was exceedingly strange, as were his later experiences with Sudanese women. "In Egypt," he ways, "it is much lovelier to be with a woman, because they do things to get you interested." Not all of the women there were circumcised, and if they were, it was far less drastic—generally a partial clitoridectomy.

"How was the experience different?" I ask.

With each of the less mutilated women, he felt he was dealing with a complete, live woman. With Sudanese women he does not feel as if he is dealing with a live woman at all. She does nothing. She lies there as if lifeless, like a block of wood.

"All of them?" I ask.

"Sometimes one acts normally," he says. "but for the most part, it is as I have said. Of course, most of the experiences have been with prostitutes. With girlfriends it is somewhat better."

"Let's talk about the girlfriends," I say.

"Well, there is only a slight difference between those."

Has he had any experience with uncircumcised women?

"No, only pharaonic or *sunna*." [There is a seeming inconsistency here between this medical practitioner's answer at this point and his initial statement that he has had sexual relations also with uncircumcised women. I have encountered this type of contradiction frequently among medical personnel in Sudan. It is an outgrowth of the fact that the most intractably severe medical and sexual problems they deal with occur in infibulated women. Because of this disparity, women who have been "merely" clitoridectomized are often thought of and referred to by them as "uncircumcised."]

Is there any difference between women letting him know when he pleases them?

"Yes, there is a big difference. The Egyptian one can tell you when she wants you and when she reaches orgasm. The Sudanese will tell you neither. She does not communicate either desire or pleasure, even when you ask her."

How does he feel about getting no feedback?

When he approaches a woman and is rebuffed, he stops, he says. Egyptian women sometimes rebuff him less strongly, and he recognizes that they really mean for him to continue, but it is different with Sudanese women.

When he does in fact have intercourse with a Sudanese woman and she refuses to acknowledge that she has desire and that he has pleased her, how does this make him feel?

He says that it is so difficult to find a woman in Sudan, that by the time you find one, whether a prostitute or a girlfriend, you are so frustrated that you don't much care. You just want sex. In Egypt it is different because women are more readily available; women are as interested as men are. You can expect a response from a woman there, because she is doing what she does because she wants to and this is already implicit in her acceptance. A girl in Sudan may want you, but still has to pretend she doesn't. Even when she has sex with you, she still has to pretend it is all for your pleasure, not her own.

Can he determine when a woman has an orgasm?

Yes, he can. He can tell by her contractions and he involuntary movements. In his personal experience, Sudanese women reach orgasm only rarely.

Is there any difference in the strength of the orgasm?

Yes there is, but the differences are individual. Some Sudanese women also have strong orgasms, just as some Egyptian women do, in spite of the extreme circumcision they have had.

When he marries, what kind of woman would he prefer?

"An uncircumcised one!" he says emphatically and without hesitation. Why? Because he knows from the medical point of view that circumcision will detract from her sexuality, no matter in what degree it exists.

Do most men in Sudan feel the way he does?

No. Most of them will disagree with him. It is a question of ignorance and lack of experience.

BIBLIOGRAPHY

Abdalla, R. M. D. (1982). *Sisters in Affliction – Circumcison and Infibulation of Women in Africa*. London: Zed Press.

Adetoro, O. O., and Ebomoyi, E. (1986). Health Implications of Traditional Female Circumcision in Pregnancy. *Asia-Oceania J. Obstet. Gynaecol.*, *12*(4), 489-492.

Ammar, H. (1954). *Growing Up in an Egyptian Village*. London: Routledge and Kegan Paul.

Assaad, M. B. (1979). *Female Circumcision in Egypt: Current Research and Social Implications*. Cairo: American University in Cairo, Social Research Centre.

Assaad, M. B. (1980). Female Circumcision in Egypt: Social Implications, Current Research and Prospects for Change. *Studies in Family Planning, 11*(1), 3-16.

Assaad, M. B. (1982). Female Circumcision in Egypt: Current Research and Social Implications. *WHO/EMRO Technical Publication: Seminar on Traditional Practices Affecting the Health of Women and Children in Africa*, p. 229. Alexandria.

Association of African Women for Research and Development. (1981). Genital Mutilation: A Statement by the Association of African Women for Research and Development. *United Nations Economic Commission for Africa, African Training and Research Centre for Women and Association of African Women for Research and Development*, p. 60. Addis Ababa. See Giorgis, B. W., *Female Circumcision in Africa*.

Baasher, T. A. (1979). Psychological Aspects of Female Circumcision, Report on a Seminar in Khartoum. *WHO/EMRO Technical Publication, 2*, 71-105.

Bakr, S. A. (1979). Circumcision and Infibulation in the Sudan. *Fifth Congress of Obstet. and Gyn.*, p. 104.

Bakr, S. A., Medical Director, Bulluk Gynecological Hospital, Omdurman, Sudan (1981). Personal interview.

Bakr, S. A. (1982). Circumcision and Infibulation in the Sudan. *WHO/EMRO Technical Publication: Seminar on Traditional Practices Affecting the Health of Women and Children in Africa*, p. 138. Alexandria.

Barker-Benfield, G. J. (1976). *The Horrors of the Half Known Life: Male Attitudes Toward Women and Sexuality in Nineteenth Century America*, p. 88-89, 96-97. New York: Harper & Row.

Becker, R. E. (March 1974). Medical Aspects of Human Sexuality. *Quiz, 8*(3), 181.

Bedri, Y., Director, Babiker Bedri Scientific Association for Women's Studies, Ahfat University, Omdurman, Sudan (1981). Personal interview.

Bergstrom, R. (June 21-26, 1981). An American Woman's Experience. *5th World Congress of Sexology*, p. 254. Jerusalem. Printed in book form: *Sexology, Sexual Biology, Behavior and Therapy*, Z. Hoch and H. I. Lief, eds., Amsterdam, Excerpta Medica, 1982.

Bettelheim, B. (1962). *Symbolic Wounds*. New York: Collier Books.

Bishaw, T. and Negash, Z. (1984). An Overview of the Prevalence of Female Circumcision and Other Traditional Practices in Selected Parts of Ethiopia. *WHO/EMRO Technical Publication: Seminar on Traditional Practices Affecting the Health of Women and Children in Africa*. Senegal.

Boddy, J. (1982). Womb as Oasis, The Symbolic Content of Pharaonic Circumcision in Rural Northern Sudan. *American Ethnologist, 9*(4), 682-698.

Bolande, R. P. (1969). Ritualistic Surgery—Circumcision and Tonsillectomy. *New England Jour. of Med., 280,* 591-596.

Bolling, D. R. (April 1976). Prevalence, Goals and Complications of Heterosexual Anal Intercourse in a Gynecologic Population. *9th Annual Meeting of the Amer. Assn. of Sex Educators, Counselors and Therapists*. Washington, D.C.

Bonaparte, M. (1950). *Notes on Excision, Psychoanalysis and the Social Sciences*. New York: International Universities Press.

Brisset, C. (Feb. 28, 1979). Trente Millions de Mutilles (The Mutilation of Thirty Million). *Le Monde*.

Bryk, F. (1928). *Neger-Eros (Negro Erotica)*. Berlin: Marcus und Weber.

Bullough, V. and Bullough B. (1977). *Sin, Sickness and Sanity*. New York: The American Library.

Christhilf, S. (June 21-26, 1981). Adverse Sequelae of Male Circumcision. *5th World Congress of Sexology*, p. 253. Jerusalem. Printed in book form: *Sexology, Sexual Biology, Behavior and Therapy*, Z. Hoch and H. I. Lief, eds., Excerpta Medica, Amsterdam, 1982.

Cloudsley, A. (1983). *Women of Omdurman: Life, Love and the Cult of Virginity*. London: Ethnographica.

Cook, R. (1979). Damage to Physical Health from Pharaonic Circumcision (Infibulation): A Review of the Medical Literature. *Background Document for the Seminar on Traditional Practices Affecting the Health of Women and Children*, p. 53-69. Khartoum.

Correa, P. et al. (1984). Excision. *WHO/EMRO Technical Publication: Seminar on Traditional Practices Affecting the Health of Women and Children in Africa*, p. 56. Senegal.

Cox, L. S. and Cox, R. K. (April/May 1982). An Alternative Circumcision Procedure. *Genesis*.

Dareer, Asma el. (1982a). *Woman Why Do You Weep?* London: Zed Press.

Dareer, Asma el. (1982b). A Study on Prevalence and Epidemiology of Female Circumcision to Date. *WHO/EMRO Technical Publication: Seminar on Traditional Practices Affecting the Health of Women and Children in Africa*, p. 312. Alexandria.

Dareer, Asma el. (1983). Epidemiology of Female Circumcision in the Sudan. *Trop. Doctor, 1*, 41-45.

David, A. (1978). *Infibulation en Republique de Djibouti (Infibulation in the Republic of Djibouti)*. Doctoral dissertation, Université de Bordeaux, Thesis No. 131, par l'Amicale des Étudiants en Medicine de Bordeaux.

Davison, J. (June 21-26, 1981). Adult Penile Circumcision: Erotosexual and Cosmetic Sequelae. *5th World Congress of Sexology*, p. 252. Jerusalem. Printed in book form: *Sexology, Sexual Biology, Behavior and Therapy*, Z. Hoch and H. I. Lief, eds., Amsterdam, Excerpta Medica, 1982.

De Villeneuve, A. (1937). Étude sur une Coutume Somalie. Les Femmes Cousues. *Journal de la Société des Africainistes*.

Dewhurst, C. J., and Michelson, A. (1964). Infibulation Complicating Pregnancy. *British Medical Jour.*, 2, 1442.

Diallo, K. (1984). Excision or Female Circumcision: Mali's Experience. *WHO/EMRO Technical Publication: Seminar on Traditional Practices Affecting the Health of Women and Children in Africa*, p. 96. Senegal.

Edwards and Masters. (1963). *Cradle of Erotica*, p. 89. New York: Julian Press.

Epelboin, S. and Epelboin, A. (1979). Special Report: Female Circumcision. *People*, 6(1), 24-29.

Eresund, P. and Tesha, N. (1979). *The Situation of Children 0-15 Years in Tanzania*, p. 12. Stockholm: SIDA Information Division.

(Author Unknown) (197?). Expectant Parents' Information Kit, #241-2811. Distributed by Pampers, Proctor and Gamble Co.

Felman, Y. M. (1979). Letter to the Editor. *N. Y. State Jour. of Med.*, 79, 1964.

Fisher, S. (1973). *The Female Orgasm*. London: Allen Lane.

Fleming, J. B. (1960). Clitoridectomy—The Disastrous Downfall of Isac Baker Brown, FRCS (1867). *J. Obstet Gyn of the British Empire*, 67, 1017-1034.

Freud, S. (1938). *Totem and Taboo*. New York: Random House. Translated by A. A. Brill.

Freud, A. (1952). *The Role of Bodily Illness in the Mental Life of Children*. New York: International University Press.

Ganesha Society. (1979). *Aspects of Indonesian Culture*. Jakarta Central Museum.

Gellis, S. (1978). Circumcision. *Am. Jour. Dis. Child.*, 132, 1169.

Giorgis, B. W. (1981). Female Circumcision in Africa. *United Nations Economic Commission for Africa, African Training and Research Centre for Women and Association of African Women for Research and Development*. Addis Ababa.

Gleviczky, A. (1980). Contribution to the Study of Female Sexual Mutilations in the East Senegal. In *Les Mutilations Sexuelles Feminines, Le Marriage Precoce*. Geneva, Switzerland: Sentinelles.

Gould, R. E. (1977). What Distinguishes "Healthy" from "Sick" Sexual Behavior? *Med. Aspects of Human Sexuality, 11*(10), 75.

Grey, S. (1983). *Beyond the Veil*, p. 206. New York: Harper & Row.

Grimes, D. (1978). Routine Circumcision of the Newborn Infant: A Reappraisal. *Am. Jour. Obstet. Gyn., 130*, 128-129.

Grossman, E., and Posner, N. A. (1981). Surgical Circumcision of Neonates, A History of its Development. *Obstet. and Gyn., 58*, 241-246.

Haas, H., Terre de Femmes, Hamburg, Germany (1979-1988). Personal interviews and correspondence.

Hakansson, T. (June 21-26, 1981). Genital and Sexual Mutilation. *5th World Congress of Sexology*, p. 255. Jerusalem. Printed in book form, *Sexology, Sexual Biology, Behavior and Therapy*, Z. Hoch and H. I. Lief, eds., Amsterdam, Excerpta Medica, 1982.

Hakim, A. S. (1982). Traditional Practices Affecting the Health of Women: Female Circumcision in Egypt. *WHO/EMRO Technical Publication: Seminar on Traditional Practices Affecting the Health of Women and Children in Africa*, p. 253. Alexandria.

Hall, L. (1963). Arthritis After Female Circumcision. *East Afr. Med J., 2*, 55-57.

Hamamsy, el L. (1973). The Daya of Egypt: Survival in a Modernizing Society. *Caltech Population Program Occasional Papers Series, 1*(8), 30.

Hansen, H. H. (1972/73). Clitoridectomy, Female Circumcision in Egypt. *Folk, 14/15*, 15-26.

Hathout, H. M. (1963). Some Aspects of Female Circumcision. *Brit. Jour. Obstet. and Gyn., 70*, 505-507.

Hayes, R. O. (1975). Female Genital Mutilation, Fertility Control, Women's Roles and the Patrilineage in Modern Sudan, A Functional Analysis. *Amer. Ethnologist, 2*(4), 627-637.

Hite, S. (1977). *The Hite Report*. New York: Dell Publishing Co.

Hosken, F. P. (1977/1978). Female Circumcision in Africa. *Victimology, 2*(3/4), 494.

Hosken, F. P. (1978). The Epidemiology of Female Genital Mutilation. *Tropical Doctor*, *8*, 150-156.

Hosken, F. P. (1979). Women and Health: Female Circumcision. *WIN News*, *4*(3), 27.

Hosken, F. P. (1982). Women and Health: Female Circumcision. *WIN News*, *7*(2), 34.

Hosken, F. P. (1982a). *The Hosken Report, Genital and Sexual Mutilation of Females*. Lexington, MA: International Network News.

Hosken, F. P. (1982b). Female Circumcision in the World Today, A Global Review. *WHO/EMRO Technical Publication: Seminar on Traditional Practices Affecting the Health of Women and Children in Africa*. Alexandria.

Huber, A.(1969). Die Weibliche Beschneidung (Female Circumcision). *Zeitschrift fur Tropenmedizin und Parasitologie*, *20*, 1-9.

Hussein, F. H. M. et al. (1982). Community Study on Female Circumcision in Somalia, Some Epidemiological Aspects. *WHO/EMRO Technical Publication: Seminar on Traditional Practices Affecting the Health of Women and Children in Africa*, p. 296. Alexandria.

Ismail, E. (1982). A Personal Testimony by Director of Health Training, Somalia. *The Hosken Report*. MA: WIN News.

Ismail, E. A. (1984). Statement on the Practice of Infibulation. *WHO/EMRO Technical Publication: Seminar on Traditional Practices Affecting the Health of Women and Children in Africa*, p. 21. Senegal.

Jensen, A. E. (1933). *Beschneidung und Reifezeremonien bei Naturvolkern (Circumcision and Initiation Rites of Primitive Peoples)*. Stuttgart: Strecher und Schreider.

Johnson, W. R. (1968). *Human Sexual Behavior and Sex Education*. Philadelphia: Lea and Febiger.

Karim, M. and Ammar, R. (1965). *Female Circumcision and Sexual Desire*. Cairo: Ain Shams University Press.

Katz, M. (1980). Letter to the Editor. *Amer. Jour. Dis. Child*, *134*, 1098.

Kenyatta, J. (1938). *Facing Mount Kenya*. London: Secker and Warburg.

Kinsey, A. C., et. al. (1953). *Sexual Behavior of the Human Female*. Philadelphia: W. B. Saunders.

Klauber, G. T. (1973). Circumcision and Phallic Fallacies, or the Case Against Routine Circumcision. *Connecticut Medicine*, 37(9), 445.

Kleida, M. H., Prof. Dept. Obstet. and Gyn., Faculty of Medicine, University of Khartoum, Khartoum (1981). Personal interview.

Koso-Thomas, O. (1987). *The Circumcision of Women: A Strategy for Eradication*. London: Zed Books Ltd.

Kouba L. and Muasher J. (1985). Female Circumcision in Africa: An Overview. *African Studies Review*, 28(1), 95-110.

Ladas, A., Whipple, B., and Perry, J. D. (1982). *The G-Spot and Other Recent Discoveries about Human Sexuality*. New York: Holt, Rinehart and Winston.

Lantier, J. (1972). *La Cité Magique (The Magic City)*. Paris: Editions Fayard.

Laycock, H. T. (1950). Surgical Aspects of Female Circumcision in Somaliland. *East Afr. Med. J.*, 27, 445-450.

Lenzi, E. (1970). Damage Caused by Infibulation and Infertility. *Acta Europea Fertilitatis*, 2(1), 47-58.

Levin, R. J. (1981). The Female Orgasm—A Current Appraisal. *Jour. Psychosomatic Research*, 25(2), 119-133.

Lightfoot-Klein, H. (August 1979). Human Rights: Crimes Against 30 Million. *New Statesman*, p. 266-268. London.

Lightfoot-Klein, H. (1983). Pharaonic Circumcision of Females in the Sudan. *Medicine and Law*, 2, 353-360.

Lightfoot-Klein, and Goebel, R.(1983). Beschwerden nach Genitalverstümmelung (Complications Arising from Genital Mutilation). *Sexualmedizin*, (8).

Lightfoot-Klein, H. (1984). Circumcision of Females (Sudan). *Jour. of Orgonomy*, 18(1), 47-57.

Linnander, M., Inter-African Committee, Geneva (1986). Personal communication.

Lowenstein, L. (1978). Attitudes and Attitude Differences to Female Genital Mutilation in the Sudan: Is There a Change on the Horizon? *Social Sci. Med.*, 2, 417-421.

MacLaine, S. (1970). *Don't Fall Off the Mountain*. New York: W. W. Norton.

Maher, M. (1981). Medical Dangers of Female Circumcision. *Int. Planned Parenthood Fed.*, 2, 1-2.

Maimonides, M. (undated). *Guide to the Perplexed.* New York: Hebrew Publishing Co. Translated by M. Friedlander.

Marino, L. J. (Nov. 17, 1980). Second Thoughts About an Old Procedure. *Newsday*, p. 8. quoted by David Zinman.

Masters, W. H., and Johnson, V. (1966). *Human Sexual Response.* Boston: Little, Brown and Co.

McLean, S. (Ed.). (1980). *Female Circumcision, Excision and Infibulation, Report No. 47.* London: Minority Rights Group.

Megafu, U. (1983). Female Ritual Circumcision in Africa: An Investigation of the Presumed Benefits Among Ibos of Nigeria. *East African Med. Jour.*, 40(11), 793-800.

Melly, J. M. (1935). Infibulation. *Lancet.* Vol. 2(1272).

Modawi, O., Director General of Obstetrics and Gynecology, Ministry of Health, Khartoum. (1981). Personal interview.

Modawi, S. (1974). The Impact of Social and Economic Changes in Female Circumcision. In *Sudan Medical Association Congress Series, No. 1.* Khartoum: Sudan Medical Association.

Moen, E. W. (1983). Genital Mutilation: Everywoman's Problem, Working Paper #22. In *Working Papers on Women in International Development.* East Lansing, MI: Michigan State Univ.

Money, J., et al. (1955). Hermaphroditism: Recommendations Concerning Assignment of Sex, and Psychologic Management. *Bull. of Johns Hopkins Hospital*, 97(4), 284-300.

Money, J. (1961). Components of Eroticism in Man, II: The Orgasm and Genital Somasthesia. *Jour. Nervous and Mental Disorders*, 132, 289.

Money, J. (June 21-26, 1981). An Institution Challenged. *5th World Congress of Sexology.* Jerusalem. Printed in book form, *Sexology, Sexual Biology, Behavior and Therapy*, Z. Hoch and H. I. Lief, eds., Amsterdam, Excerpta Medica, 1982.

Money, J. (1985). *The Destroying Angel.* Buffalo, NY: Prometheus Books.

Montague, M. F. A. (1946). Ritual Mutilation Among Primitive Peoples. *Ciba Symposia*, 8(7), 421-436.

Moorehead, Alan. (1960). *The White Nile.* New York: Harper and Brothers.

Moorehead, Alan. (1962). *The Blue Nile*. New York: Harper & Row.

Morgan, E. (1972). *The Descent of Woman*. New York: Stein and Day.

Morgan R., and Steinem, G. (March 1980). The International Crime of Genital Mutilation. *Ms.*, p. 67.

Morris, D. (1985). *Body Watching*. New York: Crown Publishers.

Munk, A., physician, Port Sudan (1979, 1981 and 1983). Personal interviews.

Mustafa, A. (1966). Female Circumcision and Infibulation in Sudan. *Jour. Obstet. Gyn.*, *173*, 305.

(July 27, 1982). President Moi Condemns Girls' Circumcision. *Nairobi Times*, p. 3.

(Nov. 1, 1982). A Sexual Rite on Trial. *Newsweek*, p. 55.

Oduntan, O., and Onadeko, M. (1984). Female Circumcision in Nigeria. *WHO/EMRO Technical Publication: Seminar on Traditional Practices Affecting the Health of Women and Children in Africa*, p. 98. Senegal.

Ogunmodede, E. (1979). End This Mutilation. *People*, 6(1), 30-31.

Patel, H. (1966). The Problem of Routine Circumcision. *Jour. Canadian Medical Association*, 95(11), 577-578.

Phillip, H. L. (1974). *Trends and Religious Belief*. Westport, CT: Greenwood Press Publications.

Population Reference Bureau (1982). *1982 World Population Data*. Washington, D.C.

Price, G. (1982). Factors Related to Sudanese Families Deciding Against Female Circumcision. *WHO/EMRO Technical Publication: Seminar on Traditional Practices Affecting the Health of Women and Children in Africa*, p. 342-359. Alexandria.

Rado, S. (1959). Sexual Anesthesia in the Female. *Quarterly Review in Obstet. Gyn*, *16*, 249.

Rahim, E. T. A., Psychiatrist, Port Sudan (1979). Personal interview.

Ras-Work, B. (1984). Female Circumcision—Proposal for Eradication. *WHO/EMRO Technical Publication: Seminar on Traditional Practices Affecting the Health of Women and Children in Africa*, p. 71. Senegal.

Ravich, A. (1973). *Preventing VD and Cancer by Circumcision*. New York: Philosophical Library.

Reik, T. (1962). *Ritual: Psychoanalytic Studies*. New York: Grove.

Remondino, P. C. (1974). *History of Circumcision from the Earliest Times to the Present*. New York: AMS Press. Originally published by Davis Co., Philadelphia, 1891.

Robertson, W. O. Jr. (1974). From Comments section, *Medical Aspects of Human Sexuality, 8*(1), 48.

Rushwan, H. (1982). Female Circumcision: Present Position and Future Outlook. *Singapore J. Obstet. Gynaecol., 1*, 3-6.

Saadawi, N. (1980). *The Hidden Faces of Eve: Women in the Arab World*. London: Zed Press.

Saadawi, N.(1982). Circumcision of Girls. *WHO/EMRO Technical Publication: Seminar on Traditional Practices Affecting the Health of Women and Children in Africa*, p. 217-228. Alexandria.

Sabib, H. A. A.(1984). Islam's Attitude to Female Circumcision. *WHO/EMRO Technical Publication: Seminar on Traditional Practices Affecting the Health of Women and Children in Africa*, p. 69. Senegal.

Sami, I. R. (1986). Female Circumcision with Special Reference to the Sudan. *Annals of Tropical Paediatrics, 6*, 99-115.

Sayed, E. (1982). Reasons for and Purposes of Female Circumcision. *WHO/EMRO Technical Publication: Seminar on Traditional Practices Affecting the Health of Women and Children in Africa*, p. 156. Alexandria.

Schwartz, G. (1970). Infibulation, Population Control and the Medical Profession. *Bull. of the New York Academy of Med., 46*(11), 964.

Seaman, B. (1972). *Free and Female: The Sex Life of the Contemporary Woman*. New York: Coward, McCann and Geoghegan Inc.

Shaalan, M. (1982). Clitoris Envy: A Psychodynamic Construct Instrumental in Female Circumcision. *WHO/EMRO Technical Publication: Seminar on Traditional Practices Affecting the Health of Women and Children in Africa*, p. 271. Alexandria.

Shamma, A. A. O., et al. (1949). Female Circumcision in the Sudan. *Lancet, 1*, 545.

Shandall, A. A. (1967). Circumcision and Infibulation of Females. *Sudan Medical Journal*, *5*, 178-212.
Shandall, A. A. (1979). Circumcision and Infibulation of Females. *Les Mutilations Sexuelles Feminines Infliges aux Enfants*. Switzerland: Terre des Hommes.
Shaw, E. (1985). Female Circumcision: Perceptions of Clients and Caregivers. *American College Health*, *33*, 193-197.
Spitz, R. (1952). Authority and Masturbation. *Psychoanalytic Quarterly*, *21*(4), 503.
Spock, B. (March 29, 1976). Letter to the Editor. *Moneysworth*, p. 12.
Taba, A. H. (May 1979). Female Circumcision. *World Health*, p. 12.
Taha, M. M., Leader of Republican Brothers Political Movement, Omdurman. (1981). Personal interview.
Uddenberg, N. J. (1974). Psychological Aspects of Sexual Inadequacy in Women. *Psychosomatic Research*, *18*, 33-47.
Verkauf, B. S. (1975). Acquired Clitoral Enlargement. *Medical Aspects of Human Sexuality*, *9*(4), 134.
Verzin, J. A. (1975). Sequelae of Female Circumcision. *Tropical Doctor*, *5*, 163-169.
Wallerstein, E. (1980). *Circumcision: An American Health Fallacy*. New York: Springer Publishing Co.
Wallerstein, E. (1983). Circumcision: Ritual Surgery or Surgical Ritual? *Medicine and Law*, *2*, 85-97.
Wallerstein, E. (1985). Circumcision: The Uniquely American Medical Enigma. *Symposium on Advances in Pediatric Urology*, p. 123-132. Urology Clinics of North America.
Wallerstein, E. (1986). *Circumcision: Information, Misinformation, Disinformation*. Corte Madera, CA: National Organization of Circumcision Information, Resource Center.
Wallerstein, E. (1987). Personal correspondence.
Weiss, C. (1966). Motives for Male Circumcision among Preliterate and Literate Peoples. *Jour. of Sex Research*, *2*(2), 69-88.
Widstrand, C. G. (1965). Female Infibulation. *Studia Ethnographica Upsaliensia*, *20*, 95-124.
Williams, J., Medical Director, Khartoum Clinic, Khartoum (1979, 1981, and 1983). Personal interviews.

Worsley, A. (1938). Infibulation and Female Circumcision: A Study of a Little-Known Custom. *Jour. Obstet. Gyn. of the British Empire*, *45*, 686-91.

Wright, H. (1980). Medical Dangers of Female Circumcision. *IPPF Medical Bulletin*, *1*, 3.

Young, E. (1949). Female Circumcision in Sudan. *The Anti-Slavery Reporter and Aborigine's Friend Series, IV*, 5(1), 13.

Youseff, N. (1973). Cultural Ideals, Feminine Behavior and Kinship Control. *Comparative Studies in Society and History*, *15*(3), 326-347.

Zwang, G. (1979). Female Sexual Mutilations, Techniques and Results. *La Mutilations Sexuelles Feminines Infliges aux Enfants*. Switzerland: Terre des Hommes.

(Author Unknown) (1975). Report of the Ad Hoc Task Force on Circumcision. *Pediatrics*, *56*, 610.

(Author Unknown) (1978). Special Report on Female Circumcision. *People*, *6*(1), 28.

Index

in Africa 31
and female circumcision in Sudan 79
Population movements
in Africa, effects of 194
in Sudan
and social disorganization 157
Potency problems
in attempted penetration 11,24,96
Practitioners of female circumcision 36
Premarital sex
among circumcised women 24
Procedures
female circumcision 32-36
male circumcision 188
Professional women
position of in Sudan 67
Promiscuity
and circumcision 39,41
Property rights of women 69
Prostitutes 26,124
uninfibulated women regarded as in
Sudan 66
Khartoum 236-237
and AIDS 240
and orgasm 93
Prostitution
and Islam 94,236
in Kenya 237-240
Psychiatric problems
of circumcised women 76
of Sudanese men and women 11
Psychiatrists
conversations with 10-12,136-154
on orgasm of circumcised women 90
on pain threshold of women 61
Psychic problems
of circumcised women at various stress
points 60
Psychological trauma
at circumcision 36

Rationale for female circumcision 38-41
"Recircumcision"
definition 35
as sexual enhancement 98
as "renewed virginity" 100
Red Sea Province 28,30
Refibulation 98-102

definition 35
a modern innovation 98
as "women's business" 100
as an additional source of income for
midwives 101
Religion
role of female circumcision in 41-42
Republican Brothers 43
Restrictions on women
in Sudan 65-67
under Islam 68
Rights of women
under Islamic law 67
Romans, ancient 27

Saudi Arabia
as "brain drain" of Sudan 49
effect on Sudan 79
influence of 194
Schools
differences between those for boys and
girls 65
Senegal 36
Sex education
lack of for men 94
and male attitudes 151-152
of mothers 101
Sex signals
of Sudanese women 87-89 —
Sexual aversion
in circumcised girls 98
Sexual behavior
of Sudanese women 89-90
Sexual desire
reduction of in circumcised women 28,
81,133-134,248-249,263,275
Sexual pleasure of men
refibulation for 35,101
female circumcision believed to be
source of greater 39
Sexual response
of circumcised women 25-26,80-102
Sexual purity of women
and family honor 64
Sexual sensitivity 6
as detriment 8
hypersensitivity given as rationale for
clitoridectomy 12